THE SECOND
ELLE
Cookbook

Also in the same series

THE ELLE COOKBOOK (1981)
Mermaid paperback edition (1984)

THE SECOND ELLE Cookbook

Translated by R. F. Fullick
Photographs by A. Bouillaud
Ph. Leroy and Y. Jannes

MICHAEL JOSEPH
LONDON

First published in Great Britain by
Michael Joseph Limited
44 Bedford Square, London WC1
1985

The Second Elle cookbook.
1. Cookery, French
641.5944   TX719

Cased edition ISBN 0 7181 2560 6

Printed and bound in Spain by
Artes Gráficas Toledo. S.A.
D. L. TO: 1021 -1985

CONTENTS

The illustrations which appear between pages 6 and 15
are reproduced by kind permission of Food & Wine from France
and the Sunday Times Wine Club.

Pyrenées

St. Paulin

Bleu d'Auvergne

Bleu de Bresse

Roquefort

Grape Cheese

Emmen

Goat Cheese

Cream Cheese

Herb Cheese

Walnut Cheese

Pont l'Eveque

Carné de l'Est

Brie

Camembert

CHEESE IN THE KITCHEN AND AT THE TABLE

In his masterly and persuasive apologia for wine-drinking (the Introduction to *Stay Me with Flagons*), Maurice Healy makes the case for Divine sanction for the very existence of wine, for its place and its necessity in the life of man. It could be supposed without too much exaggeration that the separation of milk into curds and whey and the transformation of curds into cheese, making a delectable solid from a highly perishable liquid, had the same providential approval.

The production of cheese in France is so diverse and so widespread and the place of cheese in French gastronomy is so important that it would be wrong not to preface this second volume of recipes from *Elle* magazine with a section on this most essential and delightful foodstuff, cheese – and, in particular, the cheese of France.

The place of cheese at the French table is assured: until the arrival of *cuisine nouvelle*, the salad in France followed the meat course and cheese came next, before any puddings or sweet course. Nowadays, the fashion for *salade tiède*, which is really a warm appetiser with a greater or lesser salad element as part of it, has tended to displace salad from the old order of precedence, but nothing has shaken the rock-like place of 'raw' cheese in the French way of life. A cheese sauce as part of one's fish course is understandable, and almost certainly enjoyable, but who would think of nibbling his cheese and bread or biscuits between soup and fish? Cheese by its nature is the perfect coda: who had not been pressed to a little cheese 'to finish your wine with', and then with barely-concealed pleasure seen one's host slip out for another bottle of wine 'to finish the cheese with'?

CHEESE AND CHEESES

First of all, what is cheese? In the simplest possible terms, cheese is made by the coagulation of the solid matter in milk (the curds) and the draining off of all or part of the liquid matter (the whey). Beyond this lies a variety of processes – whether cow's, goat's or ewe's milk has been used, whether the milk is pasteurised or raw, whether the curd is cooked, uncooked or scalded, the rind washed or unwashed, the length and method of maturing the cheese: all these things lead to the astonishing range and variety of cheeses which are available today to almost everyone.

Even in their diversity, cheeses tend to belong to a number of major families, each of which shares certain characteristics among the many members which make it up. These families, briefly described, are the following:

The Cream Cheeses divide into two categories, the fresh or unsalted, and the salted. As their name implies, they are sold as soon as the whey has been drained from the curds, they do not go through further curing or maturing processes and they are intended to be eaten without long storage. Among the unsalted cheeses are such as petit-Suisse, almost made to be eaten with a spoon, while a well-known example of the salted varieties is Boursin.

Uncooked Pressed Cheeses are made by pressing the curds after they have separated from the whey and then curing the cheeses in cellars for three to six months. Varieties familiar in this country are the Dutch cheeses, Edam and Gouda; Port-Salut, Cantal and the various tommes from France and, best known of all, the English Cheddar.

Cooked Pressed Cheeses and here the description of 'cooked' refers to the curd preparation taking place under heat, followed by salting or soaking in brine. Gruyère and Emmenthal are typical names in this category of dense, firm and deep-coloured cheeses.

Uncooked Soft Cheeses, like cream cheeses, divide into two distinct types – those with a rind formed by natural moulds, such as Brie and Camembert, and those whose rinds are washed regularly during the curing and maturing process to produce cheese of particular colour and flavour: Pont l'Evèque is probably the most famous cheese of this second sort.

Blue Cheeses are distinctive and unmistakable. The blue-green veining which runs through the cheese is a penicillin mould and is always present. Stilton and Roquefort come first to mind when these cheeses are mentioned.

Goat's Cheese forms a category all of its own; a family with an enormous number and variety which stretches from soft cream cheeses at one extreme to the Norwegian goat's cheese which in colour and consistency resembles nothing more closely than toffee. All have the marked flavour of their basic element and, to most people in this country, it will be the small cylinders or pyramids with their natural-mould rinds which will be most readily associated with the name of goat.

Processed Cheese deserves a mention for its commercial importance, if for nothing else. Prepared from combinations of various types of cheeses, they aim for a consistency of texture and taste which can be relied upon: often they are sold under well-known brand names in individual wrapped portions and may be mixed with herbs, peppers or other flavourings. The French name of 'sandwich cheese' perhaps best describes their nature and purpose.

BUYING CHEESE

A heartening development of the past few years has been the growth in numbers of the specialist cheese shop, often in unexpected localities. While this sort of shop has existed for a long time, there are now many more, seeking through their own professional association to raise and maintain standards. Increasingly, they strive to offer to the public a widening variety of cheeses sold in peak condition. So far has the trend developed that it is now possible to read notices on shop doors proclaiming that the establishment is closed while its proprietor is absent in France replenishing his stock.

Perhaps much of the credit for all this goes back to the great supermarket chains. Their basic commercial policy of wishing to offer a wide and attractive range of foodstuffs together with their enormous buying-power has usually resulted in most major supermarkets having a large and well-stocked cheese counter. This in turn has raised the awareness and expectations of the average shopper in respect of cheese to the point where a venture such as the setting up of an independent specialist cheese shop has a good chance of commercial success. More and more, a welcome sight in English markets – as it has been for so long in France – is the stall devoted solely to the sale of cheese. A better informed, more demanding and more discerning buying public has encouraged the cheese merchants to buy well and to buy competitively, and make it less likely that one is offered only a limited range of processed cheeses, or famous cheeses that are out of condition or which have been badly handled by the shopkeeper.

The encouraging fact, therefore, is that for those who wish to take a little trouble in their cheese-buying, it has probably never been so easy. Advice and help before buying, too, are more available although it probably and unfortunately remains true that, as with wine, enlightened stocking policies of the supermarkets are not always fully supported by an adequate level of knowledge in those engaged to sell the product. The rule must be to take your ignorance to a specialist cheese shop where you are likely to be directed towards the product that will properly suit you, and take that knowledge to a supermarket or foodstore where you are likely to find, if not a bargain, at least the keenest prices. Be adventurous and be demanding and, who knows, perhaps one day even in this country it will be a common practice to snip off a small sample to allow the customers to decide for themselves whether they wish to buy from taste and texture rather than just by name and appearance across an impersonal glass barrier.

STORING CHEESE

The storage of such a changeable and sensitive product as cheese is an important matter, requiring care and attention. Ideally, one would behave like my mother-in-law's one-time French cook who would have an empty larder at the end of each meal and go out and buy what was necessary and in top condition in time for the following meal. In these days, few of us are so fortunate to be thus well served, and so the larder and the refrigerator (but never ever the freezer) must be called into play to allow us to balance quality, economy and practicality, in those proportions which each one regards as proper.

All cheeses contain a considerable amount of moisture and the two basic principles of cheese storage are the maintenance (as far as possible) of an even temperature, and the control and limitation of dehydration. The storage period should be as short as is reasonably possible so do not buy more cheese than is likely to be eaten within the next day or so. Obviously there will be exceptions such as the range of cheeses bought for a dinner party, or the Christmas treat of a Stilton or a Brie, but in these cases there is no alternative to applying a Parkinsonian law and seeing that consumption increases to match the quantity available! But for the regular purchase, reverse the law and make the quantity bought no greater than the anticipated immediate consumption.

But we are not dealing with an exact science and there will always be some remaining cheese to be stored. Commonsense will help in determining over how long a period a particular cheese is still likely to be pleasurable and this largely will be a function of the curing or maturing period. Cream and cottage cheeses have a short life; at the other end of the scale, really hard cheeses such as Parmesan, which may mature over two years, can happily be eaten at a great age. Within this, the important factor is the rate at which a particular variety of cheese develops and therefore the length of the time during which it can be served at its best.

Cream and soft cheeses, therefore, which develop rapidly when opened and cut, should be eaten as soon as possible after being bought. For these, and indeed for all cheeses being stored in a refrigerator, the best place is within the salad drawer. The enclosed storage will help control the loss of moisture from the cheese, the fundamental factor in its change of condition. Keep these cheeses closely wrapped in their original packaging and bring them out in good time, but not more than one hour before they are to be served.

The pressed cheeses must similarly be protected against moisture-loss and should be stored in plastic bags or covered in shrink-wrap or kitchen foil while in the refrigerator. Goat's cheeses do not seem to require such careful treatment and will retain their texture and flavour even if they have become a little dried out. The drier and harder types of goat's cheese will keep over a long period if immersed in olive oil and this method is extremely useful if one has taken the opportunity at the end of a holiday to stock up with cheeses at the last market visited.

Camembert, a cow's milk cheese originally from Normandy

Roquefort, a sheep's milk cheese from the Causse

An unmoist blue cheese, on the other hand, is a sorry sight and a sad experience: who has not had the misfortune to have been offered a hollowed-out Stilton, its creamy colour turned to dark orange, looking more than anything like a photograph of the inside of an exhausted stone quarry? Because these cheeses – like a Stilton at Christmas – tend to be bought in larger quantities and are, therefore, in the house over a longer period, they require particular treatment in order to remain palatable. Some experts recommend covering them with a clean damp cloth before storing them, but even this precaution cannot work miracles and, as with all other varieties of cheese, they must be watched closely and eaten up before they begin to deteriorate seriously.

CHEESE IN COOKING
The natural qualities of cheese make it an ideal ingredient in a wide variety of dishes and it is a matter of no surprise, therefore, that so many recipes in this second volume of *Elle* recipes, as well as in its predecessor, contain cheese as an important element. The additional depth of flavour which cheese can impart to a dish, the wide variety of textures available to the cook, its quality of being able to melt as it is heated and also to form a delicious crust on the top of a dish, all these things can be used to enhance or embellish what might otherwise have been a more limited use of resources.

It is hoped that a review of the different ways in which cheese can be used in the menu will be useful. In *soups*, the sprinkling on of a finely-grated hard cheese as a flavouring, then stirred into the soup as it is being drunk, will be familiar to everybody and here Parmesan is normally the choice. French fish soups are usually accompanied by small rounds of toast on which a blob of garlic sauce (*rouille*) is first put, followed by a sprinkling of coarsely-grated pressed cheese (Emmenthal or Cheddar are probably best here). These, put to float in the soup, impart their flavours and textures gradually and deliciously.

In both volumes of *Elle*, cheese in its raw, natural state frequently takes a part in *salads* and here the list of cheeses specified range from cream and soft cheeses to the pressed cheeses; the latter are usually coarse-grated but are sometimes sliced or cut into small dice. The original recipes most often call for Emmenthal or Gruyère cheese

Saint-Paulin, a rinded cheese made from cow's milk

one specified by the recipe should be chosen. Here we are not talking only of hot sauces but also of dips for parties, cold sauces served with crudités, or as one of a selection of different sauces displayed around a *fondue bourguignonne*.

Lastly, cheese can be part of the *pudding course*. The soft cream cheeses, fromage blanc, quark or cottage cheese, are normally used flavoured with sugar and fruit essences or with fresh fruit, and made into cold creamy dishes or hot tarts. The sharpness which the flavour of the cheese adds to the dish stimulates the taste and brings out the fruit flavour in mixed dishes.

Cheese is thus a universal ingredient in cooking, with the possibility of being present in every course from soup to pudding. The text section of these notes deals with cheese eaten for its own sake, as a distinct element in the menu.

THE CHEESE COURSE

To argue the different merits of the French and English ways of treating the cheese course and to come down with firm opinions on such a prickly subject, is to attempt to cross an uncharted minefield – the chances of doing so without provoking an explosion are not high. So these notes only go so far as to describe what those differences are and perhaps to attempt to see why differences exist at all: note that what is being talked about is cheese as a later course in a luncheon or dinner menu not, as practised in other parts of Europe, the serving of cheese at breakfast or other odd and unsuitable times of day.

The French, then, eat their cheese after their main course and strictly before anything sweet, while the British think that cheese should be the last course of any meal at which it is served. It used to be thought in this country that raw cheeses could not properly be served at a proper dinner party but that the correct ending to a formal meal was a savoury, frequently a cheese-based Welsh Rabbit but equally likely to be based on something other than cheese: mushrooms, chicken livers, oysters and bacon, scrambled egg and anchovy. (Why, oh why do even those who run restaurants which

for grating on to salads (in fact, these two appear most frequently as the general-purpose cooking cheese) but cheeses of similar texture and more likely to be found in the British larder, such as Cheddar, will be perfectly acceptable substitutes.

Cheese is particularly delicious as part of a *hot starter or simple dish*, generally as the only or the main protein ingredient. Frequently, these dishes take the form of one cheese or another encased in pastry or dough, or of a flan with a cheese filling; others combine cheese with vegetables, slices of ham etc. to give an extra dimension to what otherwise might have been rather a bland dish. It is not only the depth of flavour which cheese brings to these simple and straightforward preparations but also, and perhaps particularly, that marvellous quality in cheese which has already been mentioned, of changing its texture when it is heated.

When serving a hot dish in which a cheese appears, care must be taken to bring it to the table and see that it is eaten at the correct and recommended temperature. Just as cheese will change its texture while it is being heated up, so it will change again as it cools down, obviously not reverting to its original form but in many cases becoming rubbery in texture and lacking in flavour. The best advice to follow with hot cheese dishes is that they should be eaten really hot, but there are occasions when cold cheese can be delicious. Some people derive enormous pleasure from eating the crusts and spillings of grilled cheese cold from the grill-pan, regarding them as comparable in delight only with the rim of rice pudding skin scraped from around the dish, or with those swathes garnered by running the blade of a knife around the inside edge of a soufflé dish after the cheese soufflé has been served.

Another simple but very pleasurable way of eating cheese hot is to cut small cubes of cheese and either drop them into hot oil until they are brown and sizzling, or quickly grill them all over. Goat's cheeses and Camemberts respond particularly well to this, while fried Greek Halloumi is also delicious. Again, they will be much less good if allowed to cool down.

Another important use for cheese in cooking is in *sauces*. As its purpose here is to impart its flavour to the sauce, substitutes may be made according to taste or availability; however, in every case, a cheese from the same family and having characteristics similar to the

A *plateau* showing Camembert, Reblochon, Gruyère, Comté and a goat's cheese

ABOVE *Fromages de chevre*   BELOW Cheese and wine in France are never far apart

claim to epitomise the British cuisine and to use the best of native ingredients, so neglect the savoury? Perhaps the savoury – like the great British breakfast and cold bedrooms – is part of a vanishing tradition.)

The crucial element in this *franco-brittanique* dispute may be port wine. If port, on the other side of the Channel, has a place at all, it is to be white and drunk as an aperitif: what it is not is a device to allow men to dine on their own and linger excessively over their meal, or to separate at the crucial moment from their womenfolk but still linger excessively. So it may be that the Frenchman sees the purpose of cheese to extend the drinking of whatever good red wine was served with his main course while the more devious Anglo-Saxon uses cheese to prepare his palate for the drinking of port in the company of those to whom his opinions (expressed at length) will be less familiar and possibly more persuasive than his own wife finds them.

For those who do not serve port to their guests, there can be no reason to make the cheese follow the pudding since what is to be drunk with it? A sweet pudding eaten before the cheese destroys any possibility of going back to red wine because the palate could not conceivably re-adjust to it. (Going on to the richness and depth of port is entirely another matter. Anyone who doubts this should keep back a little red wine in his glass and sip it after he has drunk half a glass of port. It is certain that he will find the experience instructive.)

Another substantial difference between the French and British habits lies in the means by which the cheese is actually conveyed to the mouth. The French use a knife and fork, perhaps because one of the negative factors in French culture is an inability to fully appreciate the qualities and sheer delight of the British dry or semi-sweet biscuit. Here we see that crisp and crunchy wafer as the ideal launch-vehicle for a tasty piece of cheese, adaptable to carry cheeses of any texture, whether spread on or balanced precariously in a lump. Some Frenchmen will concede the principle (but not adopt the practice) by eating slices of French bread with their cheese.

As the reasons for acting in diverse directions possibly become clearer, let us look at another aspect of the cheese course where Anglo-Saxon influence has been the leader. This is in the practice of adding sticks of celery, and sometimes radishes, to the cheese board, or serving a basket of crisp apples at the same time as the cheese is passed round. This seems an admirable thing to do, providing a perfect foil to the cheese, clearing the palate with a sharp flavour and a contrasting texture, and preparing it for the next morsel of cheese.

Each person therefore will have to weigh up the merits and disadvantages of the two different practices, decide how far they agree with them and act accordingly. The overriding rules must be to try to serve a meal in which the courses are balanced one with another and lead on to the next with an increasing sense of appreciation, and to serve the courses in such a way that the qualities of each one are seen at their best. One suggestion which may go some way to reconciling the two cross-Channel philosophies: leave out the pudding course entirely.

WINE WITH CHEESE

One frequently sees charts which propose certain wines to match particular cheeses. The advice given will be soundly based and well thought out but perhaps would be more applicable were the main course itself cheese or cheese-based. In practical terms, most people (assuming a resolution of the question of the order of precedence of the cheese course, and the role or otherwise of port) will be content to continue with the wine of their main course; but there must be variations. The arrival of cheese may be taken as an opportunity to produce a different wine – but perhaps it ought not to be too different in character from the main course wine which will have preceded it. If a good claret has been drunk, a Beaujolais or Burgundy with the cheese might provide far too great a contrast and each wine detract from the remembered or anticipated enjoyment of the other. A Rioja of some age might, on the other hand, be an interesting supporter of cheese in this circumstance. As a simple rule, when one red is to follow another from main course to cheese, do not change the shape of the bottle.

What if the main course is fish? Here there may seem to be plenty of scope for a free choice but in fact the room for manoeuvre may be quite narrow. It must be remembered that we are looking for a wine that will go with cheese and the assumption in most cases is that the cheese wine will be red. It would be wrong to choose one of such quality that the fish wine was quite overshadowed because, in that case, the all-important balance of the meal will be lost. On the other hand, something too pedestrian will seem make-weight after a good and carefully prepared main course. Look to the better wines of the less familiar or less prestigious districts: a Chinon or Bourgeuil from the Loire, a Gigondas from the Rhône, a Barolo from Piedmont. Where a red wine might in some cases seem inappropriate, and if there is no intention of offering port, a Madeira with cheese is always worth considering. The Madeiras sold in this country have a range of dryness/sweetness which makes it simple to achieve a happy harmony between the cheese being served and this fortified wine.

The cheese course, therefore, merits as much thought and care in the planning of its place in the meal as anything else. What is indisputable is the importance of cheese in gastronomy and in good, healthy living – its enhancement of other foods when used as an additional and supporting ingredient, and its sheer pleasure as a course of its own. Each person will already have opinions of the place cheese ought to occupy in his own culinary life and it is hoped that these few discursive notes might have helped to enlarge horizons.

So, when the battle of where-the-cheese-course-comes has been fought and decided, cut your slice of Emmenthal or whatever you have chosen and settle down to debate Berthold Brecht's philosophical conundrum – where do the holes go when the cheese is finished?

WINE IN COOKING AND WINE WITH FOOD

As the recipes in the two *Elle* cookbooks so clearly demonstrate, wine and food in France are regarded as synonymous: wine is a frequent, almost universal ingredient in every sort of dish and, the food having been prepared, it is taken for granted that the dish will be supported by an appropriate bottle, or more than one bottle, of wine. In this country, cooking with wine and eating with wine are not taken so much for granted; habit, upbringing and economics all tend to be against it. The British wine drinker probably has a far greater breadth of choice open to him than his counterpart in major wine-producing countries (where the products of other countries are unlikely to be encouraged in competition with the home-grown varieties), a happy circumstance which owes much to the traditional excellence of our independent wine merchants and the growing excellence of the major supermarket chains. On the other hand, there is the corresponding disadvantage that a great variety of choice may lead to a lack of any real knowledge in depth about the wines that are drunk, their different qualities and strengths, and their relative usefulness in cooking.

The main purpose of this section is therefore to give, in introductory form only, some hints and advice on buying, storing and handling wine, on its different uses as an ingredient and on drinking it with food.

BUYING WINE
The traditional wine merchant has declined in relative importance due both to the explosion in the prices of fine wines and to rising interest rates (which have made it impossible for the independent merchants to tie up sufficient capital to finance their stocks of wine during the long periods needed for them to mature) and also to the emergence of a new breed of wine-consumer. There are some exceptions to this picture and there is evidence that the pendulum is swinging back, but the average consumer nowadays is likely to use a combination of outlets when making his purchases. These include wine clubs, merchants which are in fact part of a large distillers or brewery chain, off-licences, wine warehouses, supermarkets and, for those with an adventurous spirit and organisational flair, direct purchase from the country of origin.

Each source has some merit: *wine clubs* provide a wide range of fringe-benefits in the form of printed guides and advice, seminars and wine tours, but are likely to be more expensive than the average. *Off-licences* have the great benefit of convenience and availability, and of permitting purchases in small and mixed parcels, but these days they do not always seem to be staffed by people knowledgeable in their trade. *Wine warehouses* are able to sell at lower prices having the advantages of bulk buying, low overhead at the point of sale and rapid turnover of stock, but in the winter you are very likely to freeze while making your selection in what seems to be a disused aircraft hangar and you have to be your own delivery service; nor can you always be sure of being able to buy on a second occasion what pleased you on the first. *Supermarkets* benefit more and more from an enlightened and expert buying policy, but the customer who wants a case of a particular wine must find an empty box and make up his dozen from the shelves; getting the purchases away and into a car always seems the most difficult. *Direct importing* is a subject all on its own and beyond the scope of these outline hints.

STORING WINE
Those who have the means to store their wines below ground level are these days both in a small minority and extremely fortunate. Below ground level is the ideal: the temperature will not fluctuate greatly from the 11°C/52°F which is generally considered to be best, and the wine is less likely to be disturbed or to suffer from vibration. The great majority of people attempting to store a few cases in a modern cellar-less house or a flat will have to compromise. Try, as far as is possible, to find a place that meets the following requirements:

a) away from the general traffic of the house so that it is not disturbed or moved except when being brought to table.

b) a dark place: direct sunlight is to be avoided at all costs.

c) small variations in temperature. Do not, for example, choose a garden shed with a corrugated iron roof: this will freeze your wine in winter and bake it in summer. It is worthwhile borrowing or acquiring a

maximum-minimum thermometer: leave it for a few days in each of the places you have chosen as possibilities, and see how wide a variation in temperature there is and how far away the average is from the magical figure of 11°C/52°F.

It follows that a wine rack in an open position in the kitchen is not to be encouraged, except perhaps for spirits and liqueurs used in cooking. It is well worth spending the time needed to determine the best storage conditions you have available and so enhance the enjoyment to be had from your cellar.

SERVING WINE
Another general rule (which like all generalities has some fairly notable exceptions) is that much white wine is drunk too cold and much red wine drunk too warm. A good white Burgundy that is much lower than cellar-temperature will seem closed up while a red Beaujolais much warmer than cellar-temperature will seem syrupy and without charm. Sweet dessert wines benefit from being well-chilled as do most rosés and the highly-flavoured white wines of Alsace, while good clarets and red Burgundies should be opened in advance and left in the room in which they are to be drunk. How long before? Here there is no substitute for the advice of an expert but a wine of great age should be brought up well in advance but only opened an hour or two before serving.

Avoid, if you can, the pretentiousness of a wine-basket at table. The purpose of this piece of cellar equipment is to move a bottle which has thrown a heavy deposit, from its rack to the place where it is to be decanted and to present it at an angle which will allow the cork to be drawn without spilling the contents or at the same time disturbing the deposit. Similarly, elaborate and heavily-cut wine glasses in 'suites', much advertised these days, should be left where they belong, in the pages of Sunday supplements. Choose instead a glass with a good-sized bowl of thin, clear glass, tending to close up towards the rim. These will allow the qualities of a good wine to be appreciated to the full: first, its colour and its clarity; next, its bouquet and, finally, its taste in the mouth.

Decanting is not as important as it used to be. Modern methods of viniculture tend to produce bright, clear wines made to be drunk younger than their predecessors and which are more tolerant of less than satisfactory storage methods and serving practices. The main purpose of decanting is to ensure that the deposit does not get into the glass: a secondary benefit is to put some air into an older wine.

WINE IN COOKING
A great proportion of the recipes in the two *Elle* volumes so far published include wine (also spirits and liqueurs) as essential ingredients. *Spirits* are normally used to flame a bird or a piece of meat early in the cooking process: this will flavour the main ingredient and also help to seal it on the outside, thus reducing the loss of juices during cooking. *Wine* is there to impart a flavour to the prepared dish, in a variety of ways: it can be used to marinade and steep certain ingredients in advance, or the wine can be introduced at the appropriate stage during cooking.

It must be remembered that except when wine is an ingredient in a cold dish, cooking will drive off the alcohol content and leave behind only the aromas and flavours. It follows therefore when a particular wine has been specified for a particular recipe in this book, this has been done for a purpose, and substitutions of a different wine with another character should not be attempted. Another error sometimes made is to believe that dregs of wine left over after a meal can be amalgamated in a spare bottle and used as 'cooking wine' on some future occasion. All that is likely to happen is that the dregs will combine into a low-grade vinegar and the dish or sauce will probably be ruined.

A number of *Elle* recipes call simply for a certain quantity of 'dry white wine' to be used, without being specific about its type or provenance: where there is also at the end of the recipe a recommendation to drink a particular white wine with the dish, it will be proper to use the same one in cooking. However, where this guidance is absent, the safest choice for an all-purpose dry white wine for cooking

commended wine temperatures

Tony Laithwaite of the Sunday Times Wine Club sampling as close to the source as possible

is probably a Mâcon. A Muscadet will tend to be too green and acidic; the whites of the upper Loire will be too flowery to be completely satisfactory as an ingredient, while the whites from Provence and the lower Rhône may be too robust for the purpose. It might be felt that a wine of the quality of Mâcon is an unnecessary extravagance merely to be used up and driven off as one of the cooking ingredients. However, the increase in price over an ordinary vin-de-table which you might be tempted to use as a substitute is not likely to be very considerable which means that the marginal increase in cost of what is no doubt expected to be a particularly elegant and attractive dish, will only be a few pence a serving and be worth every penny of it in the context of producing an outstanding recipe.

If then there are simple rules to be laid down about the use of wine in cooking they are, first, as far as possible use the wine quoted in the recipe when it is specified by name or type and, secondly, without pouring your finest wines into the casserole instead of down the throats of yourself and your guests, do not exaggeratedly try to save money on an important ingredient which while perhaps less evident than others is nonetheless as essential as they are.

Marinades are a mixture, either cooked or uncooked, of wine, oil, vinegar, vegetables, and herbs and spices. They are used to soak meat or game and have two main purposes, to flavour the meat and to make it more tender. The soaking period can be an extended one, in some recipes as long as 48 hours. Often the marinade is strained off at the end of the soaking period and the liquid used to form the base of the sauce to be served with the meat. Further details about different marinades can be found in the individual recipes and there are more marinade recipes in the first *Elle Cookbook*.

Court-bouillons differ from marinades in being wine-based broths in which food, generally fish, is poached. They are traditionally a mixture of fresh vegetables such as onion, celery and carrots, herbs and wine, extended with water. The ingredients are cooked together, then strained and the liquid used for poaching. As with marinades, the court-bouillon usually becomes the base of the sauce to be served with the ingredient which has been cooked in it. It is also possible to buy prepared court-bouillon in powder or cube form: in this case, the

preparation is dissolved in wine, or a mixture of wine and water, while the poaching liquid is being heated. As always, each cook must judge between the convenience and simplicity of the prepared product against the purity and superior flavour of the fresh ingredients. Further details about court-bouillons can be found on page 15 and a court-bouillon recipe appears on page 40 of *Elle 1*.

Steeping is a more straightforward operation in which (usually but not invariably) poultry or game is soaked in brandy or another liqueur some time during the cooking process. Cooked or part-cooked meat will better absorb the tenderising and flavour-imparting qualities of the spirit.

Wines and spirits also have a further part to play in the preparation of sauces and gravies, apart from the use of marinades and court-bouillons as bases. This is the process known as *deglazing* when, after the main ingredient has finished cooking and has been removed from its pan or casserole to a warm place, the juices, residues and small pieces left are incorporated into the sauce. Wine, spirits or vermouth (whatever the recipe calls for) are poured into the pan, and the bottom vigorously scraped clean while the liquid is brought to boiling point. Although the back of a strong fork is a satisfactory tool for this operation, an ideal one is the French device known as a *cuiller magique* which is nothing more than a coil spring forming the outline of a spoon, attached to a handle. It is well worth searching one out in a good kitchen shop.

WINE WITH FOOD

As has been said many times before, the glory of French cuisine lies in its brilliant use of the complementary qualities of food and wine. It follows that both to achieve and to share the greatest possible enjoyment from one's culinary and gastronomic efforts, as many as possible of the senses need to be stimulated. Experience tells one that the heightened sense of anticipation with which one approaches a meal in a French restaurant is not all self-delusion – clean linen, sparkling glass, well laid-out cutlery, all provide a *mise-en-scène* which says: I am about to enjoy myself. And why not? And why should not this be the first aim of anyone entertaining at home? A sense of

The shape of France

anticipation is the best possible beginning for a successful dinner party and if this can be induced then the value and enjoyment of all that follows is increased.

It would be an impertinence to attempt to tell others how they should entertain their chosen guests (or even themselves) so what follows is more in the nature of observations drawn from a lifetime of enjoyable eating and drinking.

Observation 1. Very carefully time the period between the arrival of the guests and sitting down to table. Assuming that the guests have arrived with the wished-for sense of anticipation, too long a period before the food is served will blunt it and give licence for the zealous guest to become over-stimulated – invariably leading to problems.

Observation 2 follows from the first. Serving wine or wine-based drinks before a meal is better than serving spirits; it is not necessarily more hospitable to give each guest a free run of the butler's tray. What is being led up to, after all, is a decent and carefully-prepared meal accompanied by decent and carefully-chosen wines. Champagne as the sole aperitif may be in order for some special occasion but otherwise could be considered pretentious and plutocratic. Vin blanc-cassis (Kir) is still a delightful drink before a meal, while the regional habits of serving chilled Monbazillac or Muscat de Beaumes de Venise as aperitifs have a great deal of charm. That forgotten starter, sherry, is relatively inexpensive and as well made as ever it was, but for those who *must* drink spirits, the hope of some preferment just has to be weighed against civilised reluctance: no golden rule here.

Observation 3 is make the wines fit the food, whatever they are and whatever it is. There will be as much satisfaction to be had if your wish is to serve chilli con carne with a straightforward Rioja, as in pouring your best claret with a leg of Welsh spring lamb. It would pall if one were so rich as to be able to serve fine wines with everything one ate; it would be sad if there were never an occasion when something exceptional was not brought to table. The better one can educate the palate with a wide range of wines, the more instinctively one will come to know what will seem best with whatever is being put on one's plate.

Observation 4 is about afterwards. On the assumption that the company has not been ruthlessly divided into two parties of either sex in the Edwardian manner and that the table conversations and intrigues are continuing to flow and flourish, this is the time to relax the hostly discipline. Give them what they want to drink and, at this point, for that diminishing company of victims, let them smoke as well.

To conclude with *Observation 5*, wine must not be used as a social prop, nor as a means of escape but as something that can contribute greatly to the enjoyment of life. Its benign and friendly nature makes it a good companion and there must be very few people who would say that wine at some time or another had not vastly increased the pleasure of the moment. Of all the earthly delights we enjoy, none deserves less to contribute to what Evelyn Waugh has so tellingly described as the English blight – remorse.

TRANSLATOR'S NOTES

It is a source of particular pleasure and satisfaction to be writing these notes for the second volume of recipes from *Elle*. The reception given to the first volume was overwhelming and it has become clear from talking to many enthusiasts of *Elle 1* that it plays a principal role in their culinary and entertaining life.

The layout of this new book follows closely on the pattern of its predecessor. All the recipes come from the pages of *Elle* magazine and each one is again illustrated with a colour photograph of the finished dish. I know from my own experience – as well as hearing from others, many of them highly professional cooks – that this feature is extremely valuable in achieving the desired result and, however unexpectedly, the great proportion of dishes made from the book do turn out to look just like their picture. (Perhaps the Passport Office could learn something from this.)

THE RECIPES

It bears repeating in this second volume that the recipes come from a wide variety of origins (not all of them French) and the methods of preparation and the cooking habits and customs of all the originators are clearly not identical. As before, the recipe has been published in the form in which it first appeared in *Elle* magazine so the same warning must be given: do not be surprised if succeeding recipes for what appear to be broadly similar dishes use different methods. What the originator intended is what has been translated.

THE INGREDIENTS

The notes on ingredients which appeared in *Elle I* are reprinted here since they are all as valid as when they were first written. The additional notes and tips in this volume are, in some cases, in response to queries and suggestions made by users of *Elle I*.

An advance on the situation since the first volume was published is that there should now be less need to have to prepare substitutes for peculiarly French ingredients. There is a progressively wider availability of such esoterica as *crème fraîche* and *fromage blanc* although, among vegetables, *navets* seem as rarely found in this country as ever they were.

STOCKS AND SAUCE BASES
A number of *Elle* recipes require the preparation of concentrated liquids as a base for cooking or for sauces, and instructions for making them in any given recipe should preferably be followed. However, many people will find it useful to have general guidelines, either as a substitute within a given recipe – when the instructions merely specify, say, a court-bouillon or a meat stock – or when devising a special dish of one's own. Generally, the preparations which follow can be deep-frozen and kept for some considerable time. Quantities may of course be reduced proportionally when stocks are made for each occasion.

For Fish: The stocks for fish are the court-bouillons and the fumets. The first are concoctions of wine, herbs and vegetables (sometimes vinegar is substituted for wine when the fish is rich in natural oils), and the second are meatier reductions of fish heads and trimmings (always remember to ask your fishmonger to give you these), poached with vegetables in white wine.

WHITE WINE COURT-BOUILLON Put 1 litre (1¾ pints) of water and 1 litre (1¾ pints) of dry white wine in a saucepan with the following trimmed and chopped vegetables and herbs: 2 carrots, 2 onions, 1 stalk of celery, 1 sprig each of thyme and parsley, 2 cloves and 6 black peppercorns. Season, bring to the boil, simmer for 40 minutes and allow to cool before straining. Divide into portions and freeze what is not to be used at once.

FUMET Weigh out 750 g (1½ lb) of fish heads and trimmings and chop up the larger pieces. Put them in a saucepan with the following trimmed and chopped vegetables: 2 onions, 2 shallots, 2 large carrots. Add 2 lemon quarters, a bouquet garni, 1 litre (1¾ pints) of water and a glass of dry white wine. Season, bring to the boil and allow to reduce in the uncovered pan for 1 hour. Strain before using or freezing.

It is possible to buy fish stocks in cubes (like chicken or beef stock cubes) or in powder form, but they have to be searched for. They can only be substitutes in an emergency for the recipes given above.

For Meat: The following recipes are always useful to have to hand and, as with the fish stocks, can be frozen.

A BASIC MEAT STOCK This fundamental method can be adapted according to the sort of meat used in the main recipe. The use of a meat stock and the various slightly different ways to make it appears in a number of *Elle* recipes themselves, but basically the bones and trimmings of the meat or poultry being used in the recipe (with extra meat if trimmings are scarce) together with sliced onion and carrot are first lightly browned under a hot grill, then transferred to a saucepan and gently simmered over a long period. The surface of the liquid should be skimmed from time to time.

If the stock is being made in quantity, use cubes of beef with veal bones for the rich meat stock and, for a chicken stock, the carcass or the less popular pieces. The stock will benefit from a really long period of simmering, about 4 to 5 hours, and of course extra water may be added during cooking as the level falls.

MEAT GLAZE This is a rich meat stock reduced over a long, slow cooking period, with regular skimming, to the consistency of syrup. It is used as a base for sauces, for the same purposes as a meat extract might be employed, and sometimes it is used as a decoration for roast meats. When cold, it becomes jellified and can safely be stored in the refrigerator for a long period.

MEAT MISCELLANY
LARDONS As with *Elle I*, a number of meat and salad dishes in this book contain small strips of pork belly or bacon, either fried or blanched and then fried. Thickly-cut streaky bacon is generally the best to use, green where smoked has not been definitely indicated.

PORK BELLY RIND This is included in some of the slowly-cooked meat dishes. It is placed in the base of the casserole and will melt as the meat is cooked, thickening the juices which will later become the sauce to accompany the meat.

VEAL The discussion still continues about the morality of using veal which is the product of factory-farming. Those who do not wish to eat veal should be able to decide for themselves whether pork can be used instead. For any dish specifying veal escalope or boned veal chops, pork fillet cut across the grain will be an acceptable substitute.

FRUIT AND VEGETABLES
SMALL ONIONS When a recipe indicates that small white onions are required, use pickling onions rather than the heads of spring onions since they are more tightly packed and are a better shape.

RED AND GREEN PEPPERS The grilling method of peeling peppers is now fairly widely known but is probably worth repeating. Turn the peppers under a hot grill until the skins blister and scorch on all sides, then wrap the peppers in several sheets of damp newspaper. Leave for a few minutes, unwrap and you will find that the skin will peel very easily from the flesh.

YOUNG TURNIPS As mentioned in *Elle I* as well as in the introduction to this section, the very small young turnips which the French call *navets* are still difficult to find at the average greengrocer in this country. If young turnips are not available, do not be tempted to use peeled and cubed pieces of larger and older turnips since the flavour will be much too strong.

APPLES The French, depending so much as they do (but without admitting it) on a transatlantic variety, will most often specify Golden Delicious for dishes where apples are required. In this country, we ought to be more fortunate but regrettably native varieties are sometimes less available than they should be. Try Cox's, or Ellison's Pippins or James Grieve or, if you prefer a tarter flavour, try an English cooking apple such as the Bramley.

PRESERVED LEMONS *(Citrons Confits)* These are specified in certain *Elle* recipes originating in Morocco: they add a most distinctive flavour to a number of lamb and chicken dishes, or slices can be served as a sort of exotic pickle with cold meats. The good news is that preserved lemons can now be found in shops but they are quite expensive and it is quite a simple matter to prepare one's own.

The preserving liquid can be oil, brine or lemon juice but basically the method of preservation is the same: the lemon is opened up by being cut into quarters for not quite its whole length, the inside is sprinkled generously with salt and the lemon closed up again. The fruit is put into a preserving jar and left to sweat for a few days. (Some methods omit the sweating stage.) At the end of this time, the lemons are removed, the preserving jar drained and washed out, the lemons replaced together with a spoonful of coriander seeds and then covered with the preserving liquid. They should be left in a cool dark place for at least a month: they keep well.

HERBS AND SPICES

BOUQUET GARNI This is, strictly speaking, a bunch of fresh mixed herbs tied together and added to a dish during the cooking to enhance the flavour. The herbs normally used are parsley, thyme and bay leaf. Dried herbs may be used when fresh are not available but this will always reduce the intended flavour. They should be placed on a piece of muslin and tied into a ball to prevent them dispersing into the food. Two words of caution: first, remove the bouquet garni either exactly when the recipe specifies or, by tasting, before the herb flavours begin to dominate whatever is being cooked. The purpose is to accent the dish, not to dominate it. Secondly, if dried herbs are being used, be sure they are not too old. Time-expired herbs will have leached out all their essential oils and will not be able to provide the extra depth which the recipe demands.

FINES HERBES This may be taken to mean a mixture of chopped fresh herbs added to a dish at the appropriate time during cooking. The traditionalist will expect the composition to be parsley, chives, tarragon and chervil although in Provence combinations of basil, oregano, sage and fennel may also be used.

QUATRE ÉPICES This is a blend of crushed or powdered spices based on black peppercorns (about two-thirds of the final volume) with the remainder equally divided between cloves, cinnamon and nutmeg.

Another version uses white peppercorns as the base and substitutes ginger for the cinnamon. Whichever is used, the preparation is an important ingredient in the making of terrines, pâtés and sausages.

MILK PRODUCTS

CRÈME FRAÎCHE Despite its name, crème fraîche has a hint of sourness which adds a characteristic flavour to dishes in which it is an ingredient. It is increasingly easy to obtain although the following substitute, recommended by Jane Grigson, is not difficult to make and keeps well.

Slowly heat to 90°C/194°F soured cream stirred into double its quantity of whipping or double cream. Pour into a pot, cover and put into a warm place overnight. Stir again and then refrigerate. This will keep for ten days.

FROMAGE BLANC Again, this is an ingredient which has become more readily available since the publication of *Elle I*. However, in case it cannot be found, cottage cheese can be substituted although it is preferable to extend it with a little milk and pass it through a blender in order to approximate to the texture of *fromage blanc*.

FINALLY

FLOUR Unless otherwise specified, flour is always intended to be plain.

GELATINE Where this is specified in a recipe, it may be useful to have the equivalence between powdered and leaf gelatine. Count 4 leaves to 7½ g (¼ oz) of powder: leaves should be soaked in cold water for 10 minutes and drained before being added to the dish according to the recipe instructions.

VANILLA SUGAR This is now readily available in packets: the contents of the sachets in which the French sell it is usually 7½ g, the British packet a bit bigger. You can of course make your own by immersing two vanilla pods in caster sugar in a screw-top jar.

When using vanilla essence in place of vanilla sugar, increase the amount of ordinary sugar by a teaspoon.

YEAST Yeast sometimes complicates French recipes by their practice of using the same term for baking powder. Where yeast appears as an ingredient in *Elle* recipes, however, it is yeast which is intended. Most people will use either baker's (fresh) yeast or powdered active dried yeast, both of which need to be activated in lukewarm sweetened liquid.

Happily, there is now a new dried active yeast which can go straight into the flour mixture from the packet.

THE WEIGHTS AND MEASURES

In all cases, the definitive weight or volume is the one given in metric measurements as in the original French recipe. Most people will by now have a set of kitchen scales marked in both metric and avoirdupois but for those who do not, the nearest practical equivalent in imperial measurements is given in every case. You should follow either metric or imperial: they are not interchangeable.

PREPARATION AND COOKING INSTRUCTIONS

The information given at the beginning of each recipe is for guidance only. The preparation times will vary according to the expertise of the cook, and the quantities used according to the appetites of the family or guests. For dishes cooked in the oven, both oven temperatures and regulo settings are given, while expressions used for cooking on top of the stove, such as 'over a brisk heat' or 'over a very low flame' follow the original French instructions and are intended to be straightforward and self-explanatory. There may be room for personal preference in the suggestions, which again follow the original recipes, for serving some dishes at temperatures other than hot or cold.

CONCLUSION

In conclusion, we hope that this second volume of *Elle* recipes will give as much pleasure as the first one seems to have done; pleasure to the eye as well as in the preparation and eating of the dishes. As a reader of *Elle I* said: 'I can read your book in the evening and feel I have had a good meal.'
Bon Appétit!

POTAGE GLACÉ À L'AVOCAT
Chilled avocado soup

PREPARATION TIME: 15 minutes (two hours in advance)
COOKING TIME: Nil
FOR SIX

2 avocado pears
125 g (4½ oz) crème fraîche
1 tablespoon chopped chervil
1 tablespoon chopped tarragon
500 ml (17½ fl oz) skimmed
   chicken stock

salt, white pepper
tabasco
stick of French bread

Divide the avocados in two and take out the stones. Remove the flesh from the shells and purée in a blender together with the crème fraîche and the herbs. Put the purée into a bowl (metal if possible), and stir in the chicken stock; season the mixture. Shake in a few drops of tabasco sauce to taste and stir again. Put the bowl into a refrigerator to chill for at least two hours.

Cut the French loaf diagonally and gently brown the slices on both sides under a grill.

Check the seasoning, just before serving; the soup should not be bland. Serve with the toasted bread.

Elle recommends that the avocado stones should be left in the soup until just before serving. This will prevent the mixture from darkening.

SOUPE DE FÈVES PRINTANIÈRES
Broad bean soup

PREPARATION TIME: 10 minutes
COOKING TIME: 2½ hours
FOR SIX

3 kg (6½ lb) broad beans (weight
   in pod) or 2 kg (4½ lb) frozen
   beans

1 tablespoon goose fat
1 stale crusty loaf
salt, pepper

Shell the beans if you are using fresh ones. Plunge the beans, fresh or frozen, in boiling water for 3 minutes, drain and take off the outer skins, retaining only the inner kernels. Bring 5 litres (almost 9 pints) of seasoned water to the boil, put in the beans and the goose fat (pork dripping may be substituted), cover the pan and simmer for 2½ hours. The soup may be puréed if a very smooth texture is required.

Cut the bread into thin slices and put one into the bottom of each soup bowl. Pour the soup over the bread and serve immediately.

Elle advises that this soup, which comes from the Dordogne, loses none of its flavour and quality if frozen beans are used.

CRÈME DE CONCOMBRE
Cream of cucumber soup

PREPARATION TIME: 15 minutes
COOKING TIME: 20 minutes
FOR SIX

1 kg (2¼ lb) cucumbers	*50 g (scant 2 oz) butter*
500 g (generous 1 lb) potatoes	*50 g (scant 2 oz) flour*
salt, pepper	*100 g (3½ oz) crème fraîche*

Trim and peel the cucumbers, split them in half lengthways and remove the pips. Cut the flesh into dice. Blanch a heaped tablespoonful of the diced cucumber in boiling salted water for five minutes. Remove, drain and put to one side.

Peel the potatoes and also cut them into dice. Boil 2 litres (3½ pints) of water in a pan and add the uncooked diced potato and cucumber. Season and cook covered for 20 minutes. During this time, work butter and flour together into a paste with a fork. Purée the soup and then return to pan and incorporate the butter paste little by little. Put back on the heat and bring back to the boil, stirring constantly.

Pour into a soup tureen, beat in the crème fraîche, decorate with the blanched cucumber dice and serve immediately.

Elle says this delicately-flavoured soup is particularly delicious and refreshing in warm weather.

SOUPE PARFUMÉE AU POISSON
Greek fish soup

PREPARATION TIME: 20 minutes
COOKING TIME: 30 minutes
FOR SIX

1½ kg (3¼ lb) cod or other firm white fish	*2 carrots*
	1 head of celery
1 cod's head	*2 tablespoons of rice*
salt, pepper	*3 eggs, separated*
3 onions	*1 lemon*
6 potatoes	

Put 3 litres (5¼ pints) of water into a saucepan and cook the cod's head for 20 minutes. Take out the head and let the fish stock cool.

Cut the cod into steaks and put them into the cold stock. Season and bring slowly to the boil. Take out the fish and put to one side.

Peel and trim the vegetables: chop up the onions and cut the potatoes, carrots and celery into dice. Put all the vegetables together with the rice into the fish stock and cook over a brisk heat for 20 minutes. Remove from the heat.

In a mixing bowl, whip the egg whites to the stage where they are not quite stiff. Fold in the beaten egg yolks and the juice of the lemon. With the pan off the heat, carefully stir this egg and lemon mixture into the soup, spoonful by spoonful. Serve at once.

Elle says that the cooked fish should be eaten cold as a separate sauce, accompanied either by a mayonnaise, or an oil and lemon vinaigrette.

SOUPE DE HARICOTS
Bean soup

PREPARATION TIME: 15 minutes, plus soaking overnight
COOKING TIME: 3½ hours
FOR SIX

500 g (generous 1 lb) white beans	50 g (scant 2 oz) bacon
2 leeks	1 tablespoon flour
4 large potatoes	1 large onion
salt, pepper	12 small potatoes
a blade of salt pork	

The day before, put the beans into a large bowl, amply cover with cold water and let them soak overnight. Drain, put the beans into a large saucepan and cover with fresh water. Trim and slice the leeks, peel the large potatoes and cut them into small pieces. Add these vegetables to the saucepan, season lightly, cover and bring to the boil. Add the blade of pork, previously soaked for an hour in fresh water. Continue cooking for 3½ hours altogether.

An hour before serving, prepare the fricassée. Cut the bacon into small dice and sauté them in a pan over a gentle heat. Add the finely-chopped onion and cook, stirring frequently, until the onion is lightly browned. Sift on the flour and let the roux cook for a few minutes. Moisten with two ladles of bean liquid, stir and pour the mixture into the soup pan. Add the peeled small potatoes and continue cooking for the allotted time.

Elle says the pork and potatoes should be taken out of the soup when cooking is completed. In the Dordogne, where this recipe comes from, the soup is served as a first course, and the sliced pork and potatoes follow.

POTAGE AUX FINES HERBES
Herb soup

PREPARATION TIME: 10 minutes
COOKING TIME: 15 minutes
FOR SIX

1½ litres (2½ pints) chicken stock	1 tablespoon of each of the following herbs, finely chopped: parsley, chives, tarragon, chervil
40 g (1½ oz) butter	
40 g (scant 1½ oz) flour	1 tablespoon watercress, chopped
salt, pepper	150 g (5 oz) Gouda cheese, grated

Heat the chicken stock. Take a large saucepan and make a white roux with the butter and the flour: let it cook for a few moments and then add the hot stock. Whisk the stock and the sauce together to obtain a smooth mixture.

Season, and cook for ten minutes. Add all the herbs and the watercress and continue cooking for a further 4 to 5 minutes. Remove from the heat and stir in the grated cheese; go on stirring until the cheese is completely melted and incorporated into the soup mixture. Serve at once.

Elle says that although chicken cubes may be used to make the stock, the soup will taste much better if fresh stock, skimmed of its fat, is used.

[19]

VELOUTÉ DE LAITUE
Cream of lettuce soup

PREPARATION TIME: 10 minutes
COOKING TIME: 20 minutes
FOR SIX

2 cabbage lettuces
salt, pepper
3 eggs

250 g (scant 9 oz) crème fraîche
1 sandwich loaf
20 g (generous ½ oz) butter

Trim and wash the lettuces. Cook them for 20 minutes in 2 litres (3½ pints) boiling water which has been seasoned with the salt and pepper. Purée cooked lettuce with its liquid, then replace the soup in the pan and keep hot.

Beat the eggs and put them into the tureen in which the soup will be served. Mix in the crème fraîche.

Cut 6 slices of bread, remove the crusts and cut each slice into triangles. Fry them in butter to a golden-brown colour.

When ready to serve, pour the soup slowly into the cream and egg mixture in the tureen, whisking constantly. Check the seasoning and serve at once with the triangles of fried bread.

VELOUTÉ DE MOULES
Cream of mussel soup

PREPARATION TIME: 20 minutes
COOKING TIME: 30 minutes
FOR SIX

2 litres (3½ pints) mussels
2 shallots
3 leeks (white part only)
2 carrots
2 heads of celery
1 head of fennel
1 sprig of parsley
4 cloves of garlic

2 tablespoons olive oil
2 tablespoons plain flour
2 glasses dry white wine
salt, black pepper
4 tablespoons crème fraîche
2 egg yolks
1 lemon

Scrub the mussels and wash them quickly in several changes of water, discarding any not firmly closed. Do not leave them to soak in the water. Put them in a large pan without any liquid, cover and cook over a brisk heat, shaking the pan from time to time. After 3–4 minutes, the mussels will have opened: drain off and reserve the cooking juices, take the mussels out of their shells, put to one side. Discard any that have not opened.

Trim all the vegetables and slice them into thin strips; chop the parsley and the garlic. Put the olive oil, the sliced vegetables, the parsley and the garlic into a heavy casserole and cook over a gentle heat for about five minutes, then sprinkle the flour over the mixture, stirring with a wooden spoon. Continue cooking for a further 3–4 minutes.

Pour in 1¼ litres (2¼ pints) of water, the juice from the mussels and the white wine. Season, using very little salt, and cook for 15 minutes. Then add the mussels and bring the soup to the boil; remove from the heat and stir in the cream, which has been mixed with the beaten egg yolks and the juice of the lemon. Put back to cook gently for a further five minutes, stirring constantly. Serve at once.

Elle suggests that this delicious soup makes an excellent and economical first course for a formal dinner.

GASPACHO BLANC
White gaspacho

PREPARATION TIME: 30 minutes (2–3 hours in advance)
COOKING TIME: nil
FOR SIX

6 cloves of garlic	2 red peppers
3 tablespoons stale white breadcrumbs	500 ml (17½ fl oz) milk
	1 small glass white wine vinegar
500 ml (17½ fl oz) light skimmed stock	salt, pepper
	white bread
4 firm tomatoes	oil
1 cucumber	chopped parsley
2 green peppers	

Crush the garlic and thoroughly blend it into the breadcrumbs; add a few drops of stock to bind it into a paste. Put the rest of the stock into a saucepan and stir in the garlic/breadcrumb mixture.

Cut all the vegetables into small dice, put half aside in small bowls to be served with the soup. Pass the remainder, together with the stock, through a blender. Leave the soup to stand for 2–3 hours. During this time, bring the milk to the boil, then leave it to cool thoroughly. Add the milk to the soup and make up the required volume with cold water. Stir in the vinegar and season. Just before serving, add a few spoonfuls of chopped vegetables and a tray of ice-cubes.

Dice white bread and fry in oil to make croûtons. Serve these, the chopped vegetables and the chopped parsley in small individual bowls, letting each person make his selection to add to the chilled gaspacho.

(CONTINUED)

It will save time if the stock is prepared the day before and left overnight in the refrigerator; this also makes it easier to skim off the fat. The chicken can be eaten on another occasion as a separate dish, served with the vegetables with which it has been cooked, or used for a made-up chicken dish such as croquettes.

GERMINY AUX PAILLETTES
Sorrel soup

PREPARATION TIME: 20 minutes
COOKING TIME: for the stock, 1½ hours
FOR SIX

300 g (10½ oz) fresh sorrel	1 packet frozen puff pastry
1 chicken	75 g (2½ oz) grated Parmesan cheese
500 g (generous 1 lb) carrots	
2 small turnips	30 g (1 oz) butter
2 leeks	6 tablespoons crème fraîche
2 onions	6 egg yolks
1 head of celery	salt, pepper

Make a rich chicken stock by first putting the chicken into 3 litres (5¼ pints) of cold salted water. Bring to the simmer and, as the liquid begins to bubble, add all the vegetables, sliced. Continue cooking for 1–1½ hours.

Lightly dust a pastry board with flour and roll out the puff pastry. Fold in half of the Parmesan cheese and roll out once more, to a thickness of 5 mm (a bare ¼ inch). Grease a baking sheet with some of the butter and lay the pastry on it. Using a rule and a sharp knife, slice the pastry into strips 5 mm (¼ inch) wide and 15 cm (5–6 inches) long. Sprinkle them with the remainder of the grated cheese and cook for 10 minutes in a hot oven (220°C/425°F/Gas Mark 7).

Strip the leaves of sorrel from their spines, wash them, shake off surplus moisture and roughly shred them.

Heat the remaining butter in a saucepan, add the shredded sorrel and cook gently until all the liquid has evaporated. Remove from the heat. In another saucepan, whisk together the crème fraîche and the egg yolks, then beat in 1½ litres (2½ pints) of the chicken stock and the cooked sorrel. Taste and check the seasoning and put the soup over a low heat: stir and continue to cook until the mixture coats the spoon. Serve with the cheese straws.

(CONTINUED OPPOSITE)

SOUPE AUX CHOUX DE BRUXELLES
Brussels sprout soup

PREPARATION TIME: 15 minutes
COOKING TIME: 50 minutes
FOR SIX

1 kg (2¼ lb) Brussels sprouts	*salt, pepper*
1 large onion	*white bread*
200 g (7 oz) butter	*1 egg yolk*
6 chicken stock cubes	*100 g (3½ oz) crème fraîche*

Trim the outer leaves and the stalks from the sprouts. Peel the onion, chop it finely and cook it gently in half the butter in a casserole until it is transparent; then remove the onion and put to one side.

Put the sprouts into the casserole and pour in stock made by dissolving the chicken cubes in 2½ litres (4½ pints) of boiling water. Return the cooked onion, season and cook all together over a gentle heat for 45 minutes. Purée the whole mixture in a blender and then put back on the heat to simmer slowly.

Cut slices of bread into dice and fry them in the rest of the butter. Beat the egg yolk into the crème fraîche and pour into the soup. Serve immediately with the prepared croûtons.

Elle reminds you that the soup must not boil after you have added the egg and crème fraîche mixture.

BOUILLON DE LÉGUMES À L'OEUF
Clear vegetable soup

PREPARATION TIME: 15 minutes
COOKING TIME: 50 minutes
FOR SIX

250 g (9 oz) carrots	*1 sprig each of savory and thyme*
250 g (9 oz) small turnips	*1 bay leaf*
250 g (9 oz) leeks	*1 tablespoon chopped chervil*
2 onions	*salt, pepper*
3 cloves of garlic	*6 egg yolks*
1 head of celery	

Trim, wash and slice the vegetables and put them into a saucepan with 3 litres (5¼ pints) of water. Add the savory, thyme and the bay leaf. Bring to the boil and continue cooking just on the boil for 45 minutes. Remove from the heat and leave to rest for a few minutes.

Sieve the soup to remove the vegetables and then cook the soup for a further 5 minutes, having added the chopped chervil and seasoning. Pour the liquid, still boiling, into serving bowls and into each one carefully slide the yolk of an egg.

Elle suggests that the vegetables may be served separately as a purée, the filling of an omelette or as they are, with a knob of butter.

CHOU CRÉMÉ
Creamed cabbage salad

PREPARATION TIME: 15 minutes (half an hour in advance)
COOKING TIME: nil
FOR SIX

1 green cabbage (Savoy
  cabbage is a good variety for
  this dish)
100 g (3½ oz) sliced York ham
150 g (5 oz) Gruyère cheese

1 teaspoon strong mustard
100 g (3½ oz) crème fraîche
6 tablespoons olive oil
wine vinegar
salt, pepper

Remove the coarse outer leaves of the cabbage. Strip off both the tender leaves and heart of the cabbage, wash them and trim off the stalks. Slice finely.

Dice the ham and grate the cheese coarsely. Arrange cabbage, cheese and ham in a salad bowl.

To make the sauce, begin by mixing the mustard into the crème fraîche. Add the oil, drop by drop, whipping constantly. Finally add a few drops of vinegar to taste and season.

Pour the sauce over the salad and leave to marinate in a cool place for 30 minutes.

CONCOMBRE AU CHÈVRE FERMIER
Cucumber and goat's cheese salad

PREPARATION TIME: 10 minutes (half an hour in advance)
COOKING TIME: nil
FOR SIX

750 g (generous 1½ lb)
  cucumbers
60 g (2 oz) goat's cheese (firm)

salt, white pepper
50 ml (1¾ fl oz) lemon juice
50 ml (1¾ fl oz) hazelnut oil

Trim and, if preferred, peel the cucumbers and cut them crossways into thin round slices. Put them in a colander, sprinkle with salt and let them drip for 30 minutes.

Drain the cucumber well on kitchen paper and put the slices into a bowl with the lemon juice, mix well. Then arrange the slices in six portions on separate plates, and add pepper.

Cut the goat's cheese into thin slices and add two or three to each plate of cucumber. Finally, sprinkle with hazelnut oil.

Elle says that the original recipe used a farm cheese from Sainte-Maure in Touraine. This may be unobtainable in this country but any equivalent commercial goat's cheese, the one in the form of a cylinder, will be just as good.

BAGNA CAUDA
Vegetable dip

PREPARATION TIME: **30 minutes**
COOKING TIME: **10 minutes**
FOR SIX

10 salted anchovies	1 bunch of radishes
2 heads of fennel	1 cucumber
1 head of celery	4 heads of chicory
2 peppers (1 red, 1 green)	5 peeled cloves of garlic
3 tomatoes	200 ml (7 fl oz) olive oil
6 baby globe artichokes	100 ml (3½ fl oz) double cream

Soak the anchovies for some hours to remove the salt, changing the water several times. Drain and fillet them (note: if salted anchovies cannot be found, tinned may be used, well drained of their oil and dried on kitchen paper).

Wash and break up the fennel into leaves, wash and trim the celery and cut into sticks. Clean and de-seed the peppers and cut the flesh into strips. Wash tomatoes and artichokes and, according to size, cut them either into halves or quarters. Trim the radishes and cut the cucumber into sticks. Trim the chicory and separate the leaves. Arrange all the prepared vegetables on small dishes, either mixed together or separate, as preferred.

Make the sauce in a fondue pan. Put the chopped garlic and the olive oil into the pan, bring to a simmer, add the anchovy fillets and continue cooking and stirring until a smooth sauce results. Stir in the cream and let the sauce simmer for a few minutes.

Put the fondue pan on its heated stand in the middle of the table. The prepared vegetables are dipped and eaten by each guest at will. Do not worry if the sauce separates.

Elle notes that the vegetables included in the recipe are those that would normally be found in any French or Italian market. Other raw vegetables such as carrots or cauliflower may be added or substituted. A dry Italian white wine, such as Orvieto, goes admirably with this dish.

SALADES VARIÉES
Bouquet of salads

PREPARATION TIME: **20 minutes**
COOKING TIME: **nil**
FOR SIX

1 good bunch of watercress	2 dessertspoons peanut oil
250 g (9 oz) chicory	2 dessertspoons wine vinegar
250 g (9 oz) radicchio	2 dessertspoons walnut oil
1 lettuce	2 dessertspoons cider vinegar
2 dessertspoons olive oil	salt, pepper
1 lemon	

Trim, wash and drain all the salad vegetables. Line a long flat dish with lettuce leaves. Prepare three salads in separate bowls: the white chicory leaves in a dressing of olive oil and lemon juice, the radicchio in peanut oil and wine vinegar, the watercress in walnut oil and cider vinegar. Arrange the three salads side by side on the bed of lettuce leaves, each guest choosing according to taste.

Elle says that this attractive salad is delicious with salami and other cold meats.

SALADE D'ARTICHAUTS AUX AMANDES
Artichoke and almond salad

PREPARATION TIME: 15 minutes
COOKING TIME: 20 minutes
FOR SIX

6 good globe artichokes or 6
  tinned artichoke bottoms
75 g (generous 2½ oz) blanched
  almonds
2 lemons
50 g (scant 2 oz) flour

salt, pepper
1 lettuce
200 g (7 oz) crème fraîche
50 ml (1¾ fl oz) cider vinegar
bunch of mixed fresh herbs

It is simpler and probably cheaper to use tinned artichoke bottoms in this recipe. The classic method uses fresh artichokes, in which case take off the outer leaves and, with a sharp knife, neatly trim the remaining leaves; sprinkle the bottoms with lemon juice. Mix the flour into a paste with a little water, add it to a large saucepan of salted boiling water, and put in the artichoke bottoms. Bring back to the boil and cook for about 20 minutes until tender; remove and drain. It should now be easy to remove the chokes from the artichoke bottoms. Trim off any remains of leaf or stalk and set aside to cool.

Wash and drain the lettuce and line the serving dish with the leaves; on top, arrange the artichoke bottoms. Whip the crème fraîche sufficiently to lighten it, stir in the cider vinegar and chopped mixed herbs and pour the dressing over the artichokes. Lightly grill the almonds and sprinkle on top.

From 'Le Galion' restaurant in Concarneau in Brittany: the chef recommends that a Chablis or Pouilly-Fuissé be drunk with this dish.

SALADE FRAÎCHE AUX AVOCATS
Avocado salad

PREPARATION TIME: 10 minutes
COOKING TIME: nil
FOR SIX

2 avocado pears
4 onions
6 medium-sized tomatoes
olive oil

wine vinegar
mustard
salt, pepper

Cut the avocado pears in half lengthways, remove the stones and carefully skin them. Cut them in crescent-shaped slices and arrange them in a salad bowl. Add the sliced onions and the tomatoes cut into quarters.

Make a well-spiced classic French dressing, using plenty of mustard. Pour the dressing on to the salad, and turn it over once or twice with the salad servers. Serve at once: the salad will be all the better if the ingredients have been kept in a cool place.

Elle warns that over-ripe avocado pears should be avoided.

SALAD GRENOBLOISE
Mixed cabbage salad

PREPARATION TIME: 15 minutes
COOKING TIME: nil
FOR SIX

1 small white cabbage
dry cider
2 Golden Delicious apples
2 Granny Smith apples
2 lemons
2 avocado pears
10 small white onions
100 g (3½ oz) shelled walnuts

For the sauce:
1 small pot of plain yoghurt
1 tablespoon strong mustard
6 tablespoons peanut oil
2 tablespoons cider vinegar
salt, pepper

Remove the coarse outer leaves of the cabbage, cut it into quarters, trim off the thick parts of the stalk and slice as finely as possible. Put the sliced cabbage into a dish, cover it with cider and leave it to marinate for 15 minutes. Peel and core the apples, cut them into slices and sprinkle with lemon juice. Do the same with the avocado pears. Peel, trim and slice the onions.

Drain the cabbage and put it in a salad bowl. Mix in the sliced apples, avocados, onions and walnuts. Prepare the sauce by thoroughly mixing together all its ingredients. Pour over the salad, turn it over once or twice and serve.

SALADE DE CHOU ROUGE AU LARD
Red cabbage and bacon salad

PREPARATION TIME: 15 minutes
COOKING TIME: 5 minutes
FOR SIX

1 firm red cabbage
300 g (10½ oz) streaky bacon
3 tablespoons olive oil

1 tablespoon wine vinegar
1 teaspoon mustard
salt, pepper

Strip the outer leaves from the cabbage and cut it into quarters. Trim off the stalks and, using a very sharp knife, slice the leaves as finely as possible. Plunge the bacon into boiling water, cook for three minutes, remove, drain and cut crossways into strips. Fry gently in one tablespoon of oil.

Take a salad bowl and make a French dressing in it using the rest of the oil, the vinegar, mustard, salt and pepper. Put in the sliced cabbage and turn it over until it is thoroughly covered by the dressing.

Just before serving, add the warm strips of fried bacon to the salad and pour on the hot fat from the frying pan.

Elle says that the cabbage may tend to darken after it has been sliced. It will regain its colour when the dressing has been mixed into it.

SALADE RACHEL
Chicory and walnut salad

PREPARATION TIME: 15 minutes
COOKING TIME: nil
FOR SIX

500 g (generous 1 lb) chicory
100 g (3½ oz) shelled walnuts
2 limes

200 g (7 oz) crisp eating apples
salt, pepper
200 g (7 oz) low-fat fromage
   blanc

Squeeze the limes and put their juice into a salad bowl. Remove the outer leaves from the chicory, trim the stalks and cut in half lengthways. Take out the hard core with a sharp-pointed knife and cut the rest crossways into slices about 1 cm (⅜ in) in depth. Put to one side.

Keep back a few walnuts for decoration and put the remainder through a blender. Peel and core the apples, cut them into quarters, and then into thin slices. Gently toss the apple slices in the squeezed lime juice. Remove a few which will be used for decoration. To the rest, add the crushed walnuts, salt, plenty of black pepper, the fromage blanc and the sliced chicory. Mix all the ingredients together and decorate the salad with the remaining walnuts and apple slices.

Elle suggests that those who are less diet-conscious may prefer to use crème fraîche instead of the low-fat fromage blanc.

SALADE TIÈDE DE L'ALLIER
Warm chicken salad

PREPARATION TIME: 30 minutes
COOKING TIME: 20 minutes
FOR SIX

2 chicken breasts
small bunch of watercress
2 lettuces (preferably 1 batavia
   and 1 oak leaf or radicchio)
1 curly endive
1 tomato

175 g (good 6 oz) butter
1 tablespoon olive oil
salt, pepper
500 ml (18 fl oz) wine vinegar
200 ml (7 fl oz) chicken stock

Trim and wash the salad vegetables, spin or shake out the water. Peel and de-seed the tomato and chop the flesh. Heat 60 g (2 oz) of the butter and the oil in a pan and seal the chicken breasts on both sides. As soon as they are a light golden colour, season, reduce the heat, cover the pan and cook gently for 20 minutes. (The chicken breasts should be cooked through but still tender.) Remove from the pan, cut them crossways into strips and keep in a warm place.

Pour off the cooking fat and return the pan to the heat. Add the vinegar and vigorously deglaze the pan with the back of a fork. Then add the chicken stock, stir and, over a brisk heat, reduce the sauce to a quarter of its volume. Remove from the heat and whisk in the rest of the butter, knob by knob. Occasionally warm the sauce for a few moments over a low heat during this process. Check the seasoning.

Arrange the salad vegetables, the chopped tomato and the chicken pieces in a salad bowl. Pour the sauce over it, mix well by turning it over a few times and serve at once.

Elle suggests that a chilled rosé wine from the Loire is best with this dish.

SALADE DE RIZ À L'OMELETTE
Egg and rice salad

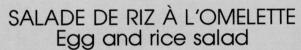

PREPARATION TIME: 15 minutes (3 hours in advance)
COOKING TIME: 15 minutes
FOR SIX

6 eggs	1 green pepper
200 g (7 oz) long grain rice	100 g (3½ oz) button mushrooms
mixed fresh herbs	1 lemon
10 tablespoons olive oil	wine vinegar
2 red peppers	salt, pepper

Wash the rice under running water and put it into a large pan of boiling salted water. Return to the boil and cook for about 15 minutes.

Beat the eggs with a pinch or two of fresh chopped herbs. Heat 4 tablespoons of oil in an omelette pan and make two separate omelettes. When the surface is just set, slide them flat onto two plates. Allow to cool.

Drain the rice and run it under cold water so that the grains are fluffy and separate. Cut the peppers in half, remove stalks and seeds and slice into thin strips lengthways. Trim the stalks of the mushrooms, slice them and sprinkle with lemon juice. Cut the omelettes into thin strips.

Arrange the rice, peppers, mushrooms and omelette strips in a salad bowl. Make a dressing to taste with the rest of the oil, the wine vinegar, salt, pepper and a pinch of chopped herbs. Mix gently together so as not to break up the omelette strips: put in a cool place for at least three hours.

Just before serving, sprinkle the salad with the rest of the chopped herbs.

SALADE BRESSANE
Chicken-liver salad

PREPARATION TIME: 30 minutes
COOKING TIME: 20 minutes
FOR SIX

12 chicken livers	750 ml (generous 1¼ pints)
4 large artichokes or 6 tinned	peanut oil (plus 2 extra
artichoke bottoms (see p. 25)	tablespoons)
1 lemon	2 egg yolks
500 g (generous 1 lb) lamb's	mustard
lettuce	1 teaspoon brandy
salt, pepper	1 tablespoon port
10 g (a good knob) butter	2 tablespoons tomato ketchup

If using fresh artichokes, remove their leaves and chokes with a thin sharp knife. Cook the bottoms in boiling salted water, to which the lemon juice has been added, for 15–20 minutes. They will be ready when the point of a knife penetrates them easily. Drain, allow to cool, neatly trim off any remains of leaf or choke and put to one side. Wash and drain the lamb's lettuce and also put aside.

Season the chicken livers, cut into bite-sized pieces and cook them over a brisk heat in the butter and the two tablespoons of oil, turning them constantly.

Line individual dishes with lamb's lettuce and divide the hot chicken livers and cut pieces of artichoke bottom among them. Serve at once, accompanied by a mayonnaise made in the classic fashion, of egg yolks, mustard and oil. When it is stiff, fold in the brandy, port and the ketchup.

From the 'Hostellerie de la Caillère' in Candé-sur-Beuvron in the Loire region: the chef recommends that a local white wine be drunk with it

CHAMPIGNONS AUX ÉPINARDS
Mushroom and spinach salad

PREPARATION TIME: 15 minutes
COOKING TIME: nil
FOR SIX TO EIGHT

300 g (10½ oz) button
 mushrooms
150 g (5 oz) fresh spinach
50 ml (1¾ fl oz) lemon juice

salt, pepper
6 dessertspoons peanut oil
chives

Trim the stalks of the mushrooms, wipe and slice them. Sprinkle lemon juice over them and season.

Tear the stalks from the spinach, wash and thoroughly drain the leaves, taking care to remove all surplus moisture. Line a salad dish with spinach leaves and arrange the sliced mushrooms on them. Put in a cool place.

Just before serving, dress the salad with peanut oil and sprinkle with chopped chives.

SALADE D'ÉPINARDS AUX POMMES
Spinach and apple salad

PREPARATION TIME: 15 minutes
COOKING TIME: 10 minutes
FOR SIX

350 g (12½ oz) fresh spinach
500 g (generous 1 lb) firm eating
 apples
olive oil
vinegar

salt, pepper
2 shallots, chopped
6 chicken livers
1 tablespoon grilled peanuts

Make a simple dressing with 4 tablespoons of olive oil, 1 tablespoon of vinegar and seasoning. Strip the stalks entirely from the spinach, wash the leaves and drain them thoroughly. Arrange the spinach and the chopped shallots in a salad bowl, sprinkle with dressing.

Peel and core the apples and cut them into dice and lightly brown them quickly in a pan in 3 tablespoons of oil. Put to one side.

Split the chicken livers and cook them in 2 tablespoons of oil. Remove when still slightly pink in the centre and cut up into pieces. Arrange apples, chicken livers and the peanuts in the spinach salad, mix and serve at once.

Elle emphasises that for a really successful salad, only the youngest and tenderest leaves of spinach should be used.

SALADE D'ORANGES
Orange and olive salad

PREPARATION TIME: 15 minutes
COOKING TIME: nil
FOR SIX

6 oranges
100 g (3½ oz) black olives
6 small white onions
olive oil

1 lemon
1 teaspoon paprika
1 pinch cayenne pepper
salt, pepper

Peel the oranges neatly, divide into segments and remove skin and pith. Arrange in a serving dish with the olives and the onions, cut into slices.

Make a dressing with olive oil, the juice of the lemon, paprika, cayenne pepper and seasoning. Pour it over the salad and serve chilled.

Elle says this is a splendid hot-weather salad.

SALADE PAYSANNE
Country salad

PREPARATION TIME: 20 minutes
COOKING TIME: nil
FOR SIX

6 potatoes (boiled in their skins)
2 red peppers
2 onions (red if possible)
4 tomatoes
200 g (7 oz) salami
2 hard-boiled eggs

100 ml (3½ fl oz) olive oil
2 tablespoons vinegar
fresh mixed herbs
salt, pepper
100 g (3½ oz) black olives

When the potatoes are cold, peel and slice them in rounds. With a sharp-pointed knife, remove the stalk, seeds and membranes from the peppers and slice them into rings. Peel and slice the onions and cut the tomatoes into quarters. Slice the salami, remove the skin and cut each slice into strips. Peel the eggs, chop them finely and pass them through a sieve.

Make a dressing with oil, vinegar, chopped mixed herbs and seasoning. Arrange all the salad ingredients in a large bowl, pour on the dressing and turn the salad until the dressing is thoroughly mixed in. Decorate with black olives and sieved egg.

Elle advises that either cider or white wine vinegar should be used so the potatoes do not become discoloured.

OEUFS EN COCOTTE ALBERT
Baked Eggs Albert

PREPARATION TIME: 10 minutes
COOKING TIME: 15 minutes
FOR SIX

12 eggs
75 g (2½ oz) small button
   mushrooms
150 g (5 oz) peeled prawns
75 g (2½ oz) butter

3 shallots
1 small glass of brandy
125 g (4½ oz) crème fraîche
salt, pepper

Wipe the mushrooms, remove the stalks and cut into slices. Cut the prawns into small pieces. Heat three-quarters of the butter in a frying pan and quickly cook prawns and mushrooms together. Chop up the shallots, add them to the pan and continue cooking until they are just transparent. Pour in the brandy and flame the mixture, then stir in the crème fraîche. Season.

Remove the prawns and mushrooms from the pan and keep in a warm place. Reduce the sauce left in the pan until it has a smooth, thick consistency.

Butter individual fireproof dishes and break two eggs into each one. Arrange them in a flat pan containing hot water and cook for 3–4 minutes or until the eggs are just cooked, but still soft. Mix prawns, mushrooms and sauce together, pour over the eggs and serve at once.

From the 'Restaurant Longchamp' in the Paris-17ᵉ Hôtel Méridien: the chef recommends that a Chablis be drunk with this dish.

OEUFS À LA MOUTARDE
Eggs in mustard sauce

PREPARATION TIME: 10 minutes
COOKING TIME: 20 minutes
FOR SIX

6 hard-boiled eggs
50 g (scant 2 oz) strong mustard
400 g (14 oz) crème fraîche

150 g (5 oz) grated Gruyère
   cheese
pepper

Divide each hard-boiled egg in two and arrange the halves, cut-side downwards, in a well-buttered fireproof dish.

To make the sauce, mix the mustard and the crème fraîche together and stir in 100 g (3½ oz) of the grated cheese. Season. Pour this sauce over the eggs and sprinkle the remainder of the cheese evenly over the surface. Cook in a very hot oven (230°C/450°F/Gas Mark 8) for 20 minutes. Serve hot.

Elle points out that no salt should be added since ample is provided by the mustard.

[31]

OEUFS AU CIDRE
Eggs in cider

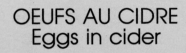

PREPARATION TIME: 15 minutes
COOKING TIME: 15 minutes
FOR SIX

9 eggs
5 large onions
50 g (scant 2 oz) butter
35 g (generous 1 oz) flour
500 ml (17½ fl oz) still dry cider

3 tablespoons strong mustard
100 g (3½ oz) crème fraîche
salt, pepper
chopped chives

Hard-boil the eggs. Peel the onions and chop them finely. Melt the butter in a heavy casserole and slowly cook the chopped onion until it is transparent. Sprinkle on the flour and moisten gradually with the cider, mixing everything together. Cook over a low heat for a further 10 minutes, stirring constantly and making sure that the mixture does not boil.

Mix the mustard and the crème fraîche together and add them to the sauce in the casserole. Stir together and season.

When the eggs are done, run them under cold water to make peeling easier. Cut them in half and arrange them in a warmed serving dish, cut-side upwards. Cover with the sauce and sprinkle with chopped chives. Serve hot.

Elle advises that chopped parsley can be used if chives are unobtainable. Cider as used in the cooking should be drunk with this dish.

OEUFS POCHÉS AUX PETITS LÉGUMES
Poached eggs with vegetables

PREPARATION TIME: 20 minutes
COOKING TIME: 25 minutes
FOR SIX

12 new-laid eggs
250 g (9 oz) carrots
150 g (5 oz) young turnips
250 g (9 oz) French beans
4 shallots

150 ml (5 fl oz) wine vinegar
300 g (10½ oz) butter
salt, white pepper
150 g (5 oz) crème fraîche

Trim all the vegetables and cut the carrots and turnips into strips about the same size as the French beans. Cook each vegetable separately for about 10 minutes in boiling salted water. Drain, run cold water through them and drain again. Put to one side.

Peel and chop the shallots and put them in a pan with 100 ml (3½ fl oz) of wine vinegar. Cook until the liquid has evaporated; these should be set aside as well.

Mix the first vegetables together and heat them through in 50 g (scant 2 oz) butter. Season and keep in a warm place.

Next prepare the butter sauce. Put the shallots on a gentle heat, stir in the crème fraîche and cook very slowly until the mixture thickens. On a very low heat, beat in the rest of the butter knob by knob, until a smooth sauce results. Season and keep the sauce just warm in a double-boiler.

Put the remainder of the wine vinegar into 1 litre (1¾ pints) of water, bring to the boil and carefully break the eggs separately into it. Keep just on the boil for 3 minutes, then remove the eggs and drain them on kitchen paper.

Arrange the vegetables on warmed individual plates, put two poached eggs on each and cover with the sauce (which should first be passed through a sieve). Serve at once.

From 'Le Gambetta' restaurant in Houilles outside Paris: the chef suggests that a Sancerre be drunk with this dish.

BOUILLABAISSE BORGNE
Eggs provençale

PREPARATION TIME: 20 minutes
COOKING TIME: 30 minutes
FOR SIX

12 new-laid eggs	100 ml (3½ fl oz) olive oil
5 tomatoes	bouquet garni
1 kg (2¼ lb) potatoes (use a firm variety)	2 sprigs of fennel (fresh or dried)
	grated peel of 1 orange
2 onions	½ teaspoon of powdered saffron
5 cloves of garlic	salt, pepper
4 leeks	stick of French bread

Peel the tomatoes, cut them into quarters and remove the pips. Peel the potatoes, the onions and the garlic and trim the leeks to leave only the white part. Chop up the leeks and onions. Wipe any moisture from the peeled potatoes (which should not have been washed) and cut them into round slices about 5 mm (¼ inch) thick.

Heat the oil in a heavy casserole and begin by slowly cooking the chopped leek and onion. When the onion is transparent, add tomatoes, crushed garlic, the bouquet garni, fennel and grated orange peel. Pour in 1¼ litres (2¼ pints) of water into which the saffron has been stirred. (Note: the colour if not the flavour may be achieved by substituting powdered turmeric.) Finally add the slices of potatoes, and season; bring to the boil and cook uncovered over a brisk heat for 15 minutes.

When the potatoes are cooked, remove all the vegetables with a perforated spoon and arrange them on a warmed serving dish. Break the eggs one at a time into a cup and slide each one carefully into the boiling soup: let them poach for 3–4 minutes and remove them in turn and put them with the vegetables on the serving dish.

Cut the French stick into thin slices and toast under the grill. Place them in the bottom of the soup bowls and pour the soup over them. Poached eggs and vegetables are served separately.

CRÊPES AU SARRASIN À L'OEUF
Buckwheat pancakes with eggs

PREPARATION TIME: 10 minutes (2 hours in advance)
COOKING TIME: about 2 minutes for each pancake
FOR FIFTEEN PANCAKES

250 g (9 oz) buckwheat flour	The filling:
3 eggs	15 eggs
250 ml (9 fl oz) milk	100 g (3½ oz) grated Gruyère
250 ml (9 fl oz) water	cheese
oil, pinch of salt	

Sieve the flour into a mixing bowl, make a well and break 3 eggs into it. Beat together and extend the mixture little by little with the milk, the water, a tablespoon of oil and the salt, until the batter is smooth. It should be a little thicker than ordinary pancake batter. Cover the bowl with a cloth and leave for 2 hours.

Heat a pancake griddle which has been greased with a ball of kitchen paper dipped in oil. Pour a measure of batter into the centre of the griddle and, using a circular motion, spread it to the edges with a pancake fork or spatula. After about half a minute, the pancake will come away from the surface of the griddle; turn it over and break an egg onto the pancake, keeping back some of the white if possible. Sprinkle with grated cheese and when the yolk of egg has taken, fold two outer edges of pancake over it. Leave on the griddle for a few seconds more and then serve at once.

Elle recommends a dry cider as the best accompaniment to this Breton dish.

[33]

SOUFFLÉS AUX OEUFS
Surprise soufflés

PREPARATION TIME: 25 minutes
COOKING TIME: 15 minutes
FOR SIX

6 new-laid eggs	*grated nutmeg*
50 g (scant 2 oz) butter	*3 eggs, separated*
50 g (scant 2 oz) flour	*50 g (scant 2 oz) grated Gruyère*
250 ml (9 fl oz) milk	*cheese*
salt, pepper	

Melt the butter in a medium saucepan, add the flour and cook for 3 minutes, stirring frequently. Pour in all the cold milk and bring to the boil, whisking constantly. Season with salt, pepper and nutmeg and remove the pan from the heat at the first bubble.

Leave the mixture to stand for 1 minute, then stir in 3 egg yolks, one by one, and then the grated cheese. The 3 egg whites should have been beaten until quite stiff: fold them in and season the mixture to taste.

Butter six individual soufflé dishes generously, and pour in the mixture to the depth of 3 cm (a good inch). Make a well in each with the back of a spoon and break a new-laid egg into each. Fill the dishes with the remainder of the mixture: an icing bag with a large nozzle is excellent for this operation.

Cook in a pre-heated oven (200°C/400°F/Gas Mark 6) for 15 minutes. If you feel it necessary to check the progress of your soufflés, wait at least 10 minutes into the cooking before opening the oven door.

OMELETTE AUX LÉGUMES
Vegetable omelette

PREPARATION TIME: 25 minutes
COOKING TIME: 30 minutes
FOR SIX

3 tomatoes	*parsley*
3 aubergines	*mixed herbs (parsley, chives,*
1 green pepper	*tarragon, chervil)*
1 red pepper	*cooking salt, sea salt, pepper*
2 onions	*tabasco*
oil	*12 eggs*

Peel the tomatoes, remove the seeds and cut into pieces. Trim the aubergines and cut them into dice, sprinkle with a handful of sea salt and leave for 20 minutes. Take the stalk and pips out of the peppers and cut them into rings. Peel and finely chop the onions.

Heat 100 ml (3½ fl oz) of oil in a heavy pan and gently cook the chopped onion until it is transparent. Then add the tomatoes and peppers and leave to cook for 15 minutes more.

Rinse the aubergines in running cold water, drain and dry on kitchen paper and cook them separately in 100 ml (3½ oz) of oil for 20 minutes. Drain them well and add to the other cooked vegetables; sprinkle with chopped parsley and the mixed herbs and cook together for 3 more minutes over a low heat. Season and add a few drops of tabasco to taste; the mixture should have a distinct and spicy flavour.

Beat the eggs with a little salt and pepper. One or two large omelettes may be made or a number of smaller ones, according to wish and the availability of omelette pans. Slide the omelettes on to the serving dishes or plates, spread the filling on one side and fold the other side over. Serve at once.

Elle says that this omelette is also quite delicious eaten cold and is ideal for picnics.

CHARLOTTE FROMAGÈRE
Cheese Charlotte

PREPARATION TIME: 15 minutes
COOKING TIME: 40 minutes
FOR SIX

400 g (14 oz) Morbier cheese (or
  Gruyère)
1 stick of French bread
6 eggs
1 litre (1¾ pints) milk

salt, pepper
1 pinch of paprika
1 pinch of grated nutmeg
30 g (1 oz) butter

Cut the cheese into small thin slices and also thinly slice the bread. Butter a soufflé dish, or similar ovenproof dish, and fill it with alternate layers of bread and cheese.

Beat the eggs and boil the milk. Pour the beaten egg slowly into the milk, stirring constantly. Season with a little salt and pepper, paprika and nutmeg. Pour this mixture over the bread and cheese layers and leave to soak for ten minutes, occasionally loosening the edges with a spatula. Dot the surface with knobs of butter and cook in a hot oven (230°C/450°F/Gas Mark 8) for 40 minutes.

Elle suggests that this country dish from the French Alps make a satisfying light meal when accompanied by a salad.

PAIN PERDU FROMAGÉ
Cheese delights

PREPARATION TIME: 15 minutes
COOKING TIME: 15 minutes
FOR SIX

100 g (3½ oz) grated Emmenthal
  cheese
50 g (scant 2 oz) butter
16 slices from a small white loaf

4 eggs
salt, pepper
nutmeg
500 ml (17½ fl oz) milk

Butter a gratin dish and put the bread in two layers into it. Beat the eggs with pepper, a little salt, some grated nutmeg and three-quarters of the cheese. Warm the milk and mix it with the egg mixture. Pour over the bread and leave for a few minutes until it has been completely absorbed. Sprinkle the rest of the cheese over the surface and bake in a very hot oven (230°C/450°F/Gas Mark 8) for 15 minutes. Serve at once.

Elle says this delicious dish is not only quick to make but also very economical.

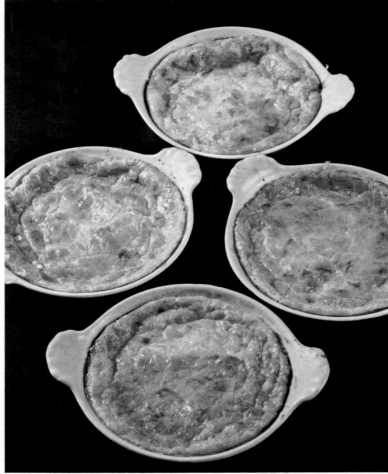

CROQUETTES DE CAMEMBERT
Camembert puffs

PREPARATION TIME: 25 minutes
COOKING TIME: 3 minutes per batch
FOR SIX

1 Camembert cheese	*100 g (3½ oz) crème fraîche*
25 g (scant 1 oz) butter	*2 eggs*
20 g (¾ oz) flour	*1 stale white loaf*
250 ml (9 fl oz) milk	*additional flour*
salt, pepper, nutmeg	*cooking oil*

Melt the butter in a pan, add the flour and whisk into a roux. Cook for 2 minutes, whisking constantly. Remove from heat and beat in half of the cold milk. Put the pan back on the heat and bring very slowly to the boil. Add the rest of the milk very gradually, beating until a thick sauce is obtained. Season and grate in nutmeg to taste. Continue cooking for 10 minutes. Cool thoroughly.

Carefully remove the outer crust of the Camembert and put the cheese into a mixing bowl. Add equal parts of the cold sauce and the crème fraîche and mix all three ingredients together very thoroughly. Check seasoning. Put the mixture into an icing bag. Lightly flour a pastry board and squeeze little balls of mixture on to it. They should be about the size of a walnut.

Beat the eggs thoroughly. Remove the crusts from the loaf and put the bread into a blender to make fine breadcrumbs. Take each ball of mixture and roll it first in flour, then in the beaten egg, and finally in breadcrumbs. Put six at a time in a wire basket and plunge them into cooking oil which should be hot, but not smoking. When lightly browned, remove, drain quickly on kitchen paper and serve hot.

From the restaurant 'Au Caneton' in Orbec in Normandy: the chef recommends that sparkling cider be drunk with the cheese puffs.

BONHOMME
Cheese batter

PREPARATION TIME: 5 minutes
COOKING TIME: 20 minutes
FOR SIX

75 g (generous 2½ oz) grated	*salt, pepper*
Emmenthal cheese	*nutmeg*
40 g (scant 1½ oz) flour	*500 ml (17½ fl oz) milk*
6 eggs	

Sieve the flour into a bowl, make a well and break in the eggs. Season and add a pinch of grated nutmeg. Beat the eggs and the flour together and moisten with the warmed milk to give a smooth batter free of lumps.

Butter individual baking dishes, pour in the mixture and sprinkle grated cheese over each one. Cook in a very hot oven (230°C/450°F/ Gas Mark 8) for 15–18 minutes. Serve at once.

Elle says that this batter can be also made in a single large dish.

ASPERGES AU GRATIN
Gratin of asparagus

PREPARATION TIME: 20 minutes
COOKING TIME: 30 minutes
FOR SIX

2 kg (4½ lb) asparagus
50 g (scant 2 oz) butter
50 g (scant 2 oz) plain flour
500 ml (17½ fl oz) milk
salt, pepper

nutmeg
3 egg yolks
75 g (generous 2½ oz) crème
    fraîche

Since this dish is covered in a sauce, it is not essential to use asparagus of the best appearance and quality.

Trim the stalks of the asparagus and cook them, tied into bundles, in boiling salted water for 10–15 minutes. Remove and drain well, keeping the cooking water to one side. Cut off the asparagus tips to a length of 6–8 cm (2½–3 inches), and divide the stalks into 1-cm (½-inch) pieces. Arrange all the asparagus on a serving dish with the tips on top and put into a hot oven for 10 minutes to evaporate their liquid.

Meanwhile melt the butter in a pan and make a roux by vigorously stirring the flour into it. Extend it with the milk and 100 ml (3½ fl oz) of cooking water, season and add a little grated nutmeg.

Beat the yolks and the crème fraîche together. Having taken the pan from the heat, stir the egg mixture into the sauce. Take the serving dish from the oven, drain off any liquid and cover the asparagus with the sauce. Put the dish under a grill until the surface starts to brown, then serve at once.

Elle says that it is essential that when the sauce is poured on to the asparagus, both are hot.

ASPERGES À LA SAVOYARDE
Asparagus Savoy

PREPARATION TIME: 30 minutes
COOKING TIME: 35 minutes
FOR SIX

1½ kg (3 lb 5 oz) asparagus
3 slices York ham
5 tablespoons oil
75 g (generous 2½ oz) grated
    Parmesan cheese

40 g (scant 1½ oz) melted butter
6 eggs
salt, pepper

Trim the asparagus and tie into 3 or 4 bundles. Plunge them into a large pan of boiling salted water and let them cook for about 20 minutes. They will be ready when the sharp point of a knife passes easily through the stalk. Remove and drain well. Cut off the tips to a length of 4 cm (1½–2 inches) and divide the rest into pieces 1 cm (½ inch) long.

Cut the ham into small squares. Oil either one large or six individual ovenproof dishes and line the bottoms evenly with the ham. Cover this with the asparagus pieces and sprinkle with half of the grated Parmesan. Pour half of the melted butter over the dish and cook in a fairly hot oven (200°C/400°F/Gas Mark 6) for 10 minutes.

As soon as the dish starts to brown, fry the 6 eggs in the rest of the oil. Put them on top of the asparagus pieces and garnish with the asparagus tips. Season, sprinkle the rest of the grated cheese and pour the remainder of the melted butter over the dish and put it back in the oven just long enough to melt the cheese. Serve at once.

Elle stresses the importance of thoroughly draining the asparagus after cooking, otherwise the appearance of the dish will be spoiled. Drain off any further juices before the eggs are put in place.

CRÈME D'AUBERGINES
Aubergine purée

PREPARATION TIME: 20 minutes
COOKING TIME: 30 minutes
FOR SIX

4 medium-sized aubergines	1 handful of chopped parsley
2 lemons	1 level teaspoon salt
1 clove of garlic	olive oil
75 g (generous 2½ oz) tahini	Greek parsley

Completely wrap each aubergine in kitchen foil and put the parcels in a very hot oven (240°C/475°F/Gas Mark 9) for 20 minutes. Remove from the oven, take them out of the foil, and peel them.

Put the flesh of the aubergines into a blender, adding the juice of the two lemons, the crushed garlic, the tahini, the salt and the chopped parsley. Mix everything together well and serve, sprinkled with olive oil and garnished with sprigs of Greek parsley.

Elle says that tahini (sesame seed paste) will be found in any Greek and most Indian grocers.

TARATO
Purée of vegetables

PREPARATION TIME: 20 minutes
COOKING TIME: 30 minutes
FOR SIX

4 aubergines	salt, pepper
2 red peppers	1 pinch cayenne pepper
3 green peppers	3 tablespoons olive oil
2 small pots natural yoghurt	100 ml (3½ fl oz) water
5 peeled cloves of garlic	black olives
2 lemons	

Trim the aubergines, halve them lengthways and put them in a very hot oven (230°C/450°F/Gas Mark 8). Leave them to cook until the flesh is soft; spoon it out and put it on one side.

Put the peppers under the grill, turning them until they are blistered on all sides. Peel them and remove stalks and seeds and put the flesh through a vegetable Mouli. Then put the peppers into a blender together with the aubergine flesh, the yoghurt, the garlic, juice of the lemons, seasoning, pinch of cayenne pepper, the oil and the water. Blend to a smooth paste, fill individual serving bowls and put in the refrigerator. At the moment of serving, decorate with stoned black olives.

Elle recommends that you wrap the peppers in damp kitchen paper when they come from under the grill, and leave for 5 minutes; this will facilitate peeling.

A well-chilled rosé wine from Provence is a suitable accompaniment to this dish.

AVOCATS SURPRISE
Stuffed avocados

PREPARATION TIME: 20 minutes
COOKING TIME: nil
FOR SIX

3 large avocados	6 egg yolks
1 lemon	strong mustard
4 limes	3 tablespoons olive oil
6 tablespoons chopped tarragon	salt, pepper
6 tablespoons chopped chervil	1 tin (200 g/7 oz) tuna fish

Cut each avocado in half lengthways and remove the stone. Neatly take a thin slice from the cut surface of each of the halves (including the outer skin), sprinkle them with lemon juice to prevent darkening, and put carefully to one side. Take out the flesh of the avocados, being careful not to damage the skins, which should be kept. With a fork, mix well together the avocado flesh and the juice of two of the limes.

In another bowl, mix the chopped herbs, the egg yolks, a teaspoon of mustard, the oil and seasoning. Add the avocado flesh and the flaked tuna fish, stirring everything together well.

Fill the avocado shells with this mixture, then cover with the slices of the fruit which had been put aside. Decorate with thin slices of lime. Serve chilled.

Elle says that one or two avocado stones left in the blended flesh will prevent it blackening while the dish is being prepared. They should be removed before mixing with the eggs and fish.

(CONTINUED)

To make the sauce, chop the tarragon leaves, add to the crème fraîche with the juice of the lemons. Season and whip lightly to get a little air into the sauce. Serve terrine and sauce together, well chilled.

From the restaurant 'Le Gambetta' at Houilles outside Paris: the chef recommends that a Muscadet should be drunk with this dish.

TERRINE D'AVOCATS À L'ESTRAGON
Avocado and tarragon terrine

PREPARATION TIME: 25 minutes (3 hours in advance)
COOKING TIME: 15–20 minutes
FOR SIX TO EIGHT

8 avocados	tabasco
8 gelatine leaves	oil
8 egg yolks	
salt, pepper	For the sauce:
500 ml (17½ fl oz) milk	1 sprig of tarragon
1 lemon	500 g (generous 1 lb) crème
500 g (generous 1 lb) crème	fraîche
fraîche	2 lemons
1 tomato	salt, pepper

Cover the gelatine with cold water in order to soften it and leave for 10 minutes. Beat the egg yolks in a pan with salt and pepper. Boil the milk and pour it very slowly into the eggs. Put the pan over a very low flame, stirring constantly with a wooden spoon. It is absolutely essential that the mixture is not allowed to boil. As soon as the mixture is thick enough to coat the spoon, remove from the heat and add the gelatine, having first squeezed out as much water as possible between the hands. Mix thoroughly and leave to cool.

Divide the avocados in half lengthways, take out the stones, and sprinkle the cut surfaces with lemon juice. Put the flesh of four of the fruit into a blender together with the crème fraîche and the tomato, peeled and deseeded and cut up. Season with salt, pepper and tabasco and blend into a smooth purée. Peel the remaining avocados and cut the flesh into dice.

Take an oblong cake tin, oil it and put a layer of avocado purée in the bottom. Follow with a layer of avocado pieces then more purée and so on, alternately, until the ingredients are used up. Finish with a layer of purée and refrigerate for at least 3 hours.

(CONTINUED OPPOSITE)

FARCI CHARENTAIS
Vegetable bombe

PREPARATION TIME: 15 minutes
COOKING TIME: 2 hours
FOR SIX

1 kg (2¼ lb) unsmoked pork-
  belly
1 bunch of chives
1 large sprig of parsley
1 small bunch of sorrel
3 cloves of garlic
1 shallot

250 g (9 oz) breadcrumbs
4 eggs
salt, pepper
8–10 leaves of spinach beet (or
  Swiss chard)

Boil a pan of water and plunge the pork-belly into it and let it simmer for 5 minutes. Remove, rinse under cold running water and cut it into small dice. Chop the chives, the parsley, the sorrel, the peeled garlic and shallot. In a large bowl, mix them all with the pork-belly, the breadcrumbs and the eggs. Season.

Wash the spinach beet leaves and wipe them dry. Lay them out to form a bed of overlapping leaves about 50 cm (20 inches) square. Put the stuffing into the middle of the leaves and wrap the leaves around it, making the shape of a ball. Put it in a muslin cloth and tie it tightly around the stuffed ball.

Boil a large pan of salted water and cook the ball in it for 2 hours. Take it out, remove the cloth and cut into slices: serve immediately.

Elle says the dish may be eaten as described above or the slices may be sealed on both sides in butter in a pan.

ENDIVES GRATINÉES
Gratin of chicory

PREPARATION TIME: 20 minutes
COOKING TIME: 30 minutes
FOR SIX

6 heads of chicory
300 ml (½ pint) dry white wine
6 slices of York ham
30 g (1 oz) butter
50 ml (1¾ fl oz) milk

2 level tablespoons potato-flour
2 lumps of sugar
salt, pepper, nutmeg
1 egg yolk
100 g (3½ oz) Gruyère cheese

Trim and wash the chicory heads; if preferred, the inner core can be removed with an apple-corer. Put the white wine and an equal quantity of water into a large pan. Add salt and bring to the boil.

Arrange the chicory in the pan, cover and bring back to the boil. Cook for a further 15–20 minutes.

Remove from the heat, take out the chicory, retaining the cooking liquid. Wrap each head of chicory in a slice of ham and arrange in a buttered ovenproof dish.

Make a smooth paste with the milk and the potato-flour. Put the cooking liquid back on the heat and reduce it to half its volume. Add the two sugar lumps. Thicken it by adding the potato-flour paste bit by bit, whisking until the sauce has the consistency of béchamel. Season, add grated nutmeg and then remove from the flame. Whisk in the beaten egg yolk and pour the sauce over the chicory and ham. Sprinkle with grated cheese and dot with small knobs of remaining butter.

Cook in a very hot oven (230°C/450°F/Gas Mark 8) for 5 minutes.

Elle warns that when the beaten egg yolk is added to the sauce, it should be whisked very vigorously to avoid curdling.

ENDIVES EN PAPILLOTES
Ham stuffed with chicory

PREPARATION TIME: 20 minutes
COOKING TIME: 45 minutes
FOR SIX

12 heads of chicory	1 tablespoon of sugar
6 slices of York ham	75 g (generous 2½ oz) grated
6 slices of smoked ham	Emmenthal cheese
100 g (3½ oz) butter	

Remove any discoloured outer leaves from the chicory and wipe them with a damp cloth. If the chicory heads have any traces of sand, they should be very thoroughly washed and drained. Put them into a heavy saucepan with 75 g (generous 2½ oz) butter in knobs; sprinkle the sugar over them. Cover the pan and cook over a low heat for 15–20 minutes. Remove and drain.

Cut six pieces of kitchen foil, as large as two slices of ham laid side by side, plus an overlap all round. Place on each piece of foil one slice of York ham and one of smoked ham: put a chicory head centrally on each slice. Sprinkle grated cheese over each chicory, put in a knob of butter and roll up each ham and chicory combination. Wrap the two rolls (one smoked, one York) side by side in the kitchen foil and make a parcel enclosing both of them. Arrange the parcels in a baking tin and cook in a very hot oven (230°C/450°F/Gas Mark 8) for about 25 minutes.

CONCOMBRES FARCIS
Stuffed cucumbers

PREPARATION TIME: 20 minutes
COOKING TIME: 45 minutes
FOR SIX

3 cucumbers	1 bunch of tarragon
150 g (5 oz) smoked pork loin	150 g (5 oz) lean minced beef
35 g (generous 1 oz) bacon	powdered paprika
20 g (¾ oz) garlic cloves	salt, pepper
75 g (generous 2½ oz) shallots	3 eggs
50 g (scant 2 oz) parsley	

Wash and trim the cucumbers and divide them in half lengthways. Carefully scoop out the seeds and discard, then carefully remove the flesh, retaining the shells. Chop the flesh coarsely and put it on some layers of kitchen paper to drain off liquid.

Mince the pork loin and the bacon, and peel and chop the garlic, shallots and the herbs: put everything into a bowl with the minced beef, cucumber flesh, a good spoonful of paprika and seasoning. Break the 3 eggs into the mixture and stir well together.

Stuff the cucumber shells with the mixture, arrange them in a baking tin and cook for 45 minutes in a fairly hot oven (200°C/400°F/Gas Mark 6).

Elle says that if pork loin is not available, ham may be used.

ARTICHAUTS AUX SAINT-JACQUES
Artichokes and scallops

PREPARATION TIME: 30 minutes
COOKING TIME: 1 hour 40 minutes
FOR SIX

6 tinned artichoke bottoms (see
   p. 25)
12 scallops
fish stock (see recipe)
½ lemon
100 g (3½ oz) butter
small glass of brandy

20 g (scant ¾ oz) cornflour
2 egg yolks
2 tablespoons of crème fraîche
salt, pepper, cayenne
50 g (scant 2 oz) grated
   Emmenthal cheese

Make a fish stock by cooking the fish head and trimmings (as described on page 15) or by using a fish stock cube if available.

Drain the artichoke bottoms and cook them in boiling salted water, with lemon juice added, for 10–15 minutes. Remove, drain and keep warm. Clean the scallops and take out the flesh and coral from each. Wash under running water and dry on kitchen paper. Melt half the butter in a pan and gently cook the white meat of the scallops for a maximum of 5 minutes. Flame them in brandy, add the coral and cook together for another 2 minutes. Remove from the pan and keep in a warm place.

Into the same pan, pour 400 ml (14 fl oz) of fish stock and deglaze by stirring vigorously. Bring to the boil and cook uncovered until it has reduced by half. Work the rest of the butter and cornflour together and incorporate this paste into the sauce. Remove from the heat and whisk in the egg yolks and crème fraîche which have already been beaten together. Season and add a pinch of cayenne to taste.

Arrange the artichoke bottoms in individual ovenproof dishes. Slice the scallops and divide the slices and the coral among the artichokes. Cover with sauce and sprinkle with grated cheese: brown for 5 minutes in a very hot oven (240°C/475°F/Gas Mark 9).

FONDS D'ARTICHAUTS MIMOSA
Artichokes Mimosa

PREPARATION TIME: 15 minutes
COOKING TIME: 10 minutes
FOR SIX

1 tin containing 12 artichoke
   bottoms
4 eggs
2 bunches of watercress

1 lemon
4 tablespoons olive oil
salt, pepper
curry powder

Hard-boil the eggs, drain the artichoke bottoms, and sort and wash the watercress. Remove the stalks, weigh out 100 g (3½ oz) of the leaves and chop very finely.

Pass the eggs through a sieve or the fine disc of a Mouli. Carefully mix the egg with the chopped cress, adding in the juice of the lemon, the olive oil, seasoning and half a teaspoon of curry powder.

Arrange the artichoke bottoms on a bed of the remaining leaves of watercress and stuff them with the egg mixture.

Elle says that chopped parsley (50 g or scant 2 oz) may be substituted for the 100 g (3½ oz) of chopped cress.

GÂTEAU DE CHOU-FLEUR
Cauliflower and bacon pudding

PREPARATION TIME: 15 minutes
COOKING TIME: 25 minutes
FOR SIX

1 good cauliflower
80 g (scant 3 oz) streaky bacon
75 g (generous 2½ oz) Comté or
*   Gruyère cheese*
5 eggs
50 g (scant 2 oz) flour
salt, pepper
200 ml (7 fl oz) milk
200 g (7 oz) crème fraîche

Wash the cauliflower and break off and separate all the heads. Blanch them for 10 minutes in boiling salted water: remove, drain and rinse them in cold running water.

Remove the rind from the bacon and cut crossways in strips. Grate the cheese. Beat the eggs in a bowl and mix in the flour little by little, taking care to avoid lumps. Season, and stir in the warmed milk. Add the crème fraîche, the grated cheese and the bacon.

Butter an ovenproof dish. Arrange the cauliflower heads in it evenly and pour the mixture over it. Cook for 25 minutes in a very hot oven (230°C/450°F/Gas Mark 8). Serve hot.

CHAMPIGNONS À LA MONÉGASQUE
Mushrooms Monaco

PREPARATION TIME: 5 minutes (2 hours in advance)
COOKING TIME: 15 minutes
FOR SIX

750 g (generous 1½ lb) button
*   mushrooms*
8 salted anchovy fillets
5 tablespoons of olive oil
pepper
1 sprig of mint
juice of 2 lemons
3 tablespoons chopped parsley

Soak the anchovy fillets in fresh water for about 2 hours to remove the salt. Change the water two or three times.

Trim the stalks of the mushrooms, wash them under running water and dry them. If small, leave whole, otherwise cut in halves or quarters according to size.

Heat the oil in a heavy pan and gently cook the mushrooms. After 5 minutes, season with pepper and add the anchovy fillets, the sprig of mint and the lemon juice. Cook until the liquid is reduced.

Sprinkle with chopped parsley and serve at once with either a plain omelette or with scrambled eggs.

Elle says that if tinned anchovies are used, the two hours of soaking will not be necessary but, in this case, a little salt should be added just before cooking is completed.

CHAMPIGNONS À LA CRÈME
Baked mushrooms

PREPARATION TIME: 15 minutes
COOKING TIME: 10 minutes
FOR SIX

1 kg (scant 2¼ lb) button
  mushrooms
1 lemon
80 g (scant 3 oz) butter
4 egg yolks

250 g (scant 9 oz) crème fraîche
salt, pepper
nutmeg
100 g (3½ oz) grated Gruyère
  cheese

Trim the stalks of the mushrooms, wash them in running water and sprinkle with lemon juice to prevent discoloration, then cut into slices. Melt the butter in a frying pan and gently cook the mushrooms until all their liquid has evaporated.

In a bowl, thoroughly mix together the egg yolks and the crème fraîche. Season and add nutmeg.

Divide the mushrooms between six individual fireproof dishes, cover with the egg and crème fraîche mixture and sprinkle with the grated cheese. Cook in a very hot oven (230°C/450°F/Gas Mark 8) until browned.

Elle suggests that baked mushrooms will go well with grills or roasts, as well as being a delicious dish on their own.

CHAMPIGNONS EN PERSILLADE
Stuffed mushrooms

PREPARATION TIME: 15 minutes
COOKING TIME: 20 minutes
FOR SIX

6 large mushrooms, or 12 smaller
  ones
1 lemon
1 bulb of garlic

1 large bunch Greek parsley
6 eggs
salt, pepper

Trim the stalks and wash the mushrooms under running water. Remove the stalks and rub the crowns with the cut side of half a lemon. Arrange them in an ovenproof dish.

Peel all the cloves of garlic and chop them finely, together with the parsley and the mushroom stalks. Put them in a bowl in which the eggs have been beaten, season and mix all the ingredients thoroughly together.

Fill the bowls of the mushrooms with this mixture and cook for 20 minutes in a moderate oven (180°C/350°F/Gas Mark 4). Serve hot.

Elle suggests that with doubled quantities, this dish makes an excellent supper course.

RISOTTO AUX CHAMPIGNONS
Mushroom risotto

PREPARATION TIME: 15 minutes
COOKING TIME: 10 minutes
FOR SIX

1 kg (2¼ lb) button mushrooms	*6 slices of lean bacon*
300 g (10½ oz) rice	*1 tablespoon tomato purée*
1 lemon	*sprig of thyme*
4 tablespoons oil	*salt, pepper*
12 cocktail sausages	*chopped parsley*

Measure the volume of the rice and make a note of it. Trim the stalks of the mushrooms and wipe them in a mixture of water and lemon juice. Slice them.

Heat two tablespoons of oil in a pan and put in the rice. Cook rice for about 3 minutes, stirring constantly until it turns a milky colour.

Put the rest of the oil into another pan and cook the sausages and bacon. When ready, put them together with the sliced mushrooms into the pan on top of the rice and add water equivalent to 2½ times the volume of the rice. Stir in the tomato purée, the chopped thyme, and season. Cover the pan and cook over a low heat until the liquid has been absorbed and the rice is tender. This will take about 10 minutes.

Sprinkle with chopped parsley and serve at once.

Elle suggests that, accompanied by a salad, this risotto would make a good main course.

MOUSSE DE POISSON FUMÉ
Smoked fish mousse

PREPARATION TIME: 15 minutes
COOKING TIME: nil
FOR 500 G (ABOUT 1 LB) OF MOUSSE

3 smoked trout	*tabasco*
300 g (10½ oz) smoked salmon	*salt*
1 lemon	*300 ml (10½ fl oz) double cream*
2 teaspoons Worcester sauce	

Skin the trout and take the flesh off the bones. Put it in the blender with the slices of smoked salmon, juice of the lemon, 2–3 drops of tabasco, the Worcester sauce and salt to taste.

Blend until a smooth paste is achieved: add the cream and blend long enough to absorb it. Turn the mousse out into a terrine and chill in the refrigerator. Serve with an assortment of raw vegetables such as radishes, celery, chicory etc, and toast.

Elle suggests that there is no need to use the best smoked salmon for this dish, and trimmings will be perfectly acceptable. Alternatively, smoked eel fillets may be used instead. Elle advises also that it will be easier to slice the mousse if the knife-blade is first held under running cold water.

POMMES DE TERRE À L'ÉTOUFFÉE
Pan-fried potatoes

PREPARATION TIME: 10 minutes
COOKING TIME: 30 minutes
FOR SIX

1½–2 kg (3½–4½ lb) potatoes
2 onions
4 cloves of garlic

150 ml (5 fl oz) cooking oil
salt, pepper

Peel and wash the potatoes and cut them into very thin slices. Chop the peeled onions and garlic finely.

Heat the oil in a heavy iron casserole, add the potato slices in layers with chopped onion and garlic and seasoning in between. Cover the pan and cook over a medium to brisk heat. At the first sign of steam, take a large flat spoon or food-slice and turn the potatoes over, in sections, to cook on their other side. Do this twice, but only twice, more.

After 25–30 minutes of cooking time, serve at once with fried or grilled sausages and a green salad.

Elle says the potatoes should not be turned more than three times. If they tend to stick to the pan, reduce the heat: do not add any liquid.

TRUFFADE
Auvergne potato cake

PREPARATION TIME: 10 minutes
COOKING TIME: 1 hour
FOR SIX

1½ kg (3 lb 5 oz) potatoes
250 g (scant 9 oz) tomme
    d'Auvergne fraîche (or Cantal)
500 g (generous 1 lb) onions
300 g (10½ oz) streaky bacon

2 cloves of garlic
50 g (scant 2 oz) lard
salt, pepper
40 g (scant 1½ oz) crème fraîche

Peel and trim the onions and the potatoes and cut both into thin slices. Buy the bacon in thick slices, cut it into dice. Chop up the peeled cloves of garlic. Melt the lard in a heavy iron pan and gently cook these ingredients all together, seasoned, for about 20 minutes until the potatoes are a light golden brown.

Cut 200 g (7 oz) of the cheese into strips and add it, with the cream, to the pan and continue cooking for 1 hour altogether, stirring frequently.

Halfway through the cooking, turn the dish out onto a plate and slide it back, upside-down, into the pan. In this way, it will be thoroughly cooked through. Serve from the pan with sliced ham or a green salad.

From 'Le Buron de Chaudefour' restaurant in Murol in the Auvergne: the chef recommends that a local rosé or Saint-Pourçain should be drunk with this dish.

RIZ À LA CARINA
Rice with sausages

PREPARATION TIME: 15 minutes
COOKING TIME: 30 minutes
FOR SIX

400 g (14 oz) long grain rice
12 chipolata sausages
2 green peppers
4 onions
250 g (scant 9 oz) unsmoked
   pork belly
3 cloves of garlic

100 ml (3½ fl oz) olive oil
1 sweet chilli pepper
salt, pepper
1 bouquet garni
100 g (3½ oz) grated Parmesan
   cheese

With a sharp-pointed knife, remove the stalks, membranes and seeds from the green peppers. Put them under a grill until the skin blackens and bubbles up. Peel off the blackened outer skin (see p. 15), then put peppers to one side and keep warm. Peel and slice the onions, cut the pork belly into dice and crush the peeled garlic.

Put the oil, onions, garlic, pork belly and the deseeded chilli into a pan and cook gently until the onion is transparent. Then add the sausages and continue cooking until they are done. Remove and keep to one side. Measure the volume of rice and, after washing, add rice to the pan and cook until that too is transparent. Stir frequently with a spoon during the cooking.

Moisten the rice with 2½ times its own volume of boiling salted water, season, add the bouquet garni, cover the pan and continue cooking over a low flame for about 20 minutes.

When the rice is done, turn it out into a warmed serving dish. Cut the green peppers into triangles and arrange them and the chipolata sausages in the rice.

Serve accompanied by a bowl of grated Parmesan cheese.

ÉPINARDS AUX FOIES DE VOLAILLE
Chicken livers with spinach

PREPARATION TIME: 20 minutes
COOKING TIME: 5 minutes
FOR SIX

500 g (generous 1 lb) chicken
   livers
1 kg (scant 2¼ lb) fresh spinach
   or 900 g (scant 2 lb) frozen leaf
   spinach
180 g (scant 6½ oz) bacon (3
   thick slices)

1 large bunch of parsley
6 cloves of garlic
250 ml (scant 9 fl oz) wine vinegar
salt, pepper
3 tablespoons olive oil

If using fresh spinach, trim the stalks, wash the leaves, then plunge into a pan of boiling salted water for 5 minutes. Drain, leave to cool, then chop coarsely.

Cut the bacon into dice and chop the parsley and the peeled garlic. Put the vinegar and the garlic into a heavy iron pan, season and bring to the boil. Add the chicken livers and simmer for 1 minute. Remove, cut into smallish pieces and return them to the hot vinegar.

Put the diced bacon into a frying pan without any added fat and gently fry until just cooked.

Take a salad bowl and arrange the spinach. Pour in the oil, then add the chicken liver pieces straight from the hot vinegar, and the diced bacon. Serve just warm.

SPAGHETTI À LA MATRICIANA
Spaghetti with basil and cheese

PREPARATION TIME: 20 minutes
COOKING TIME: 15 minutes
FOR SIX

600 g (generous 1¼ lb) spaghetti
6 large tomatoes
100 g (3½ oz) streaky bacon
2 tablespoons olive oil
100 ml (3½ fl oz) dry white wine
salt, pepper
pinch of cayenne pepper
bunch of fresh basil
100 g (3½ oz) coarsely grated
  goat's cheese

Peel and remove the seeds of the tomatoes and chop the flesh. Put the bacon slices into boiling water, let it bubble for a few moments then remove the bacon, put it under a cold tap, drain, wipe and slice into strips across the grain.

Heat a tablespoon of oil in a pan and put in the bacon strips. When they are sizzling, pour in the wine and continue cooking until the wine is reduced to nothing. Stir in the chopped tomatoes over a gentle heat, season with salt (to taste) and cayenne pepper. Finely chop the basil and put to one side.

Cook the spaghetti in a large pan of salted boiling water to which a tablespoon of olive oil has been added. After about 10 minutes, check the texture of the cooked spaghetti. When properly cooked, the strands will retain a little firmness between the teeth (*al dente*). Remove, drain and add to the sauce in the pan. Mix in chopped basil and grated cheese, check seasoning and serve on warmed plates.

From the restaurant 'Chez Gildo' in Paris-7ᵉ: the chef suggests that a red Italian wine, such as Barolo, is the best accompaniment.

TOMATES AU CHÈVRE FRAIS
Tomatoes with goat's cheese

PREPARATION TIME: 15 minutes
COOKING TIME: 10 minutes
FOR SIX

12 firm tomatoes, about 900 g
  (scant 2 lb)
180 g (scant 6½ oz) fresh goat's
  cheese
4 eggs
2 green peppers, about 250 g
  (scant 9 oz)
3 teaspoons strong mustard
2 teaspoons paprika
salt, pepper
6 lettuce leaves

Hard-boil the eggs. Wipe the vegetables. Cut the caps off the tomatoes (stalk end) and carefully scoop out the seeds and flesh. With a sharp pointed knife, remove the stalks, membranes and seeds from the peppers and cut each one into six rings.

Chop up the peeled, hard-boiled eggs and mix them in a bowl with the goat's cheese, the mustard, the paprika and seasoning. Fill each tomato with this mixture, replace caps.

Line a serving plate with lettuce leaves, arrange the 12 rings of green pepper and place a stuffed tomato on each.

TIAN DE LÉGUMES
Vegetables provençale

PREPARATION TIME: 20 minutes (half an hour in advance)
COOKING TIME: 1 hour
FOR SIX

3 aubergines	small bunch of parsley
300 g (10½ oz) onions	1 good sprig of basil
1 green pepper	1 sprig of thyme
1 red pepper	1 bay leaf
4 courgettes	salt, pepper
4 firm tomatoes	100 g (3½ oz) grated Parmesan
6 tablespoons olive oil	cheese
2 cloves of garlic	

Trim the aubergines and cut them into thick slices, sprinkle them with salt and let them sweat for 30 minutes. Peel and slice the onions. With a sharp knife, remove the stalk, membranes and seeds from the peppers, wash them and cut them into rings. Wipe the courgettes and the tomatoes and cut into round slices. There may be too much liquid if the tomatoes are particularly juicy. In this case, reduce the number of tomatoes and make up the quantity with the other vegetables. Drain and wash the aubergine thoroughly.

Put two tablespoons of olive oil and half the sliced onions into a heavy pan and cook gently until transparent. Arrange the other vegetables in an ovenproof dish, separating the layers with a mixture of raw and cooked onion. Sprinkle with peeled, chopped garlic, chopped herbs and bay leaf. Season. Sprinkle with the rest of the oil and cook in a moderate oven (180°C/350°F/Gas Mark 4) for 1 hour.

Ten minutes before the cooking is done, cover the vegetables with grated cheese and raise the temperature to very hot (240°C/475°F/Gas Mark 9) to brown the surface and to evaporate the surplus liquid.

Elle says this vegetable casserole is a delicious accompaniment to quiche lorraine.

ESCARGOTS À LA MOUTARDE
Snails in mustard sauce

PREPARATION TIME: 10 minutes
COOKING TIME: 15 minutes
FOR SIX

6 dozen snails (3 tins,	salt, pepper
125-g/4½-oz size)	600 g (generous 1¼ lb) crème
50 g (scant 2 oz) butter	fraîche
150 ml (5 fl oz) brandy	4 tablespoons strong mustard

Wash the snails under cold running water, drain. Melt the butter in a pan and cook them gently. Add half the brandy to the pan, flame it and season.

Remove the snails and keep in a warm place. Pour off the fat from the pan and make a sauce with the crème fraîche, the mustard and the rest of the brandy. Stir vigorously with the back of a fork to deglaze the pan, and simmer until the sauce is reduced by half.

Put the snails back in the pan and stir them until they are thoroughly covered in sauce. Check the seasoning and serve very hot.

From the restaurant 'Quatre-Saisons' in Craches near Ablis: the chef recommends a Pouilly-Fuissé to accompany the snails.

ESCARGOTS AUX CHAMPIGNONS
Snails with mushrooms

PREPARATION TIME: 30 minutes
COOKING TIME: 20 minutes
FOR SIX

4 dozen snails (2 tins,
  125-g/4½-oz size)
light stock
500 g (generous 1 lb) mushrooms
2 shallots
20 g (¾ oz) butter
2 tomatoes
salt, pepper
200 g (7 oz) crème fraîche

For the garlic butter:
juice of ½ lemon
25 g (scant 1 oz) chopped
  shallots
15 g (½ oz) chopped parsley
15 g (½ oz) crushed garlic
15 g (½ oz) chopped tarragon
100 g (3½ oz) butter

Heat up the snails in stock, or in salted water. Drain and keep warm. For preference, the mushrooms should be the dried packet variety which contains girolles and cèpes; in this case, the weight given is after reconstitution according to the instructions.

Peel and chop the two shallots and cook gently in butter. When transparent, add the sliced mushrooms and let them sweat for a few minutes. Add the skinned and de-seeded tomatoes together with the snails and heat through. Season and add the crème fraîche, stirring constantly.

The garlic butter is made by incorporating all the ingredients together into the butter with a fork. Take 25 g (scant 1 oz) and add to the snails, stirring until melted. Check the seasoning and serve hot in individual dishes, accompanied by hot toast spread with the rest of the garlic butter.

(CONTINUED)

the volume is further reduced by two-thirds. Mix in the purée of watercress.

Turn out the clafoutis from the mould while it is warm onto a rimmed serving plate, pour half the sauce around it and serve the rest in a sauceboat.

CLAFOUTIS AUX PRIMEURS
Vegetable clafoutis

PREPARATION TIME: 30 minutes
COOKING TIME: 35 minutes
FOR SIX

100 g (3½ oz) butter
50 g (scant 2 oz) onion
½ green pepper
½ head of fennel
50 g (scant 2 oz) mushrooms
100 g (3½ oz) young carrots
100 g (3½ oz) baby turnips
100 g (3½ oz) shelled peas
100 g (3½ oz) tomatoes
salt, pepper

4 eggs
500 ml (17½ fl oz) single cream
grated nutmeg

For the sauce:
2 bunches of watercress
100 ml (3½ fl oz) dry white wine
50 g (scant 2 oz) shallots
250 ml (9 fl oz) double cream

Melt 90 g (3 oz) butter in a large pan and add, in the following order, the chopped onion, the green pepper cut into dice, the fennel, trimmed and also cut into dice, and the sliced mushrooms. Cook for a few minutes, mixing in each ingredient as it is put in. The carrots and turnips should be scraped and cut into dice and, together with the peas, blanched in boiling water. Skin and de-seed the tomatoes and chop them. Add all these vegetables to the pan, stir, season, cover the pan and cook over a gentle heat for 10 minutes. Put to one side.

Beat the eggs and single cream together in a bowl, season with salt, pepper and grated nutmeg. Add the cooked vegetables and mix everything together. Turn the mixture into a buttered mould, place it in a pan of water and cook in a moderate oven (180°C/350°F/Gas Mark 4) for about 35 minutes.

To prepare the sauce, begin by trimming the stalks of the watercress, wash the leaves and blanch them briefly in boiling salted water. Plunge them into cold water, drain and dry with kitchen paper. Chop and put through a sieve. Keep to one side.

Heat the wine and chopped shallots in a casserole until its volume is reduced by half. Add the double cream, stir and continue cooking until
(CONTINUED OPPOSITE)

[50]

FEUILLETÉ DE CERVELLE AU CONCOMBRE
Brains and cucumber in pastry

PREPARATION TIME: 20 minutes
COOKING TIME: 40 minutes
FOR SIX

3 calves' brains	bouquet garni
6 frozen vol-au-vent cases	1 cucumber
wine vinegar	200 g (7 oz) crème fraîche
salt, pepper	chervil and chives

Rinse the brains in a mixture of water and vinegar. Bring a litre (1¾ pints) of salted water to the boil, add pepper and the bouquet garni, then the brains. Lower the heat so the water is just simmering and cook for 10 minutes: remove from the heat and leave the brains in the cooking liquid.

Put the vol-au-vent cases in a cool oven (150°C/300°F/Gas Mark 2) to raise them. In the meantime, peel the cucumber and cut it in half lengthways: scoop out the seeds. Cut the cucumber into small dice.

Put half the crème fraîche into a small saucepan, warm it through, then add the diced cucumber. Season and cook over a gentle heat for about 15 minutes. Pass the contents of the pan through a blender and put a spoonful of the mixture into the bottom of each vol-au-vent case.

Drain the brains, wipe them with kitchen paper and cut them into large pieces. Fill each pastry case and put them in a very hot oven (230°C/450°F/Gas Mark 8) for 10 minutes to heat them through.

In the meantime, take the rest of the crème fraîche and reduce it over a gentle heat. Season, add finely-chopped chervil and chives, stir and pour the sauce over the brains. Serve, very hot, at once.

From the restaurant 'Le Jardin du Louvre' in Paris-8°: the chef recommends you to drink a well-chilled rosé wine with this dish.

TOURTE AU CANTAL
Cantal cheese pie

PREPARATION TIME: 15 minutes (2 hours in advance)
COOKING TIME: 45 minutes
FOR SIX TO EIGHT

300 g (10½ oz) Cantal cheese	For the pastry (pâte brisée):
250 g (scant 9 oz) French beans	250 g (scant 9 oz) plain flour
250 g (scant 9 oz) carrots	pinch of salt
250 g (scant 9 oz) frozen peas	125 g (4½ oz) butter
200 g (7 oz) fromage blanc	2 egg yolks
200 g (7 oz) crème fraîche	about 3¼–4 tablespoons cold
salt, pepper, nutmeg	water
5 eggs	

First prepare the pastry. Sift the flour onto a pastry board or marble slab, make a hollow and put in salt, softened butter cut into knobs, and the egg yolks. Work quickly into a dough with the fingers, moistening with the water to give a good consistency. Put dough into a bowl and leave in a cool place for 2 hours.

Prepare the vegetables by trimming the beans and peeling the carrots and cutting them into rounds. Cook these, and the frozen peas all separately in boiling salted water. Drain and put to one side.

After 2 hours, take half the pastry and roll it out sufficiently to line a pie dish. Retain the trimmings. Prick the bottom with a fork. Cut half the Cantal into very thin slices and line the bottom of the dish with it. (A good Cheddar can substitute for Cantal.)

In a separate bowl, mix the fromage blanc with the crème fraîche, a pinch of nutmeg, four of the eggs, the cooked vegetables and the rest of the cheese, grated. Season and pour the mixture into the pastry dish. Roll out the remainder of the pastry and cover the pastry dish: trim off and press the edges together. Decorate with the pastry trimmings cut into strips, and brush with remaining beaten egg. Pierce a hole in the centre of the pastry lid and cook in a fairly hot oven (200°C/400°F/Gas Mark 6) for 45 minutes.

QUICHE CATALANE
Cheese and tomato quiche

PREPARATION TIME: *pastry*: 5 minutes (2 hours in advance)
filling: 15 minutes
COOKING TIME: 1 hour
FOR SIX TO EIGHT

100 g (3½ oz) grated Emmenthal
1 kg (2¼ lb) tomatoes
1 onion
50 ml (1¾ fl oz) oil
6 eggs
200 g (7 oz) crème fraîche
salt, pepper
1 tin anchovy fillets

For the pastry:
200 g (7 oz) plain flour
pinch of salt
100 g (3½ oz) butter
200 ml (7 fl oz) cold water

Sift the flour on to a pastry board and make a well in the middle. Put in the pinch of salt, the softened butter and half the water. Rapidly work it into a dough with the fingers: if necessary, add more water to achieve a dough that is supple without being sticky. Leave to rest for 2 hours in a cool place.

Lightly flour the pastry board and roll out the pastry to a thickness of 3 mm (⅛ inch). Butter a 25-cm (10-inch) flan tin and line it with pastry: prick the bottom all over with a fork. Keep in a cool place.

Peel the tomatoes, de-seed them and chop them up. Chop the onion and cook it gently in oil. When it becomes transparent, add the chopped tomatoes and continue cooking. Beat the eggs, the crème fraîche and half the grated cheese together. Season.

Spread the cooked tomatoes in the flan dish and pour the beaten eggs over them. Arrange the anchovy fillets on the surface and sprinkle over the rest of the grated cheese. Cook for 1 hour in a very hot oven (230°C/450°F/Gas Mark 8). If the quiche browns too quickly, cover it with greaseproof paper. Remove from the oven and serve when it has cooled slightly.

FEUILLETÉ FROMAGÉ
Cheese and potato pastry

PREPARATION TIME: 35 minutes (1 hour in advance)
COOKING TIME: 35 minutes
FOR SIX TO EIGHT

1 fresh goat's cheese
2 potatoes
250 g (scant 9 oz) plain flour
salt

100 g (3½ oz) butter
150 g (5 oz) crème fraîche
2 tablespoons milk

Leave the goat's cheese to drain. Cook the potatoes in their skins in boiling salted water.

Sift the flour on to a pastry board, add a pinch of salt and, using only as much water as necessary, make a firm but elastic dough with the fingertips. Allow to rest for 1 hour.

Peel and mash the potatoes and mix in the butter: it will be softened by the heat of the potatoes. Stir in the cheese and the crème fraîche and salt liberally to taste.

Roll out the pastry on a floured board to a thickness of 15 mm (¾ inch). Put the cheese and potato mixture into the centre, fold in the four corners and roll out the pastry once more. Fold it into itself three times, rolling out each time to give a final thickness of 1 cm (½ inch). Lay out on a buttered baking sheet, brush with milk and decorate the surface with the tines of a fork. Cook for 35 minutes in a very hot oven (230°C/450°F/Gas Mark 8) for 35 minutes. Serve very hot.

Elle advises that a floury variety of potato should be used and that the potatoes should be well drained before they are peeled, mashed and the butter added.

TARTE AUX COURGETTES
Courgette flan

PREPARATION TIME: 10 minutes (2 hours in advance)
COOKING TIME: 30 minutes
FOR SIX

1 kg (2¼ lb) small courgettes	For the pastry:
salt, pepper	200 g (7 oz) plain flour
6 tablespoons olive oil	pinch of salt
3 tomatoes	100 g (3½ oz) butter
1 rusk	1 glass (5 fl oz) cold water
3 cloves of garlic	
parsley	

Make the pastry in the usual way (see p. 52). It should be supple without being at all sticky. Roll it into a ball and let it rest for 2 hours in a cool place.

During this time, wipe and trim the courgettes. Cut them into rounds, put them into a dish and sprinkle them with salt. Turn them from time to time and let them sweat while the pastry is resting.

Roll out the pastry and line a buttered 25-cm (10-inch) flan tin. Prick the bottom with a fork and prepare for blind-baking by covering with greaseproof paper and dried beans. Put into a very hot oven (240°C/475°F/Gas Mark 9) for 10 minutes.

Heat 3 tablespoons of olive oil in a pan and add the drained courgettes. Turn them to cook on both sides for a few minutes.

Take the flan dish out of the oven, remove dried beans and paper and set out a layer of courgettes on the bottom. Put in a layer of peeled and sliced tomatoes from which the seeds have been removed, season and finish with another layer of courgettes. Cover with a mixture of crushed rusk, crushed garlic and finely-chopped parsley. Spot with a few drops of oil and put back into the very hot oven for 20 minutes. Before serving, sprinkle on the remainder of the olive oil.

Elle advises that if the tomatoes are particularly juicy, they too should be allowed to sweat in salt, along with the courgettes.

FEUILLETÉS AU POIREAU
Leek puffs

PREPARATION TIME: 45 minutes
COOKING TIME: 1 hour 30 minutes
FOR SIX

8 good leeks (white part only)	300 ml (10½ fl oz) red wine
400 g (14 oz) frozen puff pastry	vinegar
400 g (14 oz) small onions	200 ml (7 fl oz) dry white wine
50 g (scant 2 oz) butter	1 good tablespoon tomato purée
3 tablespoons olive oil	coriander seeds
1 tablespoon caster sugar	salt, pepper
	1 egg

Peel and trim the onions and put them in a saucepan together with 20 g (¾ oz) butter, the oil and the sugar. Put over the heat and when the mixture is the colour of caramel, deglaze with the wine vinegar, reduce it, add the white wine and continue to reduce the liquid to half its volume. Add the tomato purée and the crushed coriander seeds. Season, cover the saucepan and continue cooking gently for 1 hour, stirring from time to time.

Trim and wash the leeks and cut them into pieces 5 cm (2 inches) long. Plunge them into boiling salted water and bring back to simmer for 3–4 minutes. Drain very well.

Melt the remaining butter in a pan, add the drained leeks. Season, cover the pan and cook gently for 45 minutes. The leeks should not be allowed to brown.

Roll out the puff pastry on a lightly-floured board, to a thickness of 5 mm (about ¼ inch). Divide into six equal oblongs and firm up the edges by pressing all around with the points of the back of a fork. Brush with beaten egg and cook in a very hot oven (230°C/450°F/Gas Mark 8) for 15 minutes.

When they are cooked, remove from the oven, put them on a wire rack and split in half, to make a top and bottom. Put a layer of cooked onion, then a layer of cooked leek, onto each bottom half, cover with the top halves and serve very hot.

QUICHE AUX MORILLES
Morel quiche

PREPARATION TIME: 15 minutes (2 hours in advance)
COOKING TIME: 45 minutes
FOR SIX

250 g (scant 9 oz) fresh morels (if
  unobtainable, 1 packet dried
  morels)
1 lemon
150 g (5 oz) sliced ham
20 g (¾ oz) butter
20 g (¾ oz) plain flour
250 ml (scant 9 fl oz) milk
2 egg yolks

30 g (1 oz) crème fraîche
salt, pepper

For the pastry:
200 g (7 oz) plain flour
salt
100 g (3½ oz) butter
1 glass (5 fl oz) cold water

If, as is probable, you are using dried fungi, soak them in cold water for 1 hour. Drain, and wipe them with kitchen paper.

To make a short pastry, sift the flour onto a pastry board. Heap it up, make a well in the middle and put in a pinch of salt, the butter cut into knobs and half the glass of water. With the fingers work all the ingredients together quickly into a dough; moisten as much as is necessary to give a pastry which is supple but not sticky. Mould it into a ball and leave to rest in a cool place for 2 hours.

If using fresh fungi, trim the ends of the stalks and wipe all over with a mixture of lemon and water. Cut the ham into strips.

Roll the pastry out on a lightly-floured pastry board and line a 25-cm (10-inch) buttered flan tin. Fill the pastry case with ham and morels.

Make a white sauce with 20 g (1 oz) butter, 20 g (1 oz) flour and the milk, whisking vigorously to prevent lumps. Remove the pan from the heat and beat in the egg yolks and the crème fraîche. Season and pour the sauce into the quiche. Bake in a fairly hot oven (200°C/400°F/Gas Mark 6) for 45 minutes. Serve immediately it is ready.

<u>Elle suggests</u> that this quiche can also be made in individual dishes. Cut the morels into halves or quarters if they are particularly large.

PÂTÉ DE POMMES DE TERRE
Potato pie

PREPARATION TIME: 30 minutes (2 hours in advance)
COOKING TIME: 1 hour 15 minutes
FOR SIX

1½ kg (3 lbs 5 oz) potatoes
300 g (10½ oz) smoked bacon
500 g (generous 1 lb) forcemeat
cooking oil
225 g (8 oz) spinach
salt, pepper

For the pastry:
150 g (5 oz) butter
300 g (10½ oz) plain flour
salt
½ glass cold water (2½ fl oz)

First make the pastry. Cut the butter into knobs and using the fingers work it together with the flour in a bowl. Moisten it with a little salted water, mould the pastry into a ball and put it to rest for 2 hours in a cool place.

Plunge the bacon into boiling salted water for 2 minutes. Cut it into dice and lightly brown it in a pan without any added fat. Put to one side. Warm the forcemeat through and also put to one side.

Peel and slice the potatoes, and very gently warm them through in a little oil; they should not be completely cooked. Season. Trim the stalks from the spinach and chop the leaves.

Divide the pastry ⅔/⅓ and roll out both pieces. With the larger, line a 25-cm (10-inch) flan tin and prick the bottom all over with a fork. Fill the pastry case with successive layers of potato, forcemeat, bacon and spinach. Cover with the smaller piece of pastry; moisten the edges and press them together. Cook in a very hot oven (230°C/450°F/Gas Mark 8) for 30 minutes, reduce to a moderate heat (180°C/350°F/Gas Mark 4) and continue cooking for a further 45 minutes. Serve hot.

<u>Elle suggests</u> that you should use your favourite poultry stuffing for the forcemeat.

QUICHE AU SAUMON
Smoked salmon quiche

PREPARATION TIME: 15 minutes
COOKING TIME: 30 minutes
FOR SIX

400 g (14 oz) sliced smoked
   salmon
350 g (12½ oz) frozen shortcrust
   pastry
200 g (7 oz) Cheddar cheese
1 large onion
60 g (2 oz) butter

4 eggs
250 ml (scant 9 fl oz) milk
250 g (scant 9 oz) crème fraîche
2 tablespoons chopped parsley
2 tablespoons chopped chives
pepper
200 g (7 oz) tinned asparagus tips

Roll out the pastry and line a buttered and lightly-floured 25-cm (10-in) flan tin. Prick the bottom all over with the points of a fork.

Cut the cheese into thin slices and cover the bottom of the quiche. Gently cook the chopped onion in half the butter until it is transparent. Beat eggs, milk and crème fraîche together, stir in the chopped herbs, and season with pepper. Pour a little of this mixture over the cheese and then add layers of smoked salmon and chopped onion. Fill the quiche with the remainder of the egg and cream mixture and put it in a very hot oven (240°C/475°F/Gas Mark 9) for 5 minutes, then reduce the heat (to 220°C/425°F/Gas Mark 7) for a further 25 minutes.

Drain the asparagus spears and cook them through in the rest of the butter for 5 minutes. When the quiche is done, decorate the surface with asparagus and serve immediately.

From the restaurant 'Le Petit Coin de la Bourse' in Paris-2e: the chef recommends that a dry white wine from Alsace be drunk with this quiche.

TARTE À LA MOUTARDE
Mustard flan

PREPARATION TIME: 25 minutes
COOKING TIME: 40–50 minutes
FOR SIX

strong Dijon mustard
1 packet frozen puff pastry
   (about 400 g/14 oz size)

150 g (5 oz) Gruyère cheese
4 tomatoes

Roll out the pastry to a thickness of 4 mm (⅙ inch). Butter and lightly flour a 25-cm (10-inch) flan tin and line it with the pastry, with only a thin lining around the sides of the dish. Spread a layer of mustard 10 mm (⅖ inch) thick all over the bottom of the flan. Cut the cheese into thin slices and cover the mustard layer with them.

Peel the tomatoes and cut them into quarters (not round slices). Remove the seeds and arrange the tomatoes on the cheese. Cook in a very hot oven (240°C/475°F/Gas Mark 9). Follow the progress of the cooking and remove the flan when the edges of the pastry case are quite firm.

TARTE AUX DEUX JAMBONS
Two-ham flan

PREPARATION TIME: 15 minutes
COOKING TIME: 25 minutes
FOR SIX

120 g (4 oz) cooked ham
60 g (2 oz) smoked ham
350 g (12½ oz) frozen shortcrust
 pastry
60 g (2 oz) Cheddar cheese
2 eggs

125 ml (4½ fl oz) full cream milk
1 teaspoon crushed green
 peppercorns
nutmeg
salt

Roll out the pastry on a lightly-floured board and line a buttered 25-cm (10-inch) flan tin with it.

Trim the fat from the two hams and cut into thin strips. Arrange these over the bottom of the flan. Flake the cheese into pieces about the size of an almond and layer over the ham.

Beat eggs and milk together, add the crushed peppercorns and season with a pinch of nutmeg and a little salt. Pour the mixture over the flan.

Cook in a very hot oven (240°C/475°F/Gas Mark 9) until done.

Elle says that the weights given for the two hams are after trimming off all fat.

TARTE FERMIÈRE AUX LEGUMES
Country flan

PREPARATION TIME: 30 minutes
COOKING TIME: 40 minutes
FOR SIX

150 g (5 oz) button mushrooms
4 leeks (whites only)
1 small bunch chives
4 leaves of Swiss chard
125 g (4½ oz) sorrel
60 g (2 oz) butter
3 eggs
100 g (3½ oz) cream
1 tablespoon potato flour

150 ml (5 fl oz) milk
salt, pepper
nutmeg

For the pastry:
250 g (scant 9 oz) plain flour
salt
125 g (4½ oz) butter
1 egg

Using your fingers, work together in a bowl the sifted flour, salt and the butter cut into small pieces. Add the whole egg and, if need be, a little water to give a firm but supple pastry dough. Roll it into a ball and leave it to rest in a cool place.

Rinse and slice up all the vegetables. In batches, cook them all gently in butter: the mushrooms, then the leeks and the chives together, the Swiss chard with the sorrel. Put to one side.

Roll out the pastry. Butter and lightly flour a 25-cm (10-inch) flan tin and line it with the pastry. Blind-bake the flan case by covering its base with greaseproof paper and a layer of dried beans. Cook for 10 minutes in a very hot oven (230°C/450°F/Gas Mark 8). Take it out of the oven and remove the paper and beans.

Put the eggs, cream and potato flour into a large bowl and beat them well together. Gradually whisk in the milk, season and add a pinch of nutmeg. Mix in the cooked vegetables and pour the whole mixture into the flan case. Cook in a hot oven (220°C/425°F/Gas Mark 7) for 25–30 minutes, but check the progress to avoid burning the pastry. Serve hot.

FILETS DE BARBUE AU CRESSON
Brill with watercress

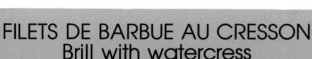

PREPARATION TIME: 20 minutes (plus 1 hour for stock)
COOKING TIME: 35 minutes
FOR SIX

1 brill weighing 2½ kg (5½ lb)	salt, pepper
1 bunch watercress	300 g (10½ oz) crème faîche
2 onions	1 teaspoon tomato purée
1 carrot	3 egg yolks
bouquet garni	25 g (scant 1 oz) butter

Ask your fishmonger to fillet the fish, but take home the head, spine and trimmings. Make a fish stock by boiling the fish head etc. with the sliced onions and carrots and the bouquet garni for 1 hour in 2 litres (3½ pints) of water in an uncovered pan. Season, pass through a sieve.

Put the brill fillets into a casserole large enough to let them lie quite flat. Cover with fish stock, bring to the boil, remove from the heat, cover the casserole and let the fish poach for 3 minutes. Remove the fish, putting the fillets on the serving dish, and keep in a warm place.

Take 500 ml (17½ fl oz) of fish stock, reduce it over a brisk heat by a third, lower the heat. Stir in the crème fraîche and the tomato purée and season to taste. Remove from the heat and vigorously whisk in the egg yolks one by one. Return to the heat to thicken the sauce: do not let it boil. Trim the stalks from the watercress, chop the leaves and gently cook a quarter of them in butter: add to the sauce.

Pour the sauce over the fish and decorate with the remaining watercress.

From 'Le Petit Laurent' restaurant in Paris-7e: the chef recommends that you drink a still champagne with this dish.

CABILLAUD DIEPPOIS
Cod with mussels

PREPARATION TIME: 30 minutes
COOKING TIME: 15 minutes
FOR SIX

1¼ kg (2¾ lb) cod	30 g (1 oz) flour
1½ litres (2½ pints) mussels	250 ml (9 fl oz) milk
1 fish stock cube if available (see p. 15)	250 ml (9 fl oz) single cream
	1 lemon
pepper	1 sprig of parsley
40 g (scant 1½ oz) butter	

Put the cod into a fish kettle, sprinkle it with the stock cube and cover with water. Cover the kettle and bring slowly to the boil, letting it just bubble for about 5 minutes. Remove from the heat and put to one side.

Thoroughly clean and wash the mussels and put them in a covered pan with a glass of water. Season with pepper and cook briskly. Discard any unopened mussels and take the rest from their shells. Keep the cooking liquid to one side.

Make a roux with the butter and flour, cook it for a few minutes, then add the liquid in which the mussels were cooked, the milk and the cream. Stir thoroughly together and cook for about 5 minutes. Add the mussels and the juice from the lemon.

Take the cod from its stock and skin it. Arrange it on a long, warmed serving dish and pour the mussel sauce over it. Decorate with chopped parsley.

Elle advises that the cooking liquid from the mussels be strained several times to remove any traces of sand.

CABILLAUD AU GROS-PLANT
Cod in wine

PREPARATION TIME: 10 minutes
COOKING TIME: 10 minutes
FOR SIX

6 cod steaks
½ bottle dry white wine (see note)
800 g (1¾ lb) potatoes
2 onions
130 g (generous 4½ oz) butter
salt, pepper
30 g (1 oz) flour
1 tablespoon crème fraîche

Peel the potatoes, peel and chop the onions. Put the fish, vegetables wine and 100 g (3½ oz) of the butter into a pressure-cooker, season, close the lid and cook over a low heat for 10 minutes, counting from the time cooking pressure is reached. Remove the cod steaks and the potatoes and arrange them on a serving dish. Keep in a warm place.

Mix the remaining butter and flour into a paste and pass the cooking liquid through a sieve into a saucepan. Over the heat, whip the butter and flour paste into the liquid little by little. Stop when the sauce is sufficiently thick. Bring to the boil, remove immediately from the heat and stir in the crème fraîche. Check the seasoning and serve separately in a sauce-boat.

Elle says that Gros-Plant is the lesser wine of the Muscadet district. However, Muscadet is more likely to be obtainable and may be used in this recipe.

MORUE AU CANTAL
Salt-cod in a cheese sauce

PREPARATION TIME: 25 minutes (plus 24 hours of soaking)
COOKING TIME: 30 minutes
FOR SIX

½ a salt-cod
250 g (scant 9 oz) Cantal cheese
2 litres (3½ pints) milk
2 onions
75 g (generous 2½ oz) butter
3 large potatoes (cooked in their skins)
pepper
2 tablespoons white breadcrumbs

Skin the salt-cod and trim off fins etc. and cut up into pieces. Put the fish into a large dish, cover with milk and leave to soak for 24 hours.

Rinse and drain the fish, put it into a pan and cover with cold water. Bring it very slowly to the boil and at the first bubble take the pan from the heat, remove the fish and flake it.

Peel and chop the onions and cook them gently in 35 g (generous 1 oz) of butter. Peel and slice the potatoes and cut the cheese into strips. Butter an ovenproof dish and arrange, in successive layers, the flaked fish, the sliced potatoes, the strips of cheese and a little of the cooked onion. Repeat and finish with a thin layer of potato. Dot with knobs of butter, season with pepper and cover with a layer of breadcrumbs. Brown in a very hot oven (230°C/450°F/Gas Mark 8) for 30 minutes.

Elle says that if fillets of salt-cod are used instead, the soaking process may be cut to 10–12 hours.

PAIN DE POISSON AU BASILIC
Provençal fish cake

PREPARATION TIME: 15 minutes
COOKING TIME: about 1 hour
FOR SIX

600 g (1 lb 5 oz) cod fillet
1 kg (scant 2¼ lb) well ripened
  tomatoes
4 cloves of garlic
4 tablespoons olive oil

6 eggs
1 good sprig of basil
salt, pepper
tabasco

Peel and de-seed the tomatoes and chop them up. Peel and crush the garlic and put it in a pan with the chopped tomato and 3 tablespoons of oil. Stir and reduce to a thick sauce.

Check the cod fillets for any lingering bones. Put the raw fish through a blender and add it, together with the beaten eggs and the chopped basil, to the sauce. Season and add tabasco to taste. Mix well.

Oil a round cake tin and spread the mixture evenly in it. Stand the tin in a pan of water and cook in a moderate oven (180°C/350°F/Gas Mark 4) for about 40 minutes. Check that the cooking is complete by inserting a skewer: it should be clean when withdrawn.

Allow to cool and turn out on to a serving dish. Garnish with tomatoes cut into quarters and serve with a lemon mayonnaise which has been flavoured with chopped basil.

Elle notes that other white fish such as hake or haddock may be substituted for cod.

ASSIETTE AU HADDOCK
Smoked haddock salad

PREPARATION TIME: 35 minutes
COOKING TIME: 25 minutes
FOR SIX

300 g (10½ oz) smoked
  haddock fillet
250 ml (9 fl oz) milk
6 large artichokes
3 lemons

salt, pepper
200 g (7 oz) carrots
50 ml (1¾ fl oz) olive oil
100 g (3½ oz) Gruyère cheese

Cut the fish into strips across the fillet, put the pieces into a saucepan and cover them with the milk. Leave to soak.

Trim the stalks and the upper parts of the leaves from the artichokes and carefully cut out the choke. (A curved grapefruit knife does this well.) Wipe in a mixture of water and some lemon juice. Into a large saucepan, put just enough water barely to cover the artichokes; add salt and the juice of 1 lemon. As soon as the water boils, plunge the artichokes in and cook for 20 minutes.

Put the saucepan with the fish onto the heat and bring the milk to the boil. Let it bubble once or twice, then remove the fish. Put to one side.

Wash and trim the carrots, then finely grate them. Divide the grated carrot between six plates and arrange it in open circles. Sprinkle with the juice of 1 lemon and a little salt. Put an artichoke in the centre of each plate, sprinkle each one with olive oil and then arrange pieces of fish and thin slices of Gruyère on each one. Grate on some black pepper and serve.

Elle says that this dish is most delicious if eaten when the fish and artichokes are still warm.

COLIN AUX POIVRONS EN PAPILLOTES
Hake with sweet peppers

PREPARATION TIME: 15 minutes
COOKING TIME: 20 minutes
FOR SIX

6 hake steaks
2 green peppers
1 red pepper

2 lemons
olive oil
salt, pepper

Heat up the grill. Put peppers under the grill, turning them so as to char all sides. Wrap them in damp kitchen paper for 5 minutes when the charred outer skins will be simple to peel off. Then remove stalks, membranes and seeds from the peppers and cut into strips. This can be done in advance.

Squeeze lemon juice over the fish steaks. Cut six sheets of aluminium foil each large enough to envelop a fish steak, and lightly oil the top surfaces. Take half the strips of pepper and make a bed in the centre of each sheet of foil: lay a fish steak on each one. Decorate the surface of the fish with a criss-cross of pepper strips, pour a few drops of oil over the fish, season and close up the foil envelope.

Cook in a fairly hot oven (200°C/400°F/Gas Mark 6) for 20 minutes. Serve with a dish of savoury rice.

LIMANDES AU CIDRE
Lemon soles in cider

PREPARATION TIME: 10 minutes
COOKING TIME: 20–25 minutes
FOR SIX

2 lemon soles or dabs, each weighing 600 g (generous 1¼ lb)
fresh tarragon, parsley and chives

200 ml (7 fl oz) still dry cider
salt, pepper
30 g (1 oz) butter
150 g (generous 5 oz) crème fraîche

Ask your fishmonger to gut the fish through the gills. Thoroughly wash the fish and, with the aid of kitchen scissors, cut off fins and tail. With a sharp knife, make three crossways incisions in the upper side of each fish. Arrange them in a buttered ovenproof dish. Chop the herbs and sprinkle generously over the fish. Pour in the cider, season and dot with knobs of butter. Cook in a fairly hot oven (200°C/400°F/Gas Mark 6) for 20–25 minutes.

Five minutes before the end of the cooking time, pour the liquid in which the fish is cooked into a saucepan. Mix in the crème fraîche and pour this sauce over the fish.

Serve, very hot, with boiled potatoes. Just before serving, sprinkle on more chopped herbs.

LIMANDES À LA MOUSSE DE PERSIL
Lemon sole in a purée of parsley

PREPARATION TIME: 15 minutes
COOKING TIME: 12 minutes
FOR SIX

3 lemon soles or dabs, each
  weighing 500 g (generous 1 lb)
salt, pepper
4 shallots

400 ml (14 fl oz) dry white wine
6 bunches of Greek parsley
100 g (3½ oz) butter
50 g (scant 2 oz) crème fraîche

Ask your fishmonger to skin and fillet the fish. Fold each fillet in half and arrange them all in a buttered ovenproof dish. Season, sprinkle with finely-chopped shallots and pour in the white wine.

Cook the fish for 6–8 minutes in a very hot oven (230°C/450°F/Gas Mark 8).

Buy the Greek (or flat-leaved) parsley. Wash it carefully, remove the stalks and plunge the leaves into boiling water for 3 minutes. Run them under the cold tap, drain and reduce them to a purée in a blender or Mouli, finally passing them through a fine sieve.

Divide the parsley purée equally between two saucepans. Put one over a low heat and whisk in the butter, knob by knob, to make a rich purée. Gently heat the contents of second pan and beat in the crème fraîche. Extend each purée with 100 ml (3½ fl oz) of the liquid in which the fish was cooked. Check seasoning.

Line the bottom of a warmed serving dish with the buttered purée, arrange the fish fillets on it and finish off with a ring of the purée with crème fraîche around the edge. Serve immediately.

From the restaurant 'Michel Pasquet' in Paris-16e: the chef recommends that a Chablis or a Sancerre is drunk with this dish.

HOMARD AUX HERBES
Lobster with herbs

PREPARATION TIME: 30 minutes
COOKING TIME: 40 minutes
FOR SIX

3 lobsters of about 800 g (1¾ lb)
  each
200 g (7 oz) onions
3 shallots
200 g (7 oz) mixed vegetables
  (carrots, celery, baby turnips)

75 g (generous 2½ oz) butter
750 g (26 oz) crème fraîche
50 ml (1¾ fl oz) brandy
1 teaspoon each of chopped
  chives and chopped tarragon
salt, pepper

Plunge the lobsters into a large pan of boiling salted water. Allow 15–20 minutes of cooking time after the water has come back to the boil. Remove and run them under cold water. Break the neck joints, then stand the lobsters on end and let them drain for about 15 minutes. Take out the flesh from the claws and the tails and put to one side.

Peel and chop the onions and the shallots. Trim the vegetables and cut them into small dice and cook all gently in half the butter. When the ingredients are well softened, stir in the crème fraîche and boil for 5 minutes. Pass the sauce through a sieve by pressing with a wooden spoon, bring the sauce back to the boil and let it reduce by half. Keep in a warm place.

Cut the lobster tails into slices crossways. Heat the rest of the butter in a pan and quickly seal the lobster pieces and the claw-meat. Pour in the brandy and flame it. Pour these cooking juices into the sauce, add the chopped herbs, stir and check the seasoning.

Arrange the lobster in a warmed serving dish and cover with the sauce.

From the 3-star Burgundian restaurant 'La Mère Blanc' in Vonnas: the chef, Georges Blanc, recommends that this special dish be accompanied by a white Burgundy such as well-chilled Chassagne-Montrachet.

POISSON AU CITRON VERT
Cod in lime juice

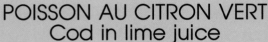

PREPARATION TIME: 15 minutes (plus 15 minutes on the previous day)
COOKING TIME: nil
FOR SIX

1¼ kg (scant 2¾ lb) cod fillet	4 tomatoes
10 limes	3 onions
parsley, chives	3 avocados
salt, pepper	tabasco

Remove any residual skin or bones from the fish and cut it into thin strips. Arrange them in a dish and cover with the juice of 8 of the limes. Season and sprinkle with the chopped herbs. Leave to marinate for 12 hours.

Cut the tomatoes into quarters, peel the onions and cut them into rings. Cut the avocados in half, remove the stone and skins, slice lengthways and sprinkle with the juice of the remaining limes. Divide the fish among individual serving dishes and decorate with tomato, onion and avocado. Stir a few drops of tabasco into the marinade and sprinkle it over the fish before serving.

MOUSSELINE DE HADDOCK
Baked smoked haddock

PREPARATION TIME: 20 minutes
COOKING TIME: 1 hour
FOR SIX

800 g (1¾ lb) smoked haddock fillet	30 g (1 oz) mint leaves
4 eggs	700 g (1 lb 9 oz) crème fraîche
	salt, pepper

Chill the blender bowl in the refrigerator. Separate the whites from the yolks of the eggs and put to one side.

Trim the smoked haddock of any residual skin or bones and reduce the fish fillets to a paste in the chilled blender. Blend in the egg whites and two-thirds of the mint, then add 300 g (10½ oz) of the crème fraîche, giving only a brief burst of the blender. Season with black pepper.

Butter six individual ramekin dishes and divide the fish mixture between them. Put them all into a pan of warm water and cook in a very hot oven (230°C/450°F/Gas Mark 8) for 1 hour. ⁃

To make the sauce, put the rest of the crème fraîche into a pan, bring to the boil and allow to reduce by half. Remove from the flame and beat in the egg yolks one by one. Salt lightly and season with pepper. Chop the remainder of the mint, add it to the sauce and serve separately.

From 'La Closerie des Lilas' restaurant in Paris-6ᵉ: the chef recommends that a Sancerre be drunk with this dish.

SALADE DE HARENGS FUMÉS
Smoked herring salad

PREPARATION TIME: 30 minutes
COOKING TIME: 5 minutes
FOR SIX

4 smoked herrings
1 litre (1¾ pints) mussels
1 large onion
250 g (scant 9 oz) tin of sweet-
    corn
1 red pepper

¼ cucumber
3 heads of chicory
French dressing flavoured with
    mustard
pinch of chopped fresh dill

Wash and scrape the mussels, discarding any that are not fresh or alive. Drop them in briskly-boiling water to open them. Drain and take the mussels out of their shells, discarding any that remain closed. Skin and fillet the smoked herrings and slice up.

Peel and slice the onion, and drain and rinse the sweetcorn. Remove stalks, membranes and seeds from the pepper and cut into strips. Peel and slice the cucumber. Divide the chicory into leaves and arrange all the ingredients in a salad bowl. Dress with the vinaigrette and finally sprinkle with chopped dill. Serve with brown bread and butter.

Elle suggests that if fresh dill cannot be found, then fronds of fennel, chopped up, may be substituted.

MARMITE DE MAQUEREAUX
Mackerel with dill

PREPARATION TIME: 10 minutes
COOKING TIME: 25 minutes
FOR SIX

3 good mackerel
3 onions
20 g (¾ oz) butter
large tin 800 g (1¾ lb) tomatoes

1 chicken stock cube
2 tablespoons chopped dill
2 tablespoons chopped parsley
½ lemon

Peel the onions and cut them into quarters. Cook them gently in butter for a few minutes: do not let them brown. Gut, wash and dry the mackerel. Put the cooked onion into an ovenproof dish and arrange the fish on top. Drain the juice from the tomatoes and put it into a bowl: dissolve the chicken cube in 250 ml (9 fl oz) of boiling water, pour this stock into the tomato juice and mix together.

Put the tomatoes around the fish, pour on the tomato stock and sprinkle with the chopped herbs. Cut the lemon into round slices and arrange these on the fish. Cook in a hot oven (220°C/425°F/Gas Mark 7) for 25 minutes. Serve with boiled potatoes.

Elle says if only small mackerel can be found, serve a larger number and reduce the cooking time to 15 minutes.

LOTTE EN BOUILLABAISSE
Provençal monkfish stew

PREPARATION TIME: 20 minutes
COOKING TIME: 20 minutes
FOR SIX

1¼ kg (2¾ lb) monkfish	For the stock:
6 slices French bread	½ teaspoon fennel seeds
300 g (10½ oz) potatoes	sea salt, pepper
300 g (10½ oz) tomatoes	1 bay leaf
200 g (7 oz) onions	3 cloves of garlic
30 g (1 oz) garlic cloves	1 onion
pinch powdered saffron	125 g (4½ oz) peeled shrimps
1 chilli pepper	1 fish head
300 g (10½ oz) mussels	

First prepare the stock. Put 1 litre (1¾ pints) water into a pan and add the fennel seeds, a tablespoon of sea salt, three twists of a black pepper mill, the bay leaf, crushed garlic, the peeled and chopped onion, the peeled shrimps and the fish head. Bring to the boil and cook, uncovered and just bubbling, for 20 minutes. Strain and put the liquid to one side.

Toast the bread, wash and peel the vegetables: cut the potatoes into thick slices, chop the tomatoes and thinly slice the onions and the garlic. Put to one side.

Cut the monkfish into 12 equal pieces. Place the fish stock over a brisk heat and, as it begins to bubble, put in the vegetables together with the saffron and the chopped chilli and cook together for 10 minutes. Add the monkfish and continue cooking for another 10 minutes.

Plunge the mussels into boiling water until they are open, remove most from their shells: keep a few half-shells as decoration. Three minutes before the fish is cooked, add the mussels to the dish. When cooking is finished, drain the liquid into a warmed tureen.

To serve, put a piece of toast in each bowl and add a portion of fish, mussels and vegetables. The liquid is added separately as desired.

STEAKS DE LOTTE AUX POIREAUX
Monkfish with leeks

PREPARATION TIME: 20 minutes
COOKING TIME: 1¾ hours
FOR SIX

1¼ kg (2¾ lb) monkfish	salt, white pepper
1 kg (2¼ lb) leeks	50 g (scant 2 oz) shallots
100 g (3½ oz) onions	100 ml (3½ fl oz) dry white wine
300 g (10½ oz) butter	300 g (10½ oz) crème fraîche
800 g (1¾ lb) sole trimmings	cayenne pepper
bouquet garni	parsley
1 lemon	

Ask your fishmonger to divide the monkfish into 6 steaks: tie each into a rounded shape with kitchen string.

Proceed to make the fish stock. Peel and chop the onions and cook them gently in 100 g (3½ oz) butter until transparent. Add the sole trimmings, the bouquet garni, half a peeled lemon and 600 ml (a generous pint) of water. Season and cook over a low heat for 1 hour until the volume is reduced by half.

Trim, wash and slice the white part of the leeks, put them in a pan and cook gently in 150 g (5 oz) butter. Season, keep in a warm place.

Butter a large fireproof dish. Peel and finely chop the shallots and line the bottom of the dish with them. Arrange the monkfish steaks, squeeze on the juice of half a lemon and pour in the white wine and the strained fish stock. Put the dish on the heat and as soon as the liquid begins to boil, move the dish into a pre-heated fairly hot oven (200°C/400°F/Gas Mark 6). Cook for 10 minutes.

Remove the fish steaks from the dish, cut off the strings and keep warm. Rapidly reduce the juices left, pour in the crème fraîche, season with cayenne and deglaze the pan by vigorously stirring with the back of a fork. Butter an ovenproof dish, line with the cooked leeks, arrange the fish steaks on top, cover with the sauce and return to the oven for 5 minutes. Just before serving, sprinkle the dish with chopped parsley.

LOTTE À LA NÎMOISE
Monkfish cooked with vegetables

PREPARATION TIME: 20 minutes
COOKING TIME: 35 minutes
FOR SIX

1½ kg (3 lb 5 oz) monkfish
1 baby turnip
2 carrots
2 sticks celery
1 leek
2 tomatoes

250 ml (9 fl oz) olive oil
4 cloves of garlic
3 sprigs thyme
1 egg yolk
salt, pepper

Divide the monkfish into pieces. Wash and trim the vegetables and cut them into thin sticks. Peel and de-seed the tomatoes and chop them up. In a heavy iron pan, gently cook all the tomatoes and all the vegetables in 2 tablespoons of oil. Add the monkfish, 1 sliced clove of garlic and the thyme. Cover the pan and cook for a further 25 minutes. Peel and crush the remaining garlic and put it in a mixing bowl with the beaten egg yolk. Season and whip in the remaining oil drop by drop, as when making mayonnaise.

Move the pieces of monkfish with a perforated spoon to a deep serving dish: keep warm. Put what remains in the cooking pan through a blender and with a fork gently fold in the garlic mayonnaise. Pour this sauce over the fish and serve immediately.

Elle says that the same dish may be made in a more ordinary but less expensive way by substituting cod for monkfish.

LOTTE AUX COURGETTES
Monkfish with courgettes

PREPARATION TIME: 20 minutes
COOKING TIME: 25 minutes
FOR SIX

1½ kg (3 lb 5 oz) monkfish
1 kg (2¼ lb) courgettes
salt, pepper
1 tablespoon peanut oil
50 g (scant 2 oz) shallots

250 ml (9 fl oz) dry white wine
1 good tablespoon crème fraîche
250 g (9 oz) butter
chives

Divide the monkfish into six equal steaks. Trim and peel the courgettes, cut them in half lengthways and divide them into pieces about 4 cm (1½ in) long and 2½ cm (1 in) thick. Round the ends to give an attractive shape. Cook for about 5 minutes in boiling salted water, drain and keep in a warm place.

Season the monkfish and arrange the steaks in an ovenproof earthenware dish. Moisten them with the peanut oil, cover with kitchen foil and cook in a very hot oven (230°C/450°F/Gas Mark 8) for about 20 minutes.

During this time, peel and finely chop the shallots. Put the shallots and the white wine into a small pan, season, and reduce over a moderate flame until the liquid has evaporated. Add the crème fraîche, bring it to the bubble briefly and remove from the heat. Beat in the butter, knob by knob, keeping the sauce hot by returning the pan to a low heat from time to time.

Arrange the fish and the courgettes on a warmed serving dish, cover with sauce and, just before serving, sprinkle with chopped chives.

From the restaurant 'Au Vieux Port' in Le Lavandou in Provence: the chef recommends that you drink a dry white wine of the region with this dish.

MULET AU VIN BLANC
Mullet in white wine

PREPARATION TIME: 15 minutes
COOKING TIME: 40 minutes
FOR SIX

1 mullet weighing 2 kg (scant 4½ lb)	1 bay leaf
5 shallots	fresh thyme
1 clove of garlic	1 litre (1¾ pints) white wine
200 g (7 oz) button mushrooms	30 g (1 oz) crème fraîche
2 lemons	150 g (5 oz) butter
salt, pepper	

Ask your fishmonger to gut and de-scale the fish. Rinse it well inside and out and lay it on a buttered fireproof dish. Peel and chop the shallots and garlic and sprinkle them over the fish. Trim the stalks of the mushrooms and wipe in a mixture of water and juice of 1½ lemons: slice and arrange around the fish. Season with salt, pepper, crushed bay leaf and the leaves of one or two sprigs of thyme. Pour in the white wine, cover with kitchen foil and cook in a very hot oven (230°C/450°F/Gas Mark 8) for 35–40 minutes. Baste the fish regularly with its own cooking liquid.

When the fish is cooked, remove it and the mushrooms from the dish and keep in a warm place. Sieve the liquid into a saucepan, reduce by half over a brisk flame, stir in the crème fraîche, let it bubble and remove from the heat. Whip in the butter, knob by knob, check the seasoning, then add the remaining lemon juice.

Arrange fish and mushrooms on a serving dish, cover with the sauce and serve.

SALADE DE MOULES AU CURRY
Mussel salad with curry dressing

PREPARATION TIME: 30 minutes
COOKING TIME: brief
FOR SIX

2 litres (3½ pints) mussels	2 tablespoons lemon juice
2 celery hearts	1 teaspoon curry powder
½ red pepper	salt, pepper
500 g (generous 1 lb) apples	6 leaves of fresh mint
6 tablespoons mayonnaise	fresh coriander leaves

Scrub the mussels and wash them under running water but do not soak them. Put them in a heavy iron pan over a brisk heat with 250 ml (9 fl oz) water until they open. Take the mussels out of their shells and put to one side.

Strain the mussel liquid through a fine sieve. Cut the celery hearts and the flesh of the red pepper into small pieces. Peel and core the apples, cut into quarters, then into thinner slices.

Thin the mayonnaise with the lemon juice and 6 tablespoons of mussel liquid. Season, mix with the curry powder and put the dressing into a salad bowl. Add the mussels, the apple, celery and red pepper and mix well together. Sprinkle with chopped mint and coriander, and serve chilled.

<u>Elle advises</u> that the red pepper will be more digestible if it is rapidly grilled and the outer skin peeled off (*see* p. 15).

MOULES AUX DEUX PÂTES
Mussels and pasta

PREPARATION TIME: 25 minutes
COOKING TIME: 20 minutes
FOR SIX

2 litres (3½ pints) mussels	40 g (scant 1½ oz) flour
4 shallots	250 g (9 oz) crème fraîche
1 sprig of parsley	3 tablespoons chopped fresh
100 ml (3½ fl oz) dry white wine	basil
salt, cayenne pepper	200 g (7 oz) plain tagliatelle
500 ml (17½ fl oz) fish stock	200 g (7 oz) green tagliatelle
120 g (scant 4½ oz) butter	

Scrape and wash the mussels in plenty of water. Put them in a pan with the peeled and chopped shallots, the chopped parsley, the white wine and a little cayenne pepper. Cook over a brisk heat until they open; discard any unopened shells. Take the mussels from their shells and put on one side.

Strain the cooking liquid through fine muslin or coffee filter papers, and add it to the fish stock. Make a white roux in a saucepan with 90 g (3 oz) butter and the flour, add the fish stock and cook for 5 minutes. Stir in the crème fraîche and heat until the sauce just bubbles. Add the mussels and the basil to the pan and gently heat through.

At the same time, the pasta should be cooked, each colour separately, in boiling salted water. When cooked to taste, drain off the water and fold in half the remaining butter into each pasta.

Divide the two pastas equally among 6 warmed plates, put a portion of mussels in sauce on each, and serve immediately.

(CONTINUED)

Divide the mussels among individual ovenproof dishes and pour in the sauce until three-quarters-full. Lay slices of toasted French bread on the top, sprinkle with grated cheese and brown quickly under the grill. Serve immediately.

GRATINÉE DE MOULES
Gratin of mussels

PREPARATION TIME: 35 minutes
COOKING TIME: 1 hour 20 minutes
FOR SIX

2 litres (3½ pints) mussels	3 sprigs fennel
2 shallots	1 bay leaf
1 sprig parsley	1 sprig thyme
30 g (1 oz) butter	salt, pepper
½ bottle of dry white wine	1 pinch saffron
150 g (5 oz) onions	4 egg yolks
100 ml (3½ fl oz) olive oil	3 tablespoons crème fraîche
2 cloves of garlic	French bread
150 g (5 oz) leeks	50 g (scant 2 oz) grated
2 fish heads (cod)	Emmenthal cheese
750 g (generous 1½ lb) tomatoes	

Scrape and wash the mussels, changing the water several times. Put them in a pan together with the peeled and chopped shallots, the parsley, butter and 250 ml (9 fl oz) white wine. Cook over a brisk heat until they open. Remove the mussels from their shells and keep in a warm place: strain the cooking liquid and put to one side.

Peel and slice the onions and cook gently in the olive oil, with chopped garlic and the leeks, trimmed, sliced and cut into strips. After 5 minutes add the fish heads and raise to a brisk heat. Add the tomatoes, chopped and de-seeded, the cooking liquid from the mussels, a glass of white wine, 2 litres (3½ pints) water and the rest of the herbs.

Cook for a good hour, strain the liquid and pick out the flesh from the fish heads. Put the pieces of fish back into the mixture and pass it all through a blender. Return to the saucepan, season, add the pinch of saffron and bring to the boil for 5 minutes.

Beat the egg yolks and fold them into the crème fraîche. Take the saucepan from the heat and stir in the crème fraîche mixture.

(CONTINUED OPPOSITE)

MOULES AUX POIREAUX
Mussels with sliced leeks

PREPARATION TIME: 40 minutes
COOKING TIME: 20 minutes
FOR SIX

3 litres (5¼ pints) mussels
3 leeks
4 shallots
50 g (scant 2 oz) butter
400 ml (14 fl oz) dry white wine

pepper
2 pinches powdered saffron
100 ml (3½ fl oz) olive oil
300 ml (10½ fl oz) crème fraîche
1 sprig of chervil

Scrub and wash the mussels under running water: do not let them soak in a bucket. Trim and wash the leeks, cut them in half crossways, then into fine strips. Peel and chop the shallots.

Put half the butter into a large heavy saucepan and gently cook the shallots until transparent; add the white wine and bring to the boil for 3 minutes. Add the mussels and season with pepper. As soon as the mussels open, remove from the pan, take them out of their shells and keep to one side in a warm place. Discard any unopened.

Strain the cooking liquid into a saucepan through a fine sieve lined with muslin. Add the saffron and, over a brisk heat, reduce the liquid by half.

Cook the sliced leeks in olive oil for 3 minutes, add the liquid from the saucepan and simmer for 5 minutes. Stir in the crème fraîche, take the pan from the heat and incorporate the rest of the butter, knob by knob, whisking to obtain a smooth, creamy sauce.

Divide the mussels among individual serving dishes, cover with sauce, sprinkle with chopped chervil and serve very hot.

From 'Le Dinanderie' restaurant in Metz: the chef suggests that a white wine from Sancerre be drunk with this dish.

ROUGETS AU FENOUIL
Red mullet with fennel

PREPARATION TIME: 20 minutes
COOKING TIME: 20 minutes
FOR SIX

3 good red mullet
500 g (generous 1 lb) fennel
300 g (10½ oz) celery
1 onion
1 tablespoon olive oil

300 g (10½ oz) butter
90 ml (3 fl oz) pastis
salt
12 leaves of fresh basil

Ask your fishmonger to de-scale and fillet the fish. Trim and wash the bulbs of fennel and reserve the fronds as decoration when serving. Trim and wash the celery, peel the onion and slice up all three vegetables. Put them all into a heavy pan in which the oil and a knob of butter have been heated and, over a brisk heat, sweat them for about 8 minutes. Reduce the heat if the vegetables begin to brown. Stir frequently and, when cooked, add a third of the pastis.

Spread the vegetables over the bottom of an ovenproof dish. Lightly salt the fish fillets and lay them on top of the vegetables, skin side upwards. Put the dish into a very hot oven (230°C/450°F/Gas Mark 8) and cook for about 6 minutes. Halfway through, decorate the fish with the fennel fronds. In the meantime chop up the basil.

Take a small saucepan and put in 30 ml (1 fl oz) of pastis and an equal amount of water. Bring it to the boil and as soon as it begins to bubble remove from the heat and whisk in the remaining butter, knob by knob. From time to time, return the pan to the heat and when all the butter has been whisked in, add the chopped basil.

Remove the fish from the oven and sprinkle with the remaining pastis. On warm plates, arrange a bed of vegetables, place a fish fillet on top and then pour on the basil sauce. Serve at once.

From the restaurant 'Chez Serge' in La Rochelle: the chef recommends that you drink either a Muscadet or a Sancerre with this dish.

TERRINE DE SAUMON
Salmon terrine

PREPARATION TIME: 30 minutes
COOKING TIME: 1 hour
FOR SIX

1 kg (2¼ lb) salmon, boned and skinned
700 g (1 lb 9 oz) whiting fillets
3 egg whites
500 g (generous 1 lb) crème fraîche
salt, pepper
butter
fresh mint

Put the whiting fillets through a blender and mix in the egg whites. Remove the fish to a cold mixing bowl and blend in half the crème fraîche, well chilled. Season.

Take a terrine mould (a deep oblong cake tin can be used) and butter it. Separate the salmon into fillets. Put a layer of whiting in the bottom, then a layer of salmon fillet, then more whiting and so on until the mould is full. End with a layer of whiting.

Cover the mould with kitchen foil and cook it in a pan of hot water in a fairly hot oven (200°C/400°F/Gas Mark 6) for 1 hour. Put a weighted board on top of the terrine, leave to cool then refrigerate until thoroughly chilled.

Turn out and serve accompanied by a sauce of whipped remaining crème fraîche seasoned with salt, pepper and chopped mint.

SAUMON À L'ANETH
Salmon in dill

PREPARATION TIME: 15 minutes
COOKING TIME: 30 minutes
FOR SIX TO EIGHT

1 salmon weighing 2 kg (4½ lb)
50 g (scant 2 oz) butter
sprigs of fresh dill
salt, pepper
200 g (7 oz) crème fraîche

Ask your fishmonger to remove the head, tail and spine of the salmon. Mix together butter and 4 tablespoons of chopped dill; season.

Wash the fish under running water and dry thoroughly with kitchen paper. Spread the herb-butter over the inside of the fish, put it on a large piece of kitchen foil and securely envelop it. Cook in a fairly hot oven (200°C/400°F/Gas Mark 6) for 30 minutes.

The dish may be served hot or cold, accompanied by new potatoes, lemon slices, a green salad and a sauce made by mixing 4 tablespoons of chopped dill and seasoning with the crème fraîche.

SARDINES À L'ESCABÈCHE
Marinated sardines

PREPARATION TIME: 15 minutes
COOKING TIME: 3–5 minutes per batch, plus 15 minutes
FOR SIX

30 sardines, weighing about 1 kg (2¼ lb)
250 ml (9 fl oz) wine vinegar
1 bulb of garlic
12 sprigs of thyme
salt, pepper
3 lemons

Gut and wash the sardines and grill them on both sides for 3–5 minutes.

Put the vinegar, the chopped garlic and the thyme into a saucepan. Season and slow-boil for 15 minutes. Pour the liquid onto the sardines while they are still warm and leave to marinate in a cool place.

Serve chilled with two pieces of quartered lemon per person.

Elle suggests that a spoonful of olive oil poured on to each portion just before serving will enhance the dish.

SARDINES AU GROS-PLANT
Sardines in white wine

PREPARATION TIME: 25 minutes
COOKING TIME: 30 minutes
FOR SIX

36 sardines
1 fish stock cube if available (see p. 15)
1 bottle white wine (Gros-Plant or Muscadet)
350 g (12½ oz) mushrooms
1 lemon
2 onions
125 g (4½ oz) butter
chives

Gut and clean the fish and arrange them in a shallow fireproof dish. Crumble over the fish stock cube, pour on half the bottle of wine and add sufficient water to cover the fish. Bring slowly to the boil, remove from the heat and leave the sardines in their liquid.

Trim the stalks of the mushrooms and wipe them in a mixture of water and lemon juice. Chop them. Peel and chop the onions, and then gently cook mushrooms and onions together in 50 g (scant 2 oz) butter. Add the rest of the white wine and 300 ml (10½ fl oz) of the liquid, strained, in which the sardines were cooked. Reduce the volume by a third over a brisk heat. Pass through a sieve, pressing the vegetables firmly with the back of a wooden spoon. Return the sauce to the heat and, knob by knob, whip in the remainder of the butter.

Drain the sardines, arrange them on a warmed serving dish, cover with sauce and chopped chives and serve.

Elle says that if you would prefer a thicker sauce, mix in a teaspoon of flour made into a paste with cold water and cook for a few minutes, stirring all the time.

SAINT-JACQUES AU RIESLING
Scallops in white wine

PREPARATION TIME: 30 minutes
COOKING TIME: 5 minutes
FOR SIX

12 scallops	wine vinegar
250 g (scant 9 oz) radicchio	salt, pepper
500 g (generous 1 lb) chicory	50 g (scant 2 oz) butter
1 bunch of watercress	150 ml (generous 5 fl oz) Riesling
peanut oil	

Remove scallops and their coral from the shells and wash them thoroughly to remove any traces of sand. Dry and trim them neatly. Put to one side.

Rinse all the salad vegetables and divide the radicchio and chicory into separate leaves. Make a dressing with 3 tablespoons of peanut oil, 1 tablespoon of wine vinegar and seasoning.

Melt the butter in a pan and cook the scallops and coral over a very gentle heat for about 3 minutes. Season.

In the meantime, put the salad vegetables in a bowl and thoroughly mix with the dressing. Divide salad and scallops into portions and arrange on individual dishes.

Pour the fat from the pan, put in the white wine. Bring to the boil while vigorously scraping the base of the pan with the back of a fork. Allow to bubble for 1–2 minutes. Pour onto the scallop salads while still warm.

Elle says it is important not to overcook the scallops or they will become tough and rubbery.

RAGOÛT DE COQUILLES
Scallop and vegetable stew

PREPARATION TIME: 40 minutes
COOKING TIME: 40 minutes
FOR SIX

24 scallops	1 egg yolk
100 g (3½ oz) carrots	100 ml (3½ fl oz) olive oil
80 g (scant 3 oz) baby turnips	200 ml (7 fl oz) fish stock
80 g (scant 3 oz) courgettes	50 ml (1¾ fl oz) white wine
60 g (2 oz) butter	200 g (7 oz) crème fraîche
100 g (3½ oz) French beans	1 lemon
100 g (3½ oz) garlic	salt, pepper

Remove the scallops and their coral from the shells and thoroughly wash and clean them. Peel carrots, turnips and courgettes and cut them into pieces 3 cm (just over 1 inch) long. Trim the ends to give each piece the rough shape of an olive. Put each vegetable in a separate saucepan and add water to half their depth. Season with salt and put 20 g (¾ oz) butter in each pan. Cook each until just tender, for about 10–15 minutes.

Trim the beans and cut them into similar lengths as above. Cook for 15 minutes in boiling salted water. As each vegetable is cooked, drain and keep in a warm place.

Make an aïoli by first crushing the cloves of garlic. Mix with the egg yolk and incorporate the oil, drop by drop, as if making a mayonnaise.

Put fish stock and white wine into a saucepan, bring to the boil and reduce volume by one-third. Mix in the crème fraîche, add a few drops of lemon juice and boil for 5 minutes. Remove from the heat, stir in the aïoli, season, pass the sauce through a sieve and return to a gentle heat, taking care that it does not boil.

Cook the scallops and coral very gently (the chef whose recipe this is cooks them in a non-stick pan without the addition of any liquid). Divide the scallops and the vegetables among individual serving dishes and cover with very hot sauce. Serve at once.

FEUILLETÉ DE SAUMON
Salmon in puff pastry

PREPARATION TIME: 15 minutes
COOKING TIME: 30 minutes
FOR EIGHT

300 g (10½ oz) smoked salmon
50 g (scant 2 oz) shallots
70 g (2½ oz) butter
125 g (4½ oz) white breadcrumbs
2 lemons
1 teaspoon pastis
5 eggs

500 g (generous 1 lb) frozen puff
 pastry
2 tins lobster bisque
2 tablespoons tomato purée
salt, pepper
cayenne pepper
2 tablespoons crème fraîche

Peel and chop the shallots and cook them gently in 30 g (1 oz) butter. Cut the salmon into small pieces and thoroughly mix in a bowl with the shallots, the rest of the butter, the breadcrumbs, the juice of the lemons, the pastis and four eggs. Leave to chill for 30 minutes.

Roll out the pastry on a lightly-floured board to a thickness of 3 mm (⅛ inch). Cut it into 16 oblongs 10 cm by 8 cm (4 inches by 3 inches approximately). Divide the salmon mixture into eight parts and put each one onto an oblong of pastry. Cover each with a second oblong and press the edges together all round. Beat the last egg with a tablespoon of water and brush the top surface of each pastry case. Cook in a very hot oven (230°C/450°F/Gas Mark 8) for 20 minutes.

To make the sauce, put the contents of the two tins of lobster bisque into a saucepan and mix with 200 ml (7 fl oz) water and tomato purée. Season, add a pinch of cayenne pepper and let it just simmer for about 10 minutes. Stir in the crème fraîche, and let it bubble for a moment.

Arrange the pastry cases on warm plates, and serve the sauce separately.

SAUMON À L'ARDENNAISE
Salmon Ardennes-fashion

PREPARATION TIME: 30 minutes (1 hour in advance)
COOKING TIME: 20 minutes
FOR SIX

2 kg (4½ lb) filleted salmon
100 ml (3½ fl oz) dry white wine
4 lemons
salt, pepper
6 slices streaky bacon (smoked)
4 tablespoons peanut oil
1 clove of garlic
thyme, savory, bay leaf
3 tablespoons chopped parsley

For the sauce:
3 shallots
180 g (scant 6½ oz) salted butter
pepper
1 lemon
1 tablespoon crème fraîche

Divide the fish into six equal portions. Put them in a dish with the white wine, the juice of half a lemon and a little black pepper. Leave to marinate for 1 hour.

Take the rind off the bacon and put two half-slices on each piece of salmon. Salt lightly. Prepare six pieces of kitchen foil large enough to fold over a fish portion: oil them and place salmon and bacon on each one.

Peel and chop the garlic, chop the leaves of three sprigs each of thyme and savory. Crumble the bay leaf and mix all these herbs with the chopped parsley. Sprinkle each fish portion with herbs and pour on a few drops of oil. Carefully close the foil envelopes and cook in a very hot oven (230°C/450°F/Gas Mark 8) for 15–20 minutes.

To make the sauce, peel and finely chop the shallots and put them in a small saucepan with the strained liquid from the marinade, and a tablespoon of water. Bring to the boil and cook until the liquid has evaporated. Remove from the heat and whisk in the butter, knob by knob, warming the pan from time to time over a low heat. Season with pepper, add a dash of lemon juice and mix in the crème fraîche. Serve the salmon with quartered lemons, and the sauce separately.

COQUILLES À LA NORMANDE
Scallops in a cream sauce

PREPARATION TIME: 20 minutes
COOKING TIME: 10 minutes
FOR SIX

24 scallops
500 g (generous 1 lb) button
  mushrooms
2 lemons
3 cloves of garlic

50 g (scant 2 oz) butter
salt, pepper
1 tablespoon flour
350 g (scant 12½ oz) crème
  fraîche

Wash scallops and coral under running water so that no trace of sand remains. Drain.

Trim the stalks of the mushrooms and wipe them in lemon juice diluted with water. Slice them and chop the garlic. Melt the butter in a large casserole and gently cook mushrooms and garlic together. When the mushrooms have given out all their juices, pour the liquid into another pan to which the scallops and coral should then be added. Season and cook over a low heat for 3–4 minutes. Remove from the heat and add the mushrooms.

Put the flour into a saucepan and work into a smooth paste with the scallops' cooking liquid. Stir in the crème fraîche, check the seasoning and put it over a low heat, stirring constantly with a wooden spoon while it thickens. Put the scallops and mushrooms into the sauce, stir and serve immediately on individual scallop shells.

<u>Elle says</u> that three scallops per person could be enough, especially for a first course.

COQUILLES PAUL BLANC
Scallops Paul Blanc

PREPARATION TIME: 15 minutes
COOKING TIME: 30 minutes
FOR SIX

18 scallops
100 g (3½ oz) button mushrooms
1 lemon
100 g (3½ oz) butter
3 shallots
salt, pepper

1 pinch powdered saffron
100 ml (3½ fl oz) white wine
250 g (scant 9 oz) crème fraîche
1 tablespoon flour
1 teaspoon pastis
2 egg yolks

Remove scallops and corals from their shells, wash them thoroughly under running water, drain. If the scallops are particularly thick, cut them in half across the grain.

Trim the mushrooms, wash in cold water, dry with kitchen paper and sprinkle with lemon juice. Chop them finely and cook gently in 20 g (¾ oz) butter. They will be cooked when they have given up their juices.

Melt 30 g (1 oz) butter in a shallow pan and cook the peeled and chopped shallots over a low heat until they are transparent. At this point, add the scallops and coral and season with salt, pepper and saffron. Add the white wine and 100 g (3½ oz) crème fraîche to the pan, stir and cook gently for about 2 minutes. Remove the scallops with a perforated spoon and keep to one side in a warm place.

Make a paste by working together a tablespoon of flour with an equal measure of butter. Reduce the liquid in the pan by one-third then beat in the paste to produce a smooth sauce. Flavour with the teaspoon of pastis.

Whisk the egg yolks and the remainder of the cream together. Just before you are ready to serve, stir this into the sauce and let it thicken without boiling. Put the scallops into the sauce and serve with rice.

[73]

FILETS DE SOLE MÂCONNAISE
Fillets of sole in red wine

PREPARATION TIME: 35 minutes
COOKING TIME: 35 minutes
FOR SIX

fillets of 3 good sole	400 g (14 oz) button mushrooms
2 carrots	1 lemon
1 onion	100 g (3½ oz) butter
750 ml (1 bottle) red wine	24 small white onions
bouquet garni	1 tablespoon caster sugar
salt, pepper	20 g (¾ oz) flour

Peel the carrots and onion and slice into rings. Put them into a saucepan, cover with the red wine. Add the bouquet garni, season, bring to the boil and cook covered for 30 minutes.

Wipe the mushrooms in lemon juice diluted with water, trim and slice them and cook gently in 50 g (scant 2 oz) butter until their juices have evaporated.

Peel the small onions and put in a pan with 30 g (1 oz) butter and the caster sugar. Pour in water until the onions are just covered. Cook covered for 20 minutes. Remove the lid and continue cooking until the water has all evaporated and the onions are caramelised.

Arrange the fillets of sole in a casserole, pour on the red wine drained from the vegetables and simmer for between 3 and 5 minutes, according to the thickness of the fish. Remove the fillets and put to one side in a warm place; reduce the red wine to half its volume.

Work the flour and the rest of the butter together into a paste, remove the red wine from the heat and mix in the paste little by little. Return the sauce to the heat occasionally for a few moments and when the sauce is quite smooth and thick enough, stop adding butter and flour paste.

Arrange the fish fillets on a warm serving dish and place the onions and mushrooms around them. Cover with sauce and serve immediately.

SOLES AU PAMPLEMOUSSE
Sole with grapefruit

PREPARATION TIME: 15 minutes
COOKING TIME: 10 minutes
FOR SIX

fillets of 3 good sole	300 g (10½ oz) cream
1 pink grapefruit	4 teaspoons honey (preferably
500 ml (17½ fl oz) fish stock	acacia)
60 g (2 oz) butter	salt, pepper

Ask your fishmonger to give you the trimmings of the filleted soles and use these to prepare the fish stock (see p.15).

Peel and divide the grapefruit, peel the segments and chop up half of them. Arrange the sole fillets, folded in half, in a pan and put a small knob of butter on each. Cover with the fish stock and add the cream, the honey and the chopped grapefruit. Season, bring to the boil and simmer for 5–6 minutes.

Remove the fish fillets and keep in a warm place. Over a brisk heat reduce the cooking liquid by half, check the seasoning, remove from heat and make the sauce by beating in the remaining butter, knob by knob. Vigorously whisk the sauce and put it back on the heat from time to time without allowing it to boil.

Arrange the sole fillets on a warmed serving dish, cover with the sauce and decorate with the remaining segments of grapefruit.

From the restaurant 'Lefebre' in Paris-7ᵉ: the chef recommends that a red Sancerre goes best with this dish.

TRUITES FARCIES À L'OSEILLE
Trout stuffed with sorrel

PREPARATION TIME: 45 minutes
COOKING TIME: 25 minutes
FOR SIX

6 trout, each about 250 g (9 oz)
200 g (7 oz) fresh sorrel
100 g (3½ oz) white bread
 without crusts
100 ml (3½ fl oz) milk
300 g (10½ oz) fillet of whiting
1 bouquet of mixed herbs

3 shallots
salt, pepper
200 ml (7 fl oz) dry white wine
200 ml (7 fl oz) dry vermouth
6 egg yolks
125 g (4½ oz) crème fraîche

Wash and trim the sorrel and cook it for 2 minutes in salted boiling water. Drain and squeeze out surplus water: chop the sorrel and put to one side.

Ask your fishmonger to fillet and gut the fish through the spine. Wash the fish thoroughly and dry with kitchen paper.

Soak the bread in the milk. Put the whiting fillets, the mixed herbs and 1 peeled shallot into a blender and mix together. Squeeze out the bread, add it to the blender, season and blend together. Stuff each trout with the mixture and arrange in an ovenproof dish, surrounded by the remainder of the shallots, peeled and chopped. Season and pour the white wine and the vermouth over the fish and cook in a very hot oven (230°C/450°F/Gas Mark 8) for 10 minutes. Remove the trout, carefully skin them and arrange on a warmed serving dish. Cover with kitchen foil and keep warm by putting them back in the oven with the heat turned off and the oven door ajar.

Pour the cooking juices into a saucepan and reduce them over a brisk heat by two-thirds. Put to one side.

In a double-boiler and using a gentle heat, whisk egg yolks and crème fraîche together until the mixture is thick enough to form an unbroken ribbon when the whisk is lifted out. Add the cooking liquid and the chopped sorrel and continue to whisk while warming through. Cover the trout with the sauce and serve immediately.

TRUITES BENDOR
Trout in pastis sauce

PREPARATION TIME: 15 minutes
COOKING TIME: 20 minutes
FOR SIX

6 trout
butter
1 litre (1¾ pints) cold fish stock
300 g (10½ oz) crème fraîche
6 egg yolks
3 teaspoons pastis

nutmeg
salt, pepper
50 g (scant 2 oz) flaked almonds
50 g (scant 2 oz) grated
 Emmenthal cheese

Gut, clean and wipe the fish. Arrange them in a buttered ovenproof dish, pour in the fish stock and cover with a buttered sheet of greaseproof paper. Cook for 10 minutes in a very hot oven (230°C/450°F/Gas Mark 8).

During this time, put the crème fraîche, the egg yolks, the pastis, a pinch of grated nutmeg and seasoning into a saucepan. Whisk all the ingredients together over a low heat and remove as soon as the sauce will coat the back of a spoon.

Drain the trout, carefully, remove the skins, and arrange them on a serving dish. Cover with sauce and sprinkle with flaked almonds and grated cheese. Put the dish under the grill for 5 minutes. Serve at once.

From 'Le Bretagne' restaurant in Saint-Omer in northern France: the chef recommends that a Sancerre be drunk with this dish.

TRUITES MARINÉES EN SALADE
Marinated trout

PREPARATION TIME: 45 minutes (8 hours in advance)
COOKING TIME: 15 minutes
FOR SIX

3 trout, each weighing about
    300 g (10½ oz)
salt, pepper
3 lemons
6 tablespoons olive oil
fresh herbs: thyme, dill, bay leaf,
    chervil and chives
1 head of celery

2 medium-sized cucumbers
375 g (generous 13 oz) French
    beans
300 g (10½ oz) button
    mushrooms
mustard powder
1½ tablespoons red wine vinegar
6 tablespoons whipping cream

Ask your fishmonger to skin and fillet the fish. Remove any residual bones and lay the fish in a flat dish. Season. Squeeze on the juice of 2 lemons and pour on the olive oil. Sprinkle with a good pinch of chopped thyme, a crushed bay leaf and a teaspoon of each of the other herbs, all chopped. Leave to marinate for 8 hours, turning the fish in the marinade from time to time. At the end of this time, divide each fillet into three equal pieces.

Wash and trim the celery and cut each stalk into thin strips about 4 cm (generous 1½ inches) long. Peel the cucumbers, cut them in half lengthways and scoop out the seeds. Cut them up also into 4 cm (1½ inch) strips. Trim the beans, cook them for 15 minutes in boiling salted water, drain and rinse in cold water. Trim the mushrooms, wipe them with a mixture of lemon juice and water and cut them also into thin slices.

Make a dressing in a bowl by mixing together a good pinch of dry mustard with the wine vinegar. Season and slowly whisk in the cream. Put all the vegetables into the bowl and mix to cover them well with dressing.

Arrange the vegetables on individual serving dishes and divide the pieces of marinated fish among them. Just before serving, sprinkle with a little chopped chives.

MOUSSELINE DE TRUITES
Trout mousse

PREPARATION TIME: 30 minutes
COOKING TIME: 35 minutes
FOR EIGHT

8 trout
150 g (5 oz) butter
8 eggs (4 separated)
500 g (generous 1 lb) crème
    fraîche
salt, pepper

4 shallots
½ bottle champagne (preferably
    blanc de blanc)
250 ml (scant 9 fl oz) fish stock
tinned truffles or jar of Danish
    lumpfish roe

Ask your fishmonger to fillet the trout. Put the fish through a blender, add 50 g (scant 2 oz) butter which has been well softened with a fork, 4 whole eggs and 4 egg yolks and blend well together.

Whisk the 4 egg whites until they are stiff and lightly whip the crème fraîche. Carefully fold these two ingredients into the blended fish, season. Butter 8 individual soufflé dishes, fill each with the fish mixture and cook covered in a pan of water on the top of the stove for 15–20 minutes.

Peel and finely chop the shallots and put them in a saucepan with the champagne. Reduce by half over a brisk heat. Stir in the fish stock and continue reducing until about ⅓ litre (12 fl oz) remains. Remove the pan from the heat, season to taste and beat in remaining butter, knob by knob.

Turn out the trout mousses on to a warmed serving dish, decorate each one with a slice of truffle (or a small spoonful of roe) and a little sauce. Serve the rest of the sauce separately. If desired, the serving dish may be garnished with glazed young vegetables.

From the restaurant 'Le Moulin du Landion' in Dolancourt: the chef recommends that the best thing to drink with this special dish is more of the champagne used in the sauce.

SALADE DE CRABE AU RHUM
Crab in rum sauce

PREPARATION TIME: 15 minutes
COOKING TIME: 5 minutes
FOR SIX TO EIGHT

1 large tin of crab (or fresh crab
  meat if available)
1 lettuce
4 tinned artichoke bottoms
juice of 2 lemons
2 avocado pears
2 sticks of celery

For the sauce:
½ liqueur glass rum
1 egg yolk
mustard
salt, pepper
olive oil
4 tablespoons crème fraîche
2 teaspoons chopped parsley

Trim, wash and drain the lettuce. Drain the artichoke bottoms, and sprinkle them with half the lemon juice. Cut into pieces.

Divide each avocado in half, remove the stone and scoop out the flesh in balls. Roll them in the remaining lemon juice. Cut the celery sticks into thin slices.

Line individual serving dishes with lettuce leaves and divide the crab meat, the artichoke bottoms and the avocado pieces among them.

To make the sauce, first prepare a stiff mayonnaise with the egg yolk, mustard and oil. Whip the crème fraîche, chopped parsley and rum together and fold the mixture into the mayonnaise. Season and serve the sauce separately.

Elle says that vinegar should not be used in making the mayonnaise or the flavour of the rum will be lost.

CHOUCROÛTE DU PÊCHEUR
Fisherman's sauerkraut

PREPARATION TIME: 20 minutes
COOKING TIME: 2½ hours
FOR SIX

800 g (1¾ lb) smoked haddock
  fillets
800 g (1¾ lb) monkfish
2 or 3 onions
60 g (2 oz) lard
1 bottle dry white wine
10 juniper berries
1 teaspoon sugar
salt, pepper
1½ kg (3¼ lb) tinned sauerkraut
200 ml (7 fl oz) milk

50 g (scant 2 oz) butter

For the sauce:
3 shallots
100 ml (3½ fl oz) wine vinegar
200 ml (7 fl oz) dry white wine
1 sugar lump
4 egg yolks
200 g (7 oz) crème fraîche
salt, pepper

Peel and chop the onions and in a large saucepan cook them gently in lard until transparent. Add the bottle of wine, the crushed juniper berries, the sugar and season. Bring to the boil for 5 minutes.

Thoroughly wash and drain the sauerkraut, break it up and add it to the pan. Cook covered over a low heat for 2½ hours. During this time, poach the smoked haddock fillets in the milk, to which some water has been added. Remove from the heat as soon as the milk begins to boil. Put the monkfish in an ovenproof dish, dot with butter and cook in a very hot oven (230°C/450°F/Gas Mark 8) for 20 minutes.

To make the sauce, peel and chop the shallots and put them with the vinegar, the wine and the sugar lump into a small saucepan, bring to the boil and reduce by half. Mix the egg yolks and the crème fraîche in a separate bowl, season. Remove the shallot pan from the flame and beat in the egg and the cream mixture. Return to a very low flame and let the sauce thicken, beating constantly. As soon as it is thick enough to coat a spoon, pour it into a sauceboat.

Arrange the sauerkraut and fish on a serving dish and garnish with boiled potatoes.

TURBOT AUX POIREAUX
Turbot and leeks

PREPARATION TIME: 20 minutes
COOKING TIME: 40 minutes
FOR SIX

a 2½-kg (5½-lb) turbot
6 large leeks
60 g (2 oz) butter
5 tablespoons crème fraîche
4 shallots

150 ml (5 fl oz) dry white wine
300 ml (10½ fl oz) fish stock
½ lemon
salt, pepper

Ask your fishmonger to skin the fish and remove the fillets.

Wash and trim the leeks and cut into thin slices. Melt 20 g (¾ oz) butter in a pan and over a low heat cook the leeks gently for 20 minutes. Stir in the crème fraîche, cook for 5 more minutes, put to one side in a warm place.

Arrange the turbot fillets in a pan, dot them with half the remaining butter, sprinkle with peeled and chopped shallots and pour in the wine and the fish stock. Bring to the boil and cook over a brisk heat for 15 minutes. Remove the fish and keep in a warm place.

Reduce the cooking liquid by half and stir in the lemon juice. Remove the pan from the heat and whisk in remaining butter, a small lump at a time. Season the sauce to taste.

Gently re-warm the leeks, spread them on the serving dish, arrange the turbot fillets on top and cover with the sauce.

From the restaurant 'Lord Gourmand' in Paris-8ᵉ: the chef suggests that either a Pouilly-Fumé from the Loire or a still champagne goes excellently with this dish.

MERLAN À LA VERACRUZ
Whiting Veracruz

PREPARATION TIME: 15 minutes
COOKING TIME: 10 minutes
FOR SIX

6 good whiting fillets
6 potatoes
4 onions
4 tomatoes

100 ml (3½ fl oz) olive oil
salt, pepper
1 red chilli
thyme, bay leaf

Cook the potatoes in boiling salted water for about 15 minutes when they should be cooked but still firm. Drain, put to one side.

Peel the onions and tomatoes and slice them into rounds. When the potatoes have cooled sufficiently, peel them and slice similarly.

Take an ovenproof dish and layer, in order, with the whiting fillets, onion rings, sliced tomato and sliced potato, until all the ingredients have been used up. Pour on olive oil, season and stick the chilli, whole, into the middle of the dish. Sprinkle with chopped thyme and the crushed bay leaf and cook in a very hot oven (230°C/450°F/Gas Mark 8) for 10 minutes.

Elle says that the chilli in its whole state will flavour the dish sufficiently. If cut up before cooking, the dish will be over-spiced. Remove before serving.

ENTRECÔTES À L'ÉCHALOTE
Steaks with shallot butter

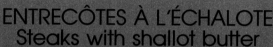

PREPARATION TIME: 5 minutes
COOKING TIME: 8–10 minutes
FOR SIX

3 good sirloin steaks	salt, pepper
150 g (5 oz) butter	oil
4 shallots	

First make the shallot butter. Use butter that has been taken out of the refrigerator in advance and softened at room temperature. Peel the shallots and chop finely in a processor. Add the butter cut into knobs, and seasoning, and blend until a smooth cream results.

Oil the steaks on both sides and cook them under a pre-heated hot grill. The cooking time will depend upon your own taste and the degree of rareness you prefer in steak; also on the thickness of the steak.

Divide the steaks into portions and put a good knob of shallot butter on each before serving.

STEAK AU POIVRE VERT
Entrecôtes with green pepper sauce

PREPARATION TIME: 5 minutes
COOKING TIME: 10 minutes
FOR SIX

6 entrecôte steaks	1 tablespoon Grand-Marnier
60 g (2 oz) butter	6 tablespoons crème fraîche
2 tablespoons oil	1 tablespoon of green
salt, pepper	peppercorns

Fry the steaks in 10 g (⅓ oz) butter and 1 tablespoon of oil. Season lightly and pour off the cooking fat. Pour the Grand-Marnier over the steaks and flame them: remove to a warmed serving plate.

Pour the crème fraîche into the pan and deglaze it by stirring with the back of a fork. Add the green peppercorns and warm through gently. Remove the pan from the heat and work the rest of the butter, cut into knobs, into the sauce. Check the seasoning and pour the sauce over the meat.

Serve at once with diced sauté potatoes.

TOURNEDOS CAMBO
Steaks with aubergines

PREPARATION TIME: 30 minutes
COOKING TIME: 30 minutes
FOR SIX

6 tournedos (trimmed fillets)
2 aubergines
1 green pepper
1 red pepper
3 shallots

peanut oil
1¼ kg (2¾ lb) small potatoes
salt, pepper
60 g (2 oz) butter

Remove stalks, seeds and membranes from the peppers and cut them into round slices. Peel and chop the shallots. In separate pans, gently cook the two vegetables in oil. Put to one side in a warm place.

Peel the potatoes and sauté them in a little oil. Cooking will take 30 minutes and the pan should be covered for the last 8 minutes of this time.

Trim the aubergines and cut six thick slices out of them. Fry them in oil on both sides until golden-brown, remove and keep warm.

Lightly oil the tournedos and quickly pan-fry them, turning them over half-way through the cooking. Season and arrange the meat on a warmed serving plate and put a slice of fried aubergine on each tournedos.

Pour any surplus fat from the frying pan and deglaze it with 100 ml (3½ fl oz) of water by vigorously scraping with the back of a fork. Reduce the sauce to half its volume, then remove from the heat and beat in the butter, knob by knob.

Cover each aubergine slice with shallots, arrange the cooked peppers around the edge of the serving dish and pour the sauce over the steaks. Serve immediately, with the satuéed potatoes.

TOURNEDOS SAUTÉS AUX MORILLES
Tournedos with morels

PREPARATION TIME: 25 minutes (24 hours in advance)
COOKING TIME: 25 minutes
FOR SIX

6 tournedos
100 g (3½ oz) dried morels
6 slices white bread
80 g (scant 3 oz) butter
4 tablespoons oil

100 g (3½ oz) pâté de foie gras
(optional)
salt, pepper
125 g (4½ oz) crème fraîche

Soak the dried fungi for a full 24 hours. Change the water frequently and rinse on each occasion to remove any sand. When beginning to prepare this dish, trim the stalks and give a final rinse. Put to one side.

Trim the slices of bread to the size of the tournedos. Fry them golden-brown in a pan in which 20 g (¾ oz) butter and 2 tablespoons of oil have been heated. Place on kitchen paper and spread each one with pâté. Put to one side.

In the same pan, put another 30 g (1 oz) butter and 2 tablespoons of oil and, over a brisk heat, seal each tournedos on both sides. Reduce the heat and continue cooking the meat to the desired degree of rareness. Season and put a tournedos on each piece of fried bread, put aside on a serving dish in a warm place. Pour off the fat from the pan and replace it with 30 g (1 oz) butter. Gently cook the morels, season and arrange around the serving dish.

Add the crème fraîche to the pan and deglaze it with the back of a fork. Let it boil until the sauce is thick enough to coat the back of a spoon.

Pour the sauce over the tournedos and serve with noodles.

From the restaurant 'A la Côte Saint-Jacques' in Joigny in Burgundy: the chef recommends that a red Burgundy, preferably a Volnay, be drunk with this dish.

FILET DE BŒUF AU POIVRE
Whole fillet in peppercorns

PREPARATION TIME: 20 minutes
COOKING TIME: 30–35 minutes
FOR SIX

whole fillet of beef weighing about 1¼ kg (2¾ lb)	1 small glass of brandy
1 tablespoon of oil	50 g (scant 2 oz) butter
salt	1 tablespoon strong mustard
2 tablespoons crushed peppercorns	125 g (4½ oz) crème fraîche

Cover the whole fillet in oil, season with salt, then roll the meat in crushed peppercorns. Heat a dry heavy iron pan and, over a brisk heat, seal the meat on all sides. Remove the meat to an ovenproof earthenware dish and put it into a pre-heated oven (230°C/450°F/Gas Mark 8) and continue the cooking for 20–25 minutes. Remove the meat to a warm place, but not so hot that it will continue cooking.

Deglaze the dish with the brandy and put these juices to one side. Melt the butter in a pan, add the mustard and the crème fraîche. Stir well together, let it bubble once or twice, then reduce the heat.

Slice the meat and add the juices from the beef and the deglazed juices to the sauce. Stir.

Arrange the meat on a warmed dish and serve with croquette potatoes and the sauce separately.

(CONTINUED)

off the heat, add this and the blanched marrow to the casserole 10 minutes before the end of cooking.

Elle says that if fresh cèpes are to be found, 200 g (7 oz) will be needed. They will of course be much more delicious.

ALOYAU AUX CÈPES
Sirloin with mushrooms

PREPARATION TIME: 15 minutes (24 hours in advance)
COOKING TIME: 1 hour 20 minutes
FOR SIX TO EIGHT

1½ kg (generous 3¼ lb) sirloin	150 g (5 oz) raw ham
50 g (scant 2 oz) dried cèpes	60 g (2 oz) butter
½ bottle red wine	1 small glass of brandy
1 tablespoon olive oil	salt, pepper
2 medium carrots	nutmeg
4 shallots	100 g (3½ oz) bone marrow
1 clove of garlic	1 tablespoon flour
bouquet garni	

The day before, put the dried fungi to soak in water. Marinate the meat in a mixture of the wine, olive oil, the peeled carrots and shallots cut into slices, the crushed garlic and the bouquet garni.

Begin cooking by cutting the ham into short strips and browning them in a casserole in half the butter. Remove the ham with a perforated spoon and replace with the fungi, cut into slices. Cook until the liquid has evaporated and they begin to brown, then remove them and keep in a warm place.

Pour the marinade into the casserole, bring to the boil and stir vigorously to blend all the ingredients together. Simmer for 20 minutes, then strain. There should be about 250 ml (9 fl oz) of sauce.

In the meantime, seal the meat in a dry pan until it is browned on each side. Put it into the casserole with the fungi and the ham, add the brandy and the marinade sauce. Season with salt, pepper and grated nutmeg, bring to the boil, lower the heat and cover the casserole. Simmer the meat for 12 minutes per 450 g (1 lb), turning the piece once during cooking.

Cut the marrow into dice and blanch it for 3 minutes in boiling salted water. Work a tablespoon of flour and remaining butter together and,
(CONTINUED OPPOSITE)

BŒUF A LA RADIGUETTE
Stuffed beef

PREPARATION TIME: 25 minutes
COOKING TIME: 3¼ hours
FOR SIX

1½ kg (generous 3¼ lb) braising
  beef in two slices
1 green cabbage
400 g (14 oz) streaky bacon
3 onions

2 tablespoons of oil
thyme
1 chicken stock cube
salt, pepper

Remove any damaged outer leaves from the cabbage, trim and wash it and cut it into quarters. Blanch it for 5 minutes in boiling salted water, remove, drain and coarsely chop it up. Cut the bacon into strips crossways, blanch them for 2 minutes in boiling water, remove, drain and run under cold water. Peel and finely chop 1 onion and mix in a bowl with the bacon and the cabbage.

Lay one slice of beef on to a board and spread it with the bacon-cabbage mixture. Lay the second slice of beef on top and tie the two halves together so the stuffing is enclosed.

Heat the oil in a casserole and seal the meat on both sides; at the same time, put 2 peeled onions into the dish. When the meat is browned, sprinkle with chopped thyme, add ⅓ litre (12 fl oz) of stock made from the chicken cube, and season.

Put the lid on the casserole and allow to simmer gently for 2½–3 hours.

To serve, remove the strings, cut the meat into slices and arrange on a warmed serving dish.

PALETTE EN CROÛTE
Beef in pastry

PREPARATION TIME: 20 minutes
COOKING TIME: 2 hours
FOR SIX

2 kg (generous 4½ lb) blade of
  beef
3–4 sprigs of tarragon
1 small jar of strong French
  mustard

salt, pepper
400 g (14 oz) frozen puff pastry
1 egg yolk

Ask your butcher to bone the joint. Stick it all over with tarragon leaves and generously coat it with mustard. Season, using salt sparingly.

Roll out the pastry into a large oblong shape and sprinkle more tarragon in the middle. Lay the joint on the pastry and fold in and press the edges together to make an enclosed pastry case. Mould and decorate the pastry to make an attractive design, remembering to leave an opening for steam to escape during cooking. Brush with beaten egg yolk.

Pre-heat the oven for 20 minutes at 230°C/450°F/Gas Mark 8 and cover the pastry with a buttered piece of greaseproof paper. Altogether, cooking should take about 2 hours.

DAUBE AUX PRUNEAUX
Braised beef with prunes

PREPARATION TIME: 20 minutes (24 hours in advance)
COOKING TIME: 3½ hours
FOR SIX

2 kg (4 lb 6 oz) neck of beef	50 ml (1¾ fl oz) Armagnac
2 carrots	2 tablespoons lard
2 onions	1 piece of pork rind
salt, pepper	4 cloves of garlic
bouquet garni	2 tomatoes
1 litre (1¾ pints) red wine	300 g (10½ oz) dried prunes

Cut the meat into large cubes and arrange them in an earthenware dish with 1 sliced carrot and 1 sliced onion. Season, add the bouquet garni and pour in the red wine and the Armagnac. Leave the meat to marinate overnight.

The next day, remove the pieces of meat with a perforated spoon and dry them on kitchen paper. Heat the lard in a frying pan and seal the meat on all sides; transfer it to a casserole and lay the pork rind on top. Pour in the marinade liquid through a fine sieve, add the peeled cloves of garlic and the remaining carrot and onion, both sliced into rings. Cover the casserole, bring the dish to the boil and continue cooking, just simmering gently for 3½ hours. Half an hour before the end of this time, add the tomatoes, which should have been peeled, de-seeded and chopped, and also the prunes previously stoned and allowed to swell for one hour in warm tea.

Serve hot with either boiled potatoes, pasta or rice.

Elle notes that this dish tastes even better if made in advance and re-heated before serving.

BŒUF AUX OIGNONS
Beef with onions

PREPARATION TIME: 15 minutes
COOKING TIME: 2½ hours
FOR SIX

1½ kg (generous 3¼ lb) neck or shoulder of beef	4 cloves of garlic
	thyme
1 kg (2¼ lb) potatoes	1 bay leaf
600 g (1 lb 5 oz) onions	6 juniper berries
cooking oil	2 cloves
salt, pepper	1 bottle white wine

Ask your butcher to cut the meat into thin slices (about 3 mm/⅛ inch thick). Peel the potatoes and onions and thinly slice them.

Brush the inside of a heavy iron casserole with cooking oil and put in first a layer of potatoes, then one of onions followed by one of meat. Continue in this order until all the ingredients have been used up, finishing with a layer of potatoes. Season each layer and sprinkle each time with chopped garlic, chopped thyme, crumbled bay leaf and crushed juniper berries. Bury the two cloves in the layers and pour in white wine up to three-quarters of the height of the top layer of potatoes. Cover the casserole, put it into a pan of hot water and cook in a hot oven (220°C/425°F/Gas Mark 7) for 2½ hours.

Elle notes that if the dish seems to be drying out during cooking, it should be moistened with a mixture of half wine and half water.

ENTRECÔTE AUX CÂPRES
Rib of beef with capers

PREPARATION TIME: 15 minutes
COOKING TIME: 45 minutes
FOR SIX

750 g (generous 1 ½ lb) boned rib
   of beef
125 g (4½ oz) smoked bacon
150 g (5 oz) onions, sliced

125 g (4½ oz) capers
150 ml (5 fl oz) sherry vinegar
salt, pepper

Trim as much as possible of the fat and gristle from the meat. Cut the bacon into strips and gently fry it in a dry, heavy iron pan. Remove and put to one side.

Put the beef and the sliced onions into the same pan and turn them frequently with a wooden spoon so that they are lightly browned all over. Drain the capers and add them to the dish, together with the fried bacon and the vinegar. Season and pour in sufficient water to cover the meat.

Simmer gently over a low heat for 45 minutes.

PÂTÉ CHAUD DE BŒUF
French steak and kidney pie

PREPARATION TIME: 35 minutes
COOKING TIME: 1½ hours
FOR SIX

800 g (1¾ lb) rump steak
500 g (generous 1 lb) calves'
   kidneys
salt, pepper
nutmeg
3 onions
parsley
40 g (scant 1½ oz) butter

300 g (10½ oz) button
   mushrooms
1 lemon
3 hard-boiled eggs
400 ml (14 fl oz) beef stock
250 g (scant 9 oz) frozen puff
   pastry
1 egg

Ask your butcher to trim the sinews from the kidneys and cut the steak into slices 1 cm (½ inch) thick. Season both with salt, pepper and grated nutmeg.

Peel the onions and finely chop both them and the parsley. Mix together. Slice the kidneys, heat 20 g (scant ¾ oz) butter in a pan and quickly seal them on both sides. Season.

Trim the stalks of the mushrooms, wipe them with a mixture of lemon juice and water and cut them into quarters. Melt the rest of the butter and gently cook the mushrooms until all their liquid is given off.

Line the bottom and sides of a pie dish with the sliced rump steak and spread the surface of the meat with the onion-parsley mixture. Pile the kidneys in the middle of the dish and cover them with the cooked mushrooms and their juices. Peel the hard-boiled eggs, cut them in half lengthways and arrange them around the kidneys and mushrooms. Moisten the whole with beef stock.

Roll out the pastry on a lightly-floured board to a size bigger than the pie dish. Cover the dish with the pastry, trim off any surplus and, with the fingers seal the pastry to the edge of the dish. Roll out the pastry trimmings, cut into thin strips and decorate the surface of the pie with a criss-cross pattern of strips.

Brush the pastry with beaten egg and cook in a fairly hot oven (200°C/400°F/Gas Mark 6) for 1½ hours. Serve as soon as ready.

POT-AU-FEU MARTINIQUAIS
Caribbean stew

PREPARATION TIME: 15 minutes
COOKING TIME: 2½ hours
FOR SIX

2 kg (generous 4¼ lb) silverside	3 baby turnips
salt, pepper	1 small head of celery
1 cabbage	2 tomatoes
1 onion	1 slice of pumpkin (if available)
1 clove of garlic	6 potatoes
3 leeks	100 g (3½ oz) vermicelli
4 carrots	

Cut up the beef, put it in a large saucepan and pour in 3 litres (5¼ pints) water. Bring to the boil, season, and cook covered for 1½ hours. Skim the surface of the cooking liquid from time to time.

Slice the heart of the cabbage, peel the onion and the garlic clove. Cut up the remaining vegetables into dice, and add all to the saucepan. Return to the boil and cook for 1 hour more. Fifteen minutes before the end of cooking time, throw in the vermicelli.

Serve very hot in warmed bowls.

Elle advises that if you prefer a spicier stew, add a good pinch of cayenne pepper during the cooking.

POT-AU-FEU MAIGRE
Slimmer's stew

PREPARATION TIME: 15 minutes
COOKING TIME: 3½ hours
FOR SIX

500 g (generous 1 lb) silverside	500 g (generous 1 lb) baby turnips
500 g (generous 1 lb) shin of beef	
1 onion	1 head of celery
300 g (10½ oz) leeks (white part only)	1 clove
	bouquet garni
750 g (generous 1½ lb) celeriac	sea salt
500 g (generous 1 lb) carrots	black peppercorns

Trim and peel all the vegetables. Stick the clove into the onion and cut the leeks into lengths. Cut the celeriac into thick slices. Put all the vegetables into a large saucepan and add the bouquet garni, salt and the peppercorns.

Add water to cover the ingredients generously, bring to the boil and put in the meat, cut into slices. Return to the boil, cover the saucepan and cook over a moderate heat for 3½ hours.

Serve accompanied by pickled gherkins and a bowl of mustard.

Elle says that the cooking liquid may be served as a soup first and, followed by a sugar-free yoghurt or a grapefruit, the whole makes an ideal slimmer's meal.

DAUBE D'ÉTÉ
Summer stew

PREPARATION TIME: 20 minutes
COOKING TIME: 2½ hours
FOR SIX

1½ kg (3 lb 5 oz) shin of beef
300 g (10½ oz) smoked bacon
1 tablespoon lard
½ bottle white wine
salt, pepper
500 g (generous 1 lb) small
  carrots
500 g (generous 1 lb) baby
  turnips

12 small potatoes
4 small celery stalks
1½ kg (generous 3¼ lb) peas in
  the pod
3 pork sausages (smoked if
  possible)
a good sprig of parsley
12 basil leaves
a sprig of thyme

Blanch the bacon for 3 minutes in boiling water, then drain. Cut the beef and bacon into large cubes.

Melt the lard in a heavy iron pan and cook the bacon until it becomes golden-brown. Remove, put to one side and replace it with the beef cubes; seal them on all sides. When this has been done, put back the bacon and pour in the half-bottle of white wine together with an equal quantity of water. Season, cover the pan and cook slowly for 2 hours.

During this time, prepare and cook each vegetable separately in boiling water for 10 minutes each, with the exception of the shelled peas which will only take 5 minutes. Drain and keep to one side in a warm place.

Prick the sausages with a sharp fork and cook them slowly in a dry frying pan until they just begin to brown. Put these to one side also. Chop or crumble all the herbs and, after the meat has been cooking for two hours, add herbs, vegetables and sausages to the dish. Continue cooking with the pan covered for a further half-hour.

STEAK TARTARE – HAMBURGER
Hamburgers raw and cooked

STEAK TARTARE: for six
PREPARATION TIME: 15 minutes
COOKING TIME: nil

900 g (scant 2 lb) fillet or sirloin
  steak, minced
6 eggs
6 teaspoons chopped mixed
  herbs
4 onions
Dijon mustard

6 tablespoons olive oil
2 lemons
125 g (4½ oz) capers
salt, pepper
Worcestershire sauce
tomato ketchup

Divide the mince into six portions and form each one into the shape of a thick hamburger. Put onto individual serving plates. Into the top of each one, press the half-shell of an egg with the yolk in it.

In separate small serving dishes, present the chopped herbs, chopped onions, mustard, oil, lemons cut into quarters, and the capers. Each guest can then prepare his or her steak tartare to taste.

Alternatively, each guest can be given a small bowl containing an oil, mustard and lemon-juice vinaigrette, into which chopped herbs and onion has been added. The capers and the 'sauces anglaises' are served separately.

HAMBURGER: for six
PREPARATION TIME: 15 minutes
COOKING TIME: 6–10 minutes

900 g (scant 2 lb) steak, minced
125 g (scant 4½ oz) butter
salt, pepper

3 chopped onions (chives if
  preferred)
6 eggs

Mould the minced steak into six hamburgers and cook to the required degree on a griddle or in a buttered frying pan; 3–4 minutes for each side will probably be enough. Season, sprinkle with chopped onion or chives and top with an egg fried in butter.

NAVARIN-PRINTANIER
Spring stew

PREPARATION TIME: 40 minutes
COOKING TIME: 2 hours
FOR SIX

boned shoulder of lamb weighing
  1½ kg (generous 3¼ lb)
25 small onions
20 small young carrots
250 g (scant 9 oz) French beans
20 small young turnips
20 small new potatoes
200 g (7 oz) shelled peas
5 tablespoons olive oil

granulated sugar
1 tablespoon flour
2–3 crushed cloves of garlic
salt, pepper
bouquet garni
50 g (2 oz) butter
parsley
chervil
tarragon

Trim and peel, where necessary, all the vegetables. Cut the meat into large cubes, heat the oil in a casserole and seal the pieces of meat on all sides. Remove and put to one side.

Place the small onions in the pan: sprinkle on a teaspoon of sugar to glaze them. Remove them and put to one side.

Roll the pieces of meat in flour and return them to the casserole. Cook them for a few moments, then stir in the crushed garlic. Season. Pour in 750 ml (26 fl oz) water, add the bouquet garni and bring the liquid to the boil. Cook for 30 minutes, remove the meat and keep it in a warm place.

Blanch the beans in boiling salted water for 5 minutes, drain and keep to one side. Heat the butter in a saucepan and toss the carrots, the turnips and the new potatoes in it. Add them all to the liquid in the casserole and continue cooking for 25 minutes. At this point add the peas, the blanched beans, the small onions and the meat and simmer the whole stew for a further hour.

Serve straight from the cooking pot, sprinkled with chopped parsley, chervil and tarragon.

From 'L'Epicurien' restaurant in Paris-6[3]: the chef recommends a red wine from the Loire, such as a Chinon, to accompany this dish.

AGNEAU BRAISÉ AUX HARICOTS ROUGES
Braised lamb with red kidney beans

PREPARATION TIME: 30 minutes
COOKING TIME: 1 hour 45 minutes
FOR SIX

boned, rolled shoulder of lamb
  weighing 1¼ kg (scant 2¾ lb)
250 g (scant 9 oz) red kidney
  beans
1 tablespoon olive oil
2 onions, chopped
bunch of parsley, chopped
white part of 4 leeks, sliced

½ bulb of fennel, sliced
bunch of mint, chopped (or 1
  tablespoon dried mint)
1 tablespoon turmeric
1 teaspoon oregano
salt, pepper
3 lemons

Put the beans in a large saucepan, cover them with cold water and bring slowly to the boil. Drain them, return them to the saucepan and add plenty of boiling salted water: bring the pan back to the boil and when it bubbles, reduce the heat so that the water is just 'shivering'. Continue cooking at this temperature for 1½ hours.

Heat the oil in a heavy pan and seal the joint on all sides. Remove it to a casserole. Replace it with the chopped onions and gently cook them, stirring frequently, until they are transparent. Add the parsley, the sliced leeks and fennel, the mint, the turmeric and the oregano. Stir it all together, season, and cook for a few moments more. Add the contents of the pan to the casserole containing the meat, moisten with 750 ml (26 fl oz) of water and bring it briskly to the boil. Cover the casserole, reduce the heat and simmer the dish for 1¼ hours.

Fifteen minutes before the end of cooking time add the juice of lemons and the drained kidney beans to the casserole.

Elle says that this deliciously flavoured dish needs only plain boiled rice as its accompaniment.

GIGOT AU PAPRIKA
Hungarian leg of lamb

PREPARATION TIME: 40 minutes
COOKING TIME: 2 hours
FOR SIX TO EIGHT

1 leg of lamb about 2 kg (4½ lb)	2 celery stalks
2 tablespoons olive oil	1 leek
1 teaspoon chopped thyme	2 onions
½ teaspoon dried sage	1 kg (scant 2¼ lb) French beans
rosemary	60 g (2 oz) butter
1 teaspoon paprika	a pinch of white pepper
tabasco	½ teaspoon savory
½ teaspoon salt	2 red peppers
2 carrots	

Ask your butcher to trim most of the fat from the leg of lamb. Put the oil in a dish and mix in the chopped thyme, the crumbled sage, a few spikes of rosemary, the paprika, a few drops of tabasco and the salt. Roll the meat in this herb mixture.

Place the joint in an ovenproof dish and add 250 ml (9 fl oz) of hot water. Cover the dish and cook in a very hot oven (230°C/450°/Gas Mark 8) for 2 hours.

Trim the carrots, the celery and the leek, peel 1 onion. Finely chop up all these vegetables, mix them together and add them to the casserole 30 minutes before the end of the joint's cooking time.

In the meantime, trim, wash and dry the French beans. Put the butter in a saucepan containing 400 ml (14 fl oz) of water, season with salt, pepper and savory and heat through. When the butter has melted, add the beans and cook them, with the liquid just on the boil, for 20 minutes. Remove the stalk, membranes and seeds from the peppers and cut them into strips; peel and slice the remaining onion and add both these vegetables to the saucepan. Continue at a simmer for 15 minutes.

Present the joint surrounded by its chopped vegetables, with the bean dish served separately.

GIGOT SAUCE ORIENTALE
Leg of lamb with pine-kernel sauce

PREPARATION TIME: 30 minutes
COOKING TIME (ON A SPIT): 12–15 minutes per 450 g (1 lb)
FOR SIX TO EIGHT

1 leg of lamb weighing 2 kg (scant 4½ lb)	cayenne pepper
80 g (scant 3 oz) pine kernels	60 g (2 oz) butter
50 g (scant 2 oz) raisins	1–2 tablespoons olive oil
100 g (3½ oz) currants	2 onions
salt, pepper	6 tablespoons dry vermouth

Soak the raisins and currants in warm water to allow them to swell. Work salt, pepper and a good pinch of cayenne into the butter. Put the leg of lamb onto the spit and smear it all over with the seasoned butter. Let it stand for 30 minutes before cooking.

Cook the joint until it is a good golden-brown all over, then stick a sharp skewer through the thickest part of the meat until it touches the bone. If, on withdrawing the skewer, the point is at all warm, remove the joint from the spit. The residual heat in the joint will soon complete the cooking sufficiently.

In the meantime, proceed to the sauce. Warm a tablespoon of olive oil in a saucepan and add the onions, finely chopped. Cook them gently until they are transparent. Brown the pine kernels separately in a few drops of oil, then add them to the onions, together with the drained currants and raisins.

Pour off surplus fat from the drip pan below the joint and deglaze it with the dry vermouth and a tablespoon of boiling water. Mix these juices into the pine-kernel mixture and keep warm. The sauce is finished off by stirring in the juices collected from the lamb as it is carved. Serve the lamb with plain boiled rice and the pine-kernel sauce.

Elle notes that while this recipe is really intended for spit-roasting, it may be adapted to the oven by preparing the joint as stated and cooking it on a trivet in a roasting-pan in the oven. Use a very hot oven (230°C/450°F/Gas Mark 8) and 15 minutes per 450 g (1 lb).

GIGOT FARCI AU RHUM
Leg of lamb with rum stuffing

PREPARATION TIME: 35 minutes
COOKING TIME: 1½ hours
FOR SIX TO EIGHT

1 leg of lamb weighing 2 kg (scant 4½ lb)	salt, pepper
200 g (7 oz) button mushrooms	100 g (3½ oz) sliced ham
1½ lemons	100 g (3½ oz) bacon
4 small lamb's kidneys	2 slices white bread
4 tablespoons olive oil	1 egg
100 ml (3½ fl oz) rum	50 g (scant 2 oz) butter

Ask your butcher to bone the leg, leaving the shank-bone.

Having trimmed the stalks, wipe the mushrooms in a mixture of water and juice of 1 lemon and slice them. Remove skin and membranes from the kidneys and cut them also into thin slices.

Heat 1½ tablespoons of oil in a pan and cook the mushrooms until all their liquid has evaporated. Remove from the pan and in the same quantity of oil, lightly cook the sliced kidneys. Return the mushrooms to the pan, stir together and heat through: pour in half the rum and flame the dish. Season.

Dice the ham and the bacon. Remove the crusts from the bread and crumble the two slices. Add these ingredients to the mushroom/kidney mixture together with a whole egg. Season, mix thoroughly together and stuff the bone cavity of the joint with it. Seal up the opening and put the joint into a meat pan and brush it all over with the remaining tablespoon of oil. Season the butter and spread this over the joint as well. Cook for 1–1¼ hours in a very hot oven (240°C/475°/Gas Mark 9).

Remove from the oven, squeeze on juice of remaining lemon and flame the joint with the remainder of the rum. Put the joint on its carving dish and deglaze the meat pan with a little hot water, scraping vigorously with the back of a fork.

Carve the joint and pour the juices released into the meat pan. Check the seasoning and serve the sauce separately.

GIGOT À LA CRÈME D'AIL
Leg of lamb with garlic cream

PREPARATION TIME: 15 minutes
COOKING TIME: 50 minutes
FOR SIX

1 leg of lamb weighing 2 kg (scant 4½ lb)	1 chicken stock cube
salt, pepper	500 g (generous 1 lb) garlic (about 18 bulbs)
thyme	1 litre (1¾ pints) single cream
100 ml (3½ fl oz) olive oil (plus 2 tablespoons)	6 slices French bread

Ask your butcher to trim as much fat as possible from the joint, to bone it and to tie it up. Make a mixture of salt, pepper and chopped thyme and rub the joint all over with it.

Heat 100 ml (3½ fl oz) olive oil in a casserole and seal the joint on all sides. During this time, dissolve the chicken stock cube in 250 ml (9 fl oz) hot water and pour it over the meat. Peel all the cloves of garlic, add them to the casserole and cook, covered, for 45 minutes, turning the meat and stirring the garlic from time to time. When the joint is done, remove it to a warmed carving dish.

Pour the cream into the casserole, bring it to the boil, keeping it there for 1–2 minutes. Remove from the heat and put the contents through a blender to make a smooth garlic cream. Strain it through a sieve and keep warm in a double boiler.

Spread a little of this cream on each slice of bread and toast them under a hot grill. Sprinkle with olive oil when done. Serve the garlic toasts and the garlic sauce with the lamb.

From the restaurant 'La Fuste' in La Fuste in Provence: the chef recommends that a red wine of the region will go best with this dish.

AGNEAU À LA LAITUE
Lamb with lettuce

PREPARATION TIME: 20 minutes
COOKING TIME: 1 hour 15 minutes
FOR SIX

1 boned and rolled shoulder of
   lamb weighing 1½ kg
   (generous 3¼ lb)
salt, pepper
80 g (scant 3 oz) butter

500 g (generous 1 lb) small
   onions
1 kg (2¼ lb) lettuce
2 eggs
1 lemon
sprig of dill

Put the joint in a casserole and cover it with cold water. Bring it to the boil, skim the surface and pour off three-quarters of the liquid. Season and add the butter, divided into lumps. Cover the casserole and cook for 1 hour over a low heat.

During this time, peel and slice the onions and blanch them in boiling salted water for 2 minutes. Remove from the water and set on one side. Trim and divide the lettuce and blanch them in the same boiling water for 5 minutes. Remove to one side and, 15 minutes before the end of the cooking time for the joint, add the lettuce and the onion.

Separate the eggs and whisk the whites until stiff. Fold in the beaten yolks, the juice of the lemon and a little of the juices from the casserole.

Put the joint on to its carving dish and arrange lettuce and onions around the edges of a warmed serving dish. Pour the beaten egg mixture into the casserole and make a sauce by briskly stirring the juices and mixture together over heat.

Carve the joint, arrange the slices in the centre of the serving dish and pour the sauce over it. Sprinkle with chopped dill and serve at once.

Elle notes that if everyone is very hungry, a boned shoulder of this size may not be enough for more than four people. In this case, a boned leg should be substituted.

ROUELLES D'AGNEAU À L'AIL CONFIT
Barnsley chops with garlic

PREPARATION TIME: 15 minutes
COOKING TIME: 20 minutes
FOR SIX

6 good Barnsley chops (also
   called butterfly chops)
75 g (generous 2½ oz) butter
30 cloves of garlic

salt, pepper
rosemary
200 ml (7 fl oz) dry vermouth

Heat the butter in a pan and gently cook the peeled garlic cloves whole. Quickly dry-seal the chops in a second pan, then put them in with the garlic. Season and sprinkle with rosemary and cook the chops on both sides for about 8 minutes altogether. Remove them to a warm serving dish.

Pour the vermouth into the pan and deglaze with the back of a fork. Pour the garlic sauce over the chops and garnish with more rosemary.

From the 'Auberge Dou Terraie' in Les Angles in the Pyrénées: the chef recommends that a red wine from the Loire be drunk with this dish, preferably a Bourgueil.

NOISETTES D'AGNEAU EN CHEVREUIL
Lamb medallions in game sauce

PREPARATION TIME: 10 minutes (the previous day)
COOKING TIME: 2 hours 10 minutes
FOR SIX

6 large, fat lamb chops	pepper
1 large onion	1 litre (1¾ pints) red wine
1 carrot	100 ml (3½ fl oz) olive oil (plus 2
2 cloves of garlic	tablespoons)
1 sprig of thyme	150 g (5 oz) butter
1 bay leaf	2 tablespoons flour
½ teaspoon sea salt	1 chicken stock cube

On the previous day, carefully bone the meat and tie each chop into a round shape, or medallion, then lay them in an earthenware dish. Retain the bones. Peel the vegetables and garlic and cut them into round slices: spread them over the meat and add the chopped thyme, the bay leaf and the bones from the chops. Season. Bring the wine to the boil and immediately pour it into the dish. Sprinkle on 100 ml (3½ fl oz) olive oil and leave the meat to marinate overnight, refrigerating the dish as soon as the wine has cooled.

The following day, remove meat and bones from the dish and drain them. Put the bones in a saucepan with a good knob of butter and gently heat them. Shake on enough flour to cover them, stir, then pour in the liquid from the marinade. Add the chicken stock cube, dissolved in 400 ml (14 fl oz) of boiling water, stir and cook over a low heat for 1½–2 hours, until the volume of liquid in the saucepan has reduced to half. Strain the sauce-base through a sieve into a small saucepan.

Cook the medallions in a frying pan in a combination of 50 g (scant 2 oz) butter and 2 tablespoons of oil for about 3–4 minutes on each side. When done, they should still be pink in the middle. Drain them of any cooking fat and arrange them on a serving dish: keep in a warm place.

(CONTINUED OPPOSITE)

LAMB CHOP
Untranslatable lamb!

PREPARATION TIME: 5 minutes
COOKING TIME: 5–15 minutes per chop, according to thickness
FOR SIX

6 chump chops, each weighing	salt, pepper
about 150 g (5 oz)	mixed (fines) herbs
150 g (5 oz) butter	1 clove of garlic

Make the savoury butter first. Blend 90 g (3 oz) of the butter with chopped herbs, seasoning and garlic. Roll it in foil to a sausage shape and firm up in the refrigerator.

For each chop, melt a knob of butter in a pan: if the pan is large enough not to let the chops touch each other, cook two at once. Each chop should be cooked on both sides: the meaty part of the chop needs less cooking than the fatty trim so from time to time press these outside parts down into the pan with the back of a fork.

Keep the serving dish hot over a pan of boiling water and remove each chop to it as soon as it is cooked to taste. Season.

Present the chops with a dish of French beans and one of sauté potatoes, and each with a slice of the savoury butter on top.

Elle says this classic but simple dish will always give pleasure to guests.

(CONTINUED)

Take the small saucepan and whisk remaining butter, knob by knob, into the sauce. Briefly return the pan to a low heat from time to time, whisking continuously. Check the seasoning, then pour the sauce over the medallions. Serve with fresh pasta which has been tossed in butter.

ESTOUFFADE DE GIGOT
Slow-cooked lamb stew

PREPARATION TIME: 15 minutes (4 hours in advance)
COOKING TIME: 3 hours
FOR SIX

1 boned leg of lamb weighing about 3 kg (6½ lb)	3 tablespoons olive oil
2 onions	400 g (14 oz) streaky bacon
4 cloves of garlic	300 g (10½ oz) pork rind
4 tomatoes	2 beef stock cubes
1 stick of celery	salt
1 orange	200 g (7 oz) flour
bouquet garni	
1 tablespoon crushed peppercorns	For the toasts:
	5 bulbs of garlic
1½ litres (generous 2½ pints) red wine	3 tablespoons olive oil
	¾ stick French bread

Cut and trim the meat into large cubes. Put it into a casserole with the chopped onions, the crushed garlic, the tomatoes (peeled, de-seeded and chopped), the trimmed and chopped celery, the sliced peel of the orange, the bouquet garni and peppercorns. Pour in the wine and olive oil and leave to marinate for 4 hours.

During this time, cut the bacon and the pork rind into strips and rinse them under running cold water.

At the end of the marinating period, add the bacon and pork rind strips, the beef stock cubes and 2–3 pinches of salt to the casserole, together with sufficient cold water to raise the level of the liquid to 2 cm (a scant inch) above the surface of the meat. Work the flour into a stiff paste with a little water and make a seal between the body and the lid of the casserole: cook for 3 hours in a pre-heated very cool oven (110°C/225°F/Gas Mark ¼).

Divide and peel the bulbs of garlic: remove the green shoot from each clove and then plunge the cloves into 2 litres (3½ pints) boiling water for 5 minutes. Repeat this operation four more times, drain the cloves and purée with 3 tablespoons of olive oil.

(CONTINUED OPPOSITE)

ÉPAULE D'AGNEAU EN SAUTÉ
Sauté of lamb

PREPARATION TIME: 20 minutes
COOKING TIME: 50 minutes
FOR SIX

1 boned shoulder of lamb weighing about 1½ kg (generous 3¼ lb)	olive oil
	1 tablespoon flour
	200 ml (7 fl oz) dry white wine
5 onions	salt, pepper
600 g (1 lb 5 oz) tomatoes	1 teaspoon powdered cinnamon
1 clove of garlic	2 tablespoons sugar
40 g (scant 1½ oz) butter	5 cloves

Peel and finely chop the onions and peel the tomatoes and garlic. Trim and cut up the meat into medium-sized cubes.

Melt the butter with 1 tablespoon of oil in a casserole and, when it is hot, seal the meat on all sides. Remove it to one side and replace it by the chopped onion: cook this gently until transparent. Roll the meat in flour and return it to the casserole, together with the crushed garlic. Stir and cook over moderate heat for a few minutes, then pour in the white wine. Season, lower the heat and continue cooking for 10 minutes.

Remove the seeds from the tomatoes, which should then be roughly chopped. Add tomatoes, cinnamon, sugar and cloves to the casserole, cover it and cook for a further 35 minutes. A little water may be added during cooking if the dish appears to be drying out.

Serve with boiled rice, decorated with chopped red pepper.

(CONTINUED)

Cut the French loaf into thin slices and lightly toast them under the grill. Spread each one with garlic purée and put back under the grill to complete the toasting. Serve the lamb stew in warmed deep bowls with garlic toasts as accompaniment.

RAGOÛT D'AGNEAU AU RHUM
Caribbean lamb stew

PREPARATION TIME: 10 minutes
COOKING TIME: 1 hour 30 minutes
FOR SIX

boned shoulder of lamb weighing
   about 1½ kg (generous 3¼ lb)
olive oil
3 onions
salt, pepper

thyme
parsley
2 cloves of garlic
cayenne pepper
2 tablespoons rum
1 tablespoon curry powder

Trim and cut the meat into large cubes; heat 3 tablespoons of oil in a casserole and rapidly seal the meat on all sides. Remove the meat to a warm place.

Peel and finely chop the onions and put them in the casserole in place of the meat. Lower the heat and cook them gently until transparent. Return the meat to the casserole, season and pour in enough hot water to half-cover the contents. Add a spoonful each of chopped thyme and parsley, the crushed garlic and a pinch of cayenne pepper. Cover the dish and let it simmer over a moderate heat for 1¼ hours.

Halfway through the cooking period, stir in the rum and the curry powder, made into a paste with 1 tablespoon of water.

Serve with boiled rice.

From 'La Grand Voile' restaurant in Fort-de-France in Martinique: the chef recommends that a good chilled rosé, a Tavel for example, will go well with this dish.

CASSOULET GRATINÉ
Mutton and bean stew

PREPARATION TIME: 25 minutes
COOKING TIME: 4 hours
FOR SIX TO EIGHT

boned shoulder of mutton
   weighing 1½ kg (generous
   3¼ lb)
1 kg (scant 2¼ lb) white haricot
   beans
100 g (3½ oz) lard or goose fat
2 onions
2 cloves of garlic

2 liqueur glasses of brandy
2 tablespoons tomato purée
bouquet garni
salt, pepper
6 'premium' pork sausages
1 piece preserved goose
   (optional)
white breadcrumbs

Put the beans and plenty of cold water into a large saucepan and bring slowly to the boil. This should take 30 minutes. As soon as the pan boils, drain the beans (retaining the cooking liquid), and put them back into the pan with plenty of boiling water, this time salted. Continue cooking at a slow boil for 1½ hours.

Cut the meat into cubes. Melt 80 g (scant 3 oz) of lard in a casserole and seal the meat on all sides. Remove the meat to one side and replace it with the chopped onions and crushed garlic and cook gently until transparent. Return the meat to the casserole and add the brandy and enough of the cooking liquid from the beans to bring the level up to the surface of the meat. Stir in the tomato purée, put in the bouquet garni and the seasoning, cover the casserole and cook over a low heat for 1½ hours. At the end of this time, add the drained beans together with a little cooking liquid if it should be necessary.

Fry the sausages in the rest of the lard. When part-cooked, cut them into thick slices and continue frying until done. Put them into the casserole with the sliced preserved goose (if available). Stir all together.

Remove the contents of the casserole to an ovenproof earthenware dish. Stir in one covering of breadcrumbs, then put a second covering on the surface. Put to brown in a hot oven (220°C/425°F/Gas Mark 7) for about 10 minutes. Serve at once.

TAJINE DE MOUTON
Eastern mutton stew

PREPARATION TIME: 30 minutes
COOKING TIME: 1½–2 hours
FOR SIX

1 shoulder of mutton weighing 2 kg (4½ lb)	150 ml (5 fl oz) olive oil
1 heaped teaspoon powdered ginger	1 kg (2¼ lb) French beans
	3 tomatoes
pinch powdered saffron	preserved lemon peel (see p. 16)
salt, pepper	1 lemon
	1 tablespoon flour

Have the shoulder divided into a dozen pieces. Arrange the meat in a casserole, sprinkle it with powdered ginger, saffron and a few pinches of salt. Pour in the oil and enough water to cover the meat completely. Bring to the boil and maintain at this heat for 10 minutes. Trim the beans, add them to the meat, cover the casserole and continue cooking over a low heat. Stir the dish from time to time, adding more water if it should be necessary.

When the beans are cooked, add the tomatoes cut into quarters, the chopped lemon peel, juice of the lemon and a level tablespoon of flour worked into a paste with a little cold water. Mix all these ingredients with the meat and beans and continue cooking for another 15 minutes.

Should there be too much gravy when cooking is complete, reduce it to a rich, thick consistency by rapid boiling. Check seasoning, add pepper if necessary, and serve at once.

TAJINE D'AGNEAU AU CUMIN
Spicy lamb stew

PREPARATION TIME: 30 minutes
COOKING TIME: 3 hours
FOR SIX

1¼ kg (2¾ lb) boned lamb shoulder	1 lemon
	1 teaspoon powdered ginger
2 cloves of garlic	½ teaspoon sweet chilli powder
1 tablespoon cumin seeds	pinch of powdered saffron
1 teaspoon coriander seeds	salt
2 preserved lemons	1 kg (2¼ lb) onions
3 tablespoons olive oil	100 g (3½ oz) black olives

This dish is properly prepared in its own special tajine pot, shown in the illustration, but any covered fireproof earthenware pot may be used.

Cut the meat into large pieces. Crush the garlic, the cumin and the coriander seeds in a pestle and mortar. Arrange the meat in its cooking pot together with pieces of preserved lemon. Moisten with 2 tablespoons of oil and the juice of the lemon and sprinkle it with the ginger, chilli powder and saffron, then add the crushed spices and garlic. Lightly season with salt, cover the pot and cook slowly for at least 3 hours after the dish comes to the boil.

Peel and slice the onions and cook them gently in the rest of the oil until they are transparent. Remove the stones from the olives and, 15 minutes before the end of cooking time, add olives and onions to the meat. Serve with boiled rice.

FILET DE PORC CHARENTAIS
Pork in vermouth

PREPARATION TIME: 10 minutes (12 hours in advance)
COOKING TIME: 1 hour 10 minutes
FOR SIX

1¼ kg (2¾ lb) boned loin of pork
20 g (¾ oz) sea salt
10 g (⅓ oz) white peppercorns
2 cloves of garlic
1 sugar lump
50 ml (1¾ fl oz) brandy
1 pinch of quatre-épices (see below)
1 sprig of thyme
1 bay leaf
150 ml (5 fl oz) dry white vermouth

Crush the salt, the peppercorns, the garlic and the sugar lump together in a pestle and mortar, and spread out the mixture in a shallow dish. Add the brandy, spices and the crumbled herbs, and roll the pork joint in the mixture. Leave the meat to marinate for 12 hours.

Put the joint in a very hot oven (240°C/475°F/Gas Mark 9) and cook for about 1 hour 10 minutes. Baste frequently with the vermouth. Remove the joint to a warmed carving-dish and slice it. Skim any fat off the cooking liquid and pour the remainder over the sliced meat. Serve at once.

Elle notes that quatre-épices is a combination of finely-ground pepper, ginger, nutmeg and cloves.

PALETTE DE PORC EN COCOTTE
Pot-roast of pork

PREPARATION TIME: 15 minutes
COOKING TIME: 1½ hours
FOR SIX

1¼ kg (2¾ lb) boned shoulder of pork
100 g (3½ oz) lard or goose fat
3 large onions
1 shallot
salt, pepper
thyme, bay leaf, savory
1 small tin tomato purée
400 ml (14 fl oz) white wine

Melt the lard in a casserole (use goose fat if possible) and seal the joint on every side to a golden-brown. Add the peeled and sliced onions and shallot, season and sprinkle the meat with the crumbled herbs.

In a bowl, whisk together the tomato purée, the white wine and 100 ml (3½ fl oz) warm water. When the meat is halfway through its cooking time, pour this mixture over it, cover the casserole and lower the heat to a simmer. From time to time, turn the joint over and baste it with the sauce.

When the joint is cooked, remove it to a warmed serving dish and cut it into slices. Taste the sauce in the casserole and if it seems too greasy, whisk in a small glass of warm water. Pour the sauce over the sliced meat and serve with grilled tomatoes and either boiled potatoes or rice.

From the 'Auberge de Senneville' in Senneville-Guerville near Paris: the chef recommends that a good Beaujolais, such as a Chiroubles, be drunk with this dish, or alternatively the dark red wine of Cahors.

CÔTES DE PORC AU CIDRE
Pork chops in cider sauce

PREPARATION TIME: 10 minutes
COOKING TIME: 25 minutes
FOR SIX

6 good pork chops	salt, pepper
3 tablespoons olive oil	1 tablespoon of cornflour
18 small onions	50 g (scant 2 oz) crème fraîche
200 ml (7 fl oz) dry cider	

Heat the oil in a large frying pan and seal the chops on both sides to a good golden-brown. Remove to a warm place. Replace them by the peeled onions, shake the pan during cooking so that the onions brown evenly. Keep these warm also.

Pour in the cider and heat it through while vigorously scraping the pan with the back of a fork. Return chops and onions to the pan, season, cover it and cook over a moderate heat for 15–18 minutes.

Stir the cornflour and crème fraîche together into a smooth mixture. Remove the chops and onions to a warmed serving dish and, off the heat, whisk the crème fraîche into the cooking liquid. Return to the heat to give just one bubble, then pour the sauce over the chops.

Serve with a dish of mashed potatoes and, to be different, baked apples.

Elle recommends that the same cider used in cooking should be drunk with this dish from Normandy.

FILETS MIGNONS AU ROQUEFORT
Sliced pork fillet in Roquefort sauce

PREPARATION TIME: 30 minutes
COOKING TIME: 1 hour
FOR SIX

1 kg (scant 2¼ lb) pork fillet	60 g (2 oz) butter
200 g (7 oz) Roquefort cheese	2 tablespoons caster sugar
1½ kg (3 lb 5 oz) baby turnips	4 shallots
300 g (10½ oz) green olives	100 ml (3½ fl oz) dry vermouth
2 tablespoons of goose fat or lard	100 g (3½ oz) crème fraîche
salt, pepper	

Trim, wash the baby turnips and wipe them dry. Using a scoop or baller, scoop out balls of turnip about the size of a large olive.

Stone the olives and blanch them in boiling water for about 2 minutes. Drain and put to one side.

Melt the goose fat in a casserole and sauté the seasoned pork fillets slowly: at the end of 45 minutes, they should be cooked through but still tender.

While the pork fillets are cooking, blanch the turnip balls in boiling water. Melt the butter in a pan and slowly cook the drained turnips to a golden-brown. When they begin to change colour, sprinkle them with sugar and continue cooking over a moderate heat until they are glazed: shake the pan frequently so that they are glazed evenly.

When the meat is cooked, put it on a plate to keep warm. Add the finely-chopped shallots to the casserole and deglaze with the vermouth: when the liquid is bubbling, add the cheese, crumbled with a fork, and the blanched olives. Season with pepper and slowly reduce the mixture. One minute before serving, stir in the cream. Check the seasoning.

Cut the fillets into slices, arrange them on a warmed serving dish, surrounded by the turnips and olives. Serve the sauce separately.

From the restaurant 'Le Trou Gascon' in Paris-12e: the chef recommends that a red Madiran should be drunk with this dish.

FILETS DE PORC RÔTIS
Roast pork fillet

PREPARATION TIME: 15 minutes (1 hour in advance)
COOKING TIME: 30 minutes
FOR SIX

1 kg (scant 2¼ lb) pork fillet	salt, pepper
dried leaves of sage	thyme
lard	

With a very sharp knife, cut 6 or 8 slits in each fillet and insert a sage leaf in each one. Season a good tablespoon of lard with salt, pepper and chopped thyme and spread it over the fillets. Put the meat into its cooking pan and leave it to stand in the lard and herbs for ¾–1 hour.

Roast the pork fillets in a fairly hot oven (200°C/400°F/Gas Mark 6) for 30 minutes. Turn the fillets from time to time.

When the pork is cooked, cut into thickish slices across the grain and serve with its own juices. Mashed potatoes, Brussels sprouts, celeriac etc. go well with the pork.

PORC ESMERALDA
Mexican pork

PREPARATION TIME: 20 minutes
COOKING TIME: 35 minutes
FOR SIX

1 kg (scant 2¼ lb) pork fillet	2 lemons
2 tins taco sauce	peanut oil
300 g (10½ oz) crème fraîche	2 aubergines
250 ml (9 fl oz) chicken stock	salt, pepper
750 g (generous 1½ lb) button mushrooms	

Mix together in a large bowl the taco sauce, the crème fraîche and the chicken stock. Season.

Trim the stalks of the mushrooms, wipe them in a mixture of lemon juice and water and slice them. In 2 tablespoons of peanut oil cook them until their liquid has been given off: drain, and put to one side.

Trim the aubergines and cut them into round slices about 1 cm (½ inch) thick. Fry them in a pan in 100 ml (3½ fl oz) of oil until they are soft. Season, drain, and put to one side.

Cut the pork into small chunks and sauté it in 3 tablespoons of oil. When it is browned all over, drain off the cooking oil and pour in one-third of the sauce mixture: mix together and warm it through over a moderate heat. At the same time, divide the remaining sauce equally and warm through the mushrooms in one portion and the aubergine slices in the other.

When everything is hot, arrange the pork in the centre of a warmed serving dish with the mushrooms and aubergines all in their sauces around it.

CÔTES DE PORC AUX CÈPES
Pork chops with mushrooms

PREPARATION TIME: 10 minutes
COOKING TIME: 25 minutes
FOR SIX

6 pork chops
1 tin of cèpes
40 g (scant 1½ oz) lard
150 ml (5 fl oz) dry white wine
100 ml (3½ fl oz) chicken stock
3 onions

2 tablespoons olive oil
salt, pepper
1 level teaspoon powdered
   cinnamon
1 clove of garlic
parsley

Fresh mushrooms may be used instead of cèpes, but it is worth taking the trouble to find them.

Rinse the cèpes in warm water and thoroughly drain them and wipe with kitchen paper.

Lightly fry the chops in lard until they are just golden-brown on both sides. Remove from the pan and deglaze it with the white wine and the chicken stock, letting it boil for 10 seconds.

Peel and chop the onions and gently cook them in oil in a heavy iron casserole until transparent. Add the cèpes and let them cook for a few minutes, then add the pork chops. Season, sprinkle with powdered cinnamon and chopped garlic, pour in the liquid from the frying pan, cover the casserole and cook over a moderate flame for 15 minutes. Sprinkle with chopped parsley and serve at once.

PORC AU LAIT
Pork chops in milk

PREPARATION TIME: 5 minutes
COOKING TIME: 40 minutes
FOR SIX

6 boned pork chops
thyme
salt, pepper

500 ml (17½ fl oz) full-cream milk
6 cloves of garlic

Sprinkle chopped thyme over both sides of each chop. Heat a heavy pan and cook the chops dry (i.e. without additional fat) until they are lightly golden-brown. Season, pour the milk over the chops, add the crushed cloves of garlic and bring to the boil. Keep it to a gentle boil for about 30 minutes, when the liquid will have reduced by two-thirds.

Remove the chops to a warmed serving dish and pour over the sauce having strained it through a sieve.

CARRÉ DE PORC AU CARAMEL
Glazed loin of pork

PREPARATION TIME: 20 minutes
COOKING TIME: 1½ hours
FOR SIX

a loin of pork weighing 2 kg
  (scant 4½ lb)
1 tablespoon oil
2 carrots
2 onions
salt, pepper
4 oranges

100 ml (3½ fl oz) dry white wine
100 g (3½ oz) caster sugar
2 tablespoons wine vinegar
250 ml (9 fl oz) chicken stock
1 teaspoon of cornflour
1 tablespoon orange marmalade
2 tablespoons orange liqueur

Heat the oil in a heavy oval casserole and seal the joint on all sides. Remove and replace with the peeled and sliced carrots and onions. Stir frequently and when the vegetables are lightly browned, put the joint back in the casserole: season and add the juice of 2 oranges and the white wine. Cover and cook in a very hot oven (240°C/475°F/Gas Mark 9) for 30 minutes. Lower the heat to a moderate oven (180°C/350°F/Gas Mark 4) and continue the cooking for a further hour.

During this time, prepare the syrup: put the sugar in a small saucepan, just cover it with water and heat until a clear syrup results. Remove from the heat and mix in the vinegar. Blanch the peel of the two remaining oranges for 3 minutes in boiling water, drain and cut into very fine strips. Divide the flesh into segments, removing the skin from each one.

When the joint is cooked, keep it warm on its serving dish. Return the casserole to the heat with the juices in which the pork was cooked plus the chicken stock and the syrup. Stirring frequently, reduce the sauce by half. Make a paste with cornflour and a little water and incorporate it into the sauce: check the seasoning and finally add the marmalade, the orange liqueur and the strips of peel.

To serve, pour part of the sauce over the joint and decorate the serving dish with orange segments. Serve the rest of the sauce separately.

CÔTES DE PORC AUX NOIX
Pork chops in walnut sauce

PREPARATION TIME: 5 minutes
COOKING TIME: 20 minutes
FOR SIX

6 pork chops
100 g (3½ oz) shelled walnuts
40 g (scant 1½ oz) butter
salt, pepper

½ lemon
cayenne pepper
200 g (7 oz) crème fraîche

Roughly chop up the walnut kernels. Heat the butter in a pan and when it foams, add the pork chops and cook them for about 7 minutes on each side. Season and remove the chops to a warm place.

Scrape the bottom of the pan to loosen the bits and put in the lemon juice, the chopped walnuts and a pinch of cayenne pepper. Mix together and, over a brisk heat and stirring constantly, add the crème fraîche. Check the seasoning, pour the sauce over the chops and serve at once.

Elle suggests that if the chops are very thick ones, it might be better to brown them only in a pan, and complete their cooking in the oven.

[99]

PORC AU CORBIÈRES
Pork chops in white wine

PREPARATION TIME: 1 hour
COOKING TIME: 20 minutes
FOR EIGHT

8 pork chops	For the sauce:
500 g (generous 1 lb) salsify	goose fat (or lard)
1 kg (2¼ lb) potatoes	pork bones and trimmings
1 kg (2¼ lb) chestnuts	1 onion
400 g (14 oz) carrots	2 carrots
100 g (3½ oz) goose fat (or lard)	200 g (7 oz) celery
200 g (7 oz) chicken livers	bouquet garni
1 onion	1 bottle white wine
2 egg yolks	30 g (1 oz) butter
olive oil	30 g (1 oz) flour

Begin with the sauce. Put a little goose fat or lard in a heavy iron casserole and sweat the pork bones and trimmings. Peel and chop the onion, the carrots and the celery and add them, with the bouquet garni, to the casserole. Pour in 500 ml (17½ fl oz) of water and an equal quantity of wine, bring to the boil and then simmer for a good hour. Skim off the fat and briskly reduce the volume of liquid by half.

Peel the salsify, potatoes, chestnuts and carrots and separately blanch them for 10 minutes in salted boiling water. Then, again separately, braise each in a little goose fat or lard.

While this is being done, cook the chicken livers in a little hot fat so they are still pink inside. Gently cook the peeled and chopped onion in fat until it is transparent. Finely chop the liver and mix liver and onion together. Make a mayonnaise with the beaten egg yolks and the oil, fold in the liver–onion mixture and put to one side.

Ten minutes before serving, fry the chops in as much of the remaining goose fat or lard as necessary. Keep in a warm place.

(CONTINUED OPPOSITE)

HAMBURGERS DE PORC
Pork hamburgers

PREPARATION TIME: 10 minutes
COOKING TIME: 20 minutes
FOR SIX

900 g (scant 2 lb) boned shoulder	thyme
of pork	12–18 thin slices of streaky
salt, pepper	bacon
bay leaf	olive oil

Finely mince the meat, season and mix in a crumbled bay leaf and 6 chopped sprigs of thyme. Divide the mixture into hamburgers. Wrap each hamburger in 2 or 3 slices of smoked bacon.

Cut squares of kitchen foil, brush them with oil and seal up each hamburger carefully.

Cook in a very hot oven (240°C/475°F/Gas Mark 9) for 20 minutes.

Elle says that the hamburgers can also be cooked over a barbecue, wrapped as above. In this case they should be turned from time to time.

(CONTINUED)

Pour off the surplus fat from the pan and deglaze it with the rest of the wine. Add the sauce, stir well and begin to reduce over a brisk heat. Thicken it with a paste made from working butter and flour together.

Arrange the braised vegetables in the centre of a warmed serving dish, put the chops round the edge and pour the sauce over it all. Serve at once with the chicken-liver mayonnaise separately.

VEAU BASQUAISE
Veal Basque

PREPARATION TIME: 20 minutes
COOKING TIME: 45 minutes
FOR SIX

1½ kg (3 lb 5 oz) loin of veal
3 aubergines
3 tomatoes
3 onions
1 kg (scant 2¼ lb) button
   mushrooms

1 lemon
3 tablespoons olive oil
1 bulb of garlic
bouquet garni
1 glass (5 fl oz) white wine
salt, pepper

Trim the aubergines and cut them up into dice, sprinkle with salt and leave to sweat for 20 minutes. Peel and de-seed the tomatoes and cut them up. Peel and slice the onions. Trim off the ends of the stalks of the mushrooms and wipe them in a mixture of water and lemon juice. Dry the aubergines on kitchen paper.

Heat the oil in a casserole and seal the joint on all sides. Add the onions, season and cook for 20 minutes. Then add the tomatoes, the aubergines, the peeled and crushed garlic, the mushrooms cut into quarters and the bouquet garni. Moisten with the white wine, season, cover the casserole and cook for another 25 minutes.

When the joint is cooked, remove it to a carving dish and arrange the vegetables around a warmed serving dish. Carve the meat and put the slices in the centre of the serving dish. Pass the juices in the casserole through a sieve and serve them separately.

QUASI DE VEAU AUX PETITS OIGNONS
Veal with onions

PREPARATION TIME: 15 minutes
COOKING TIME: 1 hour or 1½ hours (see note)
FOR SIX

1 kg (scant 2¼ lb) boned chump
   end of loin of veal
750 g (generous 1½ lb) small
   onions

4 sprigs of basil
200 ml (7 fl oz) dry white wine
salt, pepper

A pressure cooker is required for the original recipe; if you don't have a pressure cooker, follow the instructions in the Note.

Choose a lean joint of veal. Peel the small onions, put them into a pressure cooker with the sprigs of basil and the white wine. Add the loin of veal, season and cook under pressure for 1 hour.

Remove the joint, carve into thick slices and arrange on a warmed serving dish surrounded by the onions and herbs.

Note: If you do not have a pressure cooker, pre-heat your oven to 160°C/325°F/Gas Mark 3. Lightly brown the veal in a heavy casserole with a little oil and butter. Add the onions, then the white wine, basil and seasoning. Cook, covered, in the lower half of the oven for about 1½ hours, basting the meat occasionally. Serve as above.

VEAU AU PAMPLEMOUSSE
Veal with grapefruit

PREPARATION TIME: 10 minutes
COOKING TIME: 20 minutes
FOR SIX

*4 thick slices of loin of veal
   weighing about 1¼ kg (2¾ lb)
2 medium-sized grapefruit
6 carrots
75 g (generous 2½ oz) butter*

*3 tablespoons olive oil
50 ml (1¾ fl oz) brandy
100 ml (3½ fl oz) dry white wine
salt, pepper
25 g (scant 1 oz) flour*

Wash, trim and peel the carrots and cut them into round slices. Gently cook them in 50 g (scant 2 oz) butter.

Heat oil in a large pan and cook the veal slices on both sides until they are golden-brown. This should take about 10 minutes. Put aside in a warm place.

Pour off any surplus fat and deglaze the pan with the juice of one grapefruit, the brandy and the white wine. Continue until the volume of sauce is reduced by half. Season. Work the flour and remaining butter together.

Remove the pan from the heat and, little by little, incorporate the butter paste into the sauce. Return the pan to a very low heat from time to time, whisking constantly, until the sauce becomes velvety and of the desired consistency. Add the slices of veal, the carrots and their juices, the remaining grapefruit, peeled and divided into skinned segments, and cook everything together for a final 5 minutes. Serve at once.

VEAU À L'ANETH
Veal with dill

PREPARATION TIME: 15 minutes
COOKING TIME: 1½ hours
FOR SIX

*1¼ kg (2¾ lb) loin of veal
1 bunch of fresh dill
piece of larding fat
salt
allspice (crushed)*

*4 tablespoons of olive oil
50 g (scant 2 oz) butter
50 ml (1¾ fl oz) aquavit
250 g (scant 9 oz) crème fraîche
4 apples*

Roll and tie the joint but do not at this stage incorporate any larding fat. Make four or five cuts in the joint and insert a sprig of dill into each one. Mix salt and crushed allspice together and rub the mixture into the entire surface of the meat. Do this several times.

Heat 3 tablespoons of oil in a casserole and quickly seal the meat on all sides. Remove the meat, discard the oil and replace it by the butter and 1 fresh tablespoon of oil. Put the joint back in the casserole and sprinkle it with aquavit and chopped dill. Lay the larding fat over the meat, cover the casserole and cook for 1 hour over a moderate heat. Remove the lid and cook uncovered for a further 30 minutes.

Remove the joint to its warmed serving dish and carve it in slices. Deglaze the casserole with the crème fraîche, let the sauce bubble once or twice, and check the seasoning.

The carved joint is served garnished with thin slices of apple which have been fried in extra butter, with the sauce in a separate sauceboat.

Elle notes that if aquavit is not available, vodka may be substituted.

CÔTES DE VEAU AUX ÉPINARDS
Veal chops with spinach

PREPARATION TIME: 20 minutes
COOKING TIME: 20 minutes
FOR SIX

6 good thick veal chops	olive oil
6 tablespoons pre-cooked leaf spinach	20 g (¾ oz) butter
salt, pepper	100 ml (3½ fl oz) white wine
6 slices Gouda cheese (about 6 mm/¼ inch thick)	2 tablespoons double cream

Split open each veal chop along its side to make a pocket, season lightly. Stuff each one with a slice of cheese and a spoonful of leaf spinach.

Heat a little oil and the butter in a pan and cook each chop to a good golden-brown for about 7–8 minutes each side. Lower the heat towards the end of cooking. Remove the chops to a serving dish and keep in a warm place.

Deglaze the pan with the white wine, then pour in the cream and bring to a slow boil for 5 minutes. Check the seasoning and pour the sauce over the chops. Serve at once.

From the restaurant 'Le Lord Gourmand' in Paris-8e: the chef of this Left-Bank restaurant recommends that a red wine from the Loire, preferably a Sancerre, goes well with this dish.

BLANQUETTE À L'OSEILLE
Veal stew with sorrel

PREPARATION TIME: 10 minutes
COOKING TIME: 1 hour
FOR SIX

2 kg (4½ lb) breast of veal	75 g (generous 2½ oz) butter
1 chicken stock cube	40 g (scant 1½ oz) flour
200 g (7 oz) chopped sorrel	250 g (scant 9 oz) button mushrooms
½ bottle white Mâcon	2 lemons
2 onions	2 egg yolks
5 peppercorns	250 g (scant 9 oz) crème fraîche
250 g (scant 9 oz) small onions	
1 tablespoon sugar	

Cut the meat into pieces, put it into a cooking pot and sprinkle it with the crumbled stock cube. Moisten with the white wine and 1½ litres (generous 2½ pints) water. Add the peeled onions and the peppercorns, cover the pot, bring to the boil and cook at this temperature for 40–45 minutes. Remove the meat and, over a brisk flame, reduce by half the volume of the liquid in the pot. Strain the stock and set aside.

During this time, trim and peel the small onions and put them into a saucepan with the sugar, ½ glass (2½ fl oz) water and 25 g (scant 1 oz) of butter. Cover the pan, bring it to the boil and cook for 10 minutes. Remove the lid and continue the cooking until all the liquid is evaporated. Take the pan from the heat and put to one side.

Make a roux in a saucepan with the remaining butter and the flour. Slowly add the stock, whisking constantly, and let the sauce bubble for 2–3 minutes. Put the meat into the sauce together with the mushrooms which have been trimmed and wiped with a mixture of the juice of 1 lemon and water. Cover the pan and cook for 15 minutes.

In a bowl, mix together the beaten egg yolks, the crème fraîche and the juice of the second lemon. Extend it with two ladles of sauce from the meat, then pour the whole back into the meat saucepan. Add the glazed onions and chopped sorrel, check the seasoning but do not let the sauce boil.

MÉDAILLONS DE VEAU À LA SAUGE
Veal medallions with sage

PREPARATION TIME: 15 minutes
COOKING TIME: 20 minutes
FOR SIX

6 veal medallions	3 shallots
12 sage leaves	½ glass (2½ fl oz) wine vinegar
flour	1 chicken stock cube
1 tablespoon of butter	salt, pepper
1 tablespoon of olive oil	250 g (scant 9 oz) crème fraîche

Have the medallions cut from good chops and flattened. Put a sage leaf on both sides of each piece of meat. Lightly flour each one, shaking off any surplus. Heat the butter and oil in a pan and cook the medallions for 3 minutes each side. Finish the cooking with 5 minutes in a very hot oven (230°C/450°F/Gas Mark 8). Remove from the pan to a warmed serving dish.

Replace the meat in the pan by the peeled and chopped shallots and gently cook them until transparent. When done, remove to one side with a perforated spoon. Pour off any surplus fat and deglaze the pan with the vinegar, replace the shallots and continue cooking until all the liquid has evaporated.

Moisten with the chicken cube dissolved in 200 ml (7 fl oz) of hot water, bring to the boil and reduce the volume of liquid by half. Season, mix in the crème fraîche and, stirring constantly, let the sauce thicken until it coats the back of a spoon. Pour the sauce through a sieve onto the medallions.

From the restaurant 'Demornex' in Saint-Jean-de-Gonville just across the border from Geneva: the chef says a good cool Beaujolais will go best with this dish.

GRENADINS AUX AMANDES
Veal fillets with almonds

PREPARATION TIME: 10 minutes
COOKING TIME: 20 minutes
FOR SIX

6 veal fillets, each about 200 g (7 oz)	salt, pepper
350 g (scant 12½ oz) almonds	75 g (generous 2½ oz) butter
2 tablespoons flour	1 small glass (3 fl oz) dry white vermouth
2 eggs	

Tie each fillet into a round shape. Put the flour into a flat dish and beat the eggs in a bowl. Chop up the almonds. Roll each fillet first in flour, then in beaten egg and finally in chopped almond, pressing firmly with the fingertips so that the meat is evenly coated with chopped nuts. Season.

Heat the butter and cook the fillets on both sides for about 10 minutes until they are an even golden-brown. Remove to a meat pan and finish the cooking with 10 minutes in a fairly hot oven (200°C/400°F/Gas Mark 6).

Deglaze the frying pan with the vermouth, arrange the veal fillets on their serving dish and cover with sauce.

Elle notes that creamed spinach goes deliciously with the veal fillets.

SAUTÉ DE VEAU AU CITRON
Veal with lemon

PREPARATION TIME: 30 minutes
COOKING TIME: 1¾–2 hours
FOR SIX

1½ kg (3 lb 5 oz) boned veal shoulder, cut into chunks
4 lemons
cooking oil
3 tablespoons butter
flour
200 ml (7 fl oz) dry white wine
salt, pepper
bouquet garni
2 cloves of garlic
2 carrots
1 large onion
2 tablespoons tomato purée

Be sure that the meat is cut into even chunks. Heat 3 tablespoons of oil in a frying pan and quickly seal the veal on all sides to a golden-brown. Using a perforated spoon, remove the meat to a heavy casserole. Add 2 tablespoons of butter and sift in 2 tablespoons of flour. Stir, and when the flour takes colour, add the white wine, the juice of 3 lemons and enough water just to cover the meat. Stir well, scraping the bottom of the casserole with the back of a fork. Season, add the bouquet garni and 2 crushed cloves of garlic. Cover the casserole and simmer gently over a low heat.

Peel and dice the carrots, peel and slice the onion. Pour the fat off the frying pan and heat 1 tablespoon of butter and 1 tablespoon of oil and gently cook the vegetables until the onion is transparent. Stir in the tomato purée and add all the mixture to the casserole. Continue to simmer, stirring from time to time.

Remove the veal when done to a warmed serving dish. Peel the remaining lemon, remove pith and skin and cut the flesh into small chunks. Decorate the meat with lemon pieces, serve with boiled rice.

GUIAPRAKIA
Veal-stuffed cabbage

PREPARATION TIME: 30 minutes
COOKING TIME: 1 hour
FOR SIX

500 g (generous 1 lb) trimmed shoulder of veal
1 cabbage
100 g (3½ oz) risotto rice
50 g (scant 2 oz) butter
salt
1 teaspoon ground pepper
2 firm tomatoes
2 lemons

Plunge the rice into boiling water for 5 minutes. Carefully separate the cabbage leaves and, after trimming off the thick parts of the stalks, plunge these into plenty of boiling salted water also. Let it bubble two or three times, then drain the leaves and rinse them under running cold water. Keep to one side.

Mince the veal and put it in a mixing bowl with the drained rice and 40 g (scant 1½ oz) of butter. Season and mix well together. Make cylinders of veal mixture and wrap each one in a cabbage leaf, then arrange them side by side in an ovenproof dish. Season again with salt and dot with knobs of remaining butter. Peel and de-seed the tomatoes, chop them up and spread them over the stuffed cabbage. Squeeze the juice of 2 lemons over the dish and add 200 ml (7 fl oz) water.

Cook in a moderate oven (180°C/350°F/Gas Mark 4) for about 1 hour. Serve hot.

Elle advises that the smaller the Guiaprakia are, the better they will taste. Trim the cabbage leaves to size to suit the amount of stuffing being used.

ESCALOPES ROULÉES AU PAPRIKA
Veal birds with paprika

PREPARATION TIME: 20 minutes
COOKING TIME: 40 minutes
FOR SIX

6 large veal escalopes	12 rashers smoked streaky
3 onions	bacon
olive oil	2 long potatoes
1 tablespoon of paprika	salt, pepper
strong mustard	200 g (7 oz) crème fraîche

Have the escalopes well flattened. Peel and slice the onions and cook them gently in 3 tablespoons of oil until they are transparent. When they are done, stir in the paprika, remove from the heat and put to one side.

Spread each escalope with a thin layer of mustard, lay two rashers of bacon, trimmed of rind, side by side on top, followed by a thin slice of potato. Lightly season and roll up the escalope and bacon around the potato slice: use a toothpick to keep the roll closed.

Arrange the veal rolls in an ovenproof dish, add 200 ml (7 fl oz) water, cover the dish and cook in a moderate oven (180°C/350°F/Gas Mark 4) for 30 minutes. When cooked, remove the veal to a serving dish and vigorously stir the crème fraîche into the cooking juices. Let it bubble once or twice, pour the sauce over the meat and serve at once.

VEAU JARDINIÈRE
Veal stew with young peas

PREPARATION TIME: 20 minutes
COOKING TIME: 2½ hours
FOR SIX

1½ kg (3¼ lb) breast of veal	500 g (generous 1 lb) small
75 ml (2½ fl oz) oil	onions
bouquet garni	600 g (generous 1¼ lb) young
salt, pepper	carrots
3 kg (6½ lb) peas in pod	2 sugar lumps
	50 g (scant 2 oz) butter

Trim and cut the meat into cubes. Heat the oil in a pan and, when it is hot, seal the meat on all sides. Remove meat into a casserole together with the bouquet garni and seasoning. Add enough boiling water to cover the meat, cover the casserole and simmer over a low heat for 1½ hours.

During this time, shell the peas and trim and peel the other vegetables. Add them all to the casserole with 2 lumps of sugar and, with the pot still covered, continue cooking over a very low heat for a further 1 hour. Take out the bouquet garni and stir in the butter. Keep the casserole warm but do not allow its contents to boil again.

Elle says this dish can be equally good in winter when only tinned peas and tinned small carrots are available. It also re-heats very well.

GÂTEAUX DE FOIES DE VOLAILLE
Chicken-liver terrine

FOIES DE VOLAILLE EN BROCHETTES
Chicken-liver kebabs

PREPARATION TIME: 35 minutes (part the day before)
COOKING TIME: 1¾ hours
FOR SIX

250 g (scant 9 oz) chicken livers	120 g (scant 4½ oz) turkey
125 ml (4½ fl oz) sherry	escalopes
thyme	1 teaspoon mixed black and
bay leaf	white peppercorns
3 cloves of garlic	3 eggs
120 g (scant 4½ oz) shallots	40 g (scant 1½ oz) parsley
300 g (10½ oz) button	40 g (scant 1½ oz) chervil
mushrooms	40 g (scant 1½ oz) chives
	1 teaspoon salt

Trim and clean the chicken livers and marinate them overnight in sherry with thyme and bay leaf. Stir from time to time.

Peel the garlic and the shallots, trim the mushrooms and wipe them. Blend all three together and put to one side.

Drain the livers from their marinade and put them and the turkey through the blender. Stir the two mixtures thoroughly together and fold in the marinade after straining out the herbs. Crush the peppercorns and beat the eggs and incorporate these ingredients also, together with the fresh chopped herbs. Season.

Line six individual moulds with kitchen foil and divide the chicken-liver mixture between them. Place the moulds in a pan of water and cook for 1¾ hours in a cool oven (150°C/300°F/Gas Mark 2).

Refrigerate the terrines in their moulds: to serve, turn them out, chilled, onto a serving plate decorated with lettuce leaves and chopped aspic.

PREPARATION TIME: 30 minutes
COOKING TIME: 30 minutes
FOR SIX

500 g (generous 1 lb) chicken	2 or 3 leaves of sage
livers	salt, pepper
50 g (scant 2 oz) butter	18 thin rashers smoked streaky
1 teaspoon chopped thyme	bacon

Melt the butter over a very low heat with the chopped thyme and crushed leaves of sage. Allow time for the aroma of the herbs to be absorbed, then put in the trimmed and cleaned chicken livers. Raise the heat to seal the livers but leave them undercooked inside. Remove from the heat, season and let them cool.

Cut the livers into 18 even pieces and wrap each one in bacon. Divide them in six and thread on barbecue skewers. Put them under a heated grill and turn from time to time: the kebabs will be ready when the bacon is evenly cooked.

Serve with polenta made into a flat cake and lightly browned in the pan. Dot with butter. Grated cheese may be sprinkled on the polenta if desired.

Elle notes that packet streaky bacon, which is usually cut very thin, is ideal for this dish.

FOIE DE VEAU À LA BANANE
Calves' liver and banana

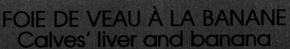

PREPARATION TIME: 15 minutes
COOKING TIME: 5 minutes
FOR SIX

*6 slices of calves' liver each
about 100 g (3½ oz)
750 g (generous 1½ lb) bananas*

*1 kg (scant 2¼ lb) oranges
1 bunch of watercress
salt, pepper*

Peel the bananas and cut them into round slices. Squeeze the juice from the oranges. Wash and dry the watercress and remove the stalks from the leaves.

In a very hot frying pan, without any fat, seal each piece of liver on both sides. Remove from the pan and keep in a warm place.

Deglaze the pan with the orange juice. Let it bubble once or twice, season, reduce the heat and add the sliced bananas. Cook slowly for 3 minutes, turning from time to time. Remove the bananas, raise the heat and return the liver to the pan. Allow 2 more minutes of cooking to leave the liver pink in the middle.

Serve with the fried banana and decorate with watercress.

Elle says that since the recipe contains the luxury of calves' liver, it is well worth the trouble to use freshly-squeezed oranges and not be tempted to use commercial 'fresh orange juice'.

FOIE DE VEAU À LA MENTHE
Calves' liver in a mint sauce

PREPARATION TIME: 10 minutes
COOKING TIME: 10–12 minutes
FOR SIX

*6 slices of calves' liver each
about 100 g (3½ oz)
4 oranges
1 lemon
salt, pepper*

*100 g (3½ oz) flour
100 g (3½ oz) butter
300 g (10½ oz) crème fraîche
15 leaves of fresh mint (plus extra
for decoration)*

Peel the oranges and the lemon, finely slice the peel and blanch it for 3 minutes in boiling water. Drain. Squeeze the oranges and reserve their juice.

Season the liver and roll it in flour, shaking each piece to remove any surplus. Heat half the butter in a pan and cook the liver to the extent preferred; put to one side in a warm place.

Pour the fat from the pan and deglaze it with the orange juice. Bring the sauce to the boil and reduce its volume by half. Stir in the cream and the blanched lemon and orange peels and the chopped mint: continue cooking, stirring constantly, until a smooth and velvety sauce results. Check the seasoning, remove the pan from the heat and whisk in the remaining butter, knob by knob.

Serve decorated with leaves of mint set aside.

From the restaurant 'La Caillère' at Condé-sur-Beuvron: the chef recommends that a chilled rosé from the Loire be drunk with this dish.

ROGNONS AUX CÈPES
Calves' kidneys and cèpes

PREPARATION TIME: 20 minutes
COOKING TIME: 15 minutes
FOR SIX

3 calves' kidneys weighing about
   900 g (2 lb)
1 kg (scant 2¼ lb) cèpes
100 g (3½ oz) smoked bacon

3 tablespoons olive oil
100 g (3½ oz) butter
3 shallots
salt, pepper

Trim the kidneys of fat and membrane and cut them into largish pieces. Put the bacon into boiling water for 3 minutes, remove and run it under a cold tap, then cut it into strips across the grain.

Trim the fungi, separating the stalks from the caps. Slice the caps and cook them gently in 1 tablespoon of oil and 25 g (scant 1 oz) of butter until their liquid has been given off.

Peel and chop the shallots and cook them until transparent in the same quantities of oil and butter. Add the sliced mushroom stalks to the shallots and continue cooking until the juices evaporate.

Fry the bacon strips to a light golden-brown in the final tablespoon of oil. Remove from the pan, melt the remainder of the butter and cook the kidneys for about 4 minutes, according to taste. Add the bacon, season sparingly.

To serve, mix the kidneys and the caps of the fungi together and sprinkle with the shallot/stalk mixture.

Elle says that if you do not have a source of fresh cèpes (boletus), they may be bought dried in packets and reconstituted according to the directions.

ROGNONS AU VINAIGRE
Kidneys in wine vinegar

PREPARATION TIME: 5 minutes
COOKING TIME: 20 minutes
FOR SIX

900 g (2 lb) calves' kidneys
100 ml (3½ fl oz) wine vinegar
olive oil
salt, pepper

2 onions
50 g (scant 2 oz) butter
1 beef stock cube

Trim the kidneys of fat and membrane and cut them into largish pieces. Put 3 tablespoons of oil into a pan and when it is smoking hot, quickly seal half the kidneys, stirring so they cook on all sides. Season, remove with a perforated spoon to a warm place, and repeat with the remaining kidneys.

Peel and finely chop the onions and cook them gently in the juices from the kidneys, to which the butter has been added. Add the vinegar and scrape the pan with the back of a fork so that everything is incorporated.

Dissolve the beef cube in 200 ml (7 fl oz) of boiling water and pour the stock over the onions. Bring to the boil and reduce the sauce: return the kidneys to the pan and heat the dish through without letting the sauce boil again. Check the seasoning.

Serve hot, with sauté potatoes or French beans.

RISOTTO AUX ROGNONS
Kidney risotto

PREPARATION TIME: 5 minutes
COOKING TIME: 25 minutes
FOR SIX

2 calves' kidneys about 600 g
   (generous 1¼ lb)
250 g (9 oz) long grain rice
2 medium-sized onions
130 g (generous 4½ oz) butter
olive oil

bouquet garni
1 chicken stock cube
salt, pepper
200 ml (7 fl oz) white wine
1 tablespoon flour

Measure and note the volume of the rice. Trim the kidneys of fat and membrane. Peel and finely chop the onions and cook them gently in 60 g (2 oz) butter and 3 tablespoons of oil. When the onion is transparent, pour in the rice and stir with a wooden spoon. When the rice has become milky-white, add three times its volume of water, the bouquet garni and the crumbled chicken cube. Cover the pan and continue the cooking over a low heat for about 20 minutes. The rice will be done when all the water has been absorbed.

Cut up the kidneys and seal them quickly in a hot pan in which 60 g (2 oz) butter has been melted. Season, pour in the wine, reduce the heat and cook slowly for 5 minutes.

Make a paste from the flour and the rest of the butter. Remove the kidneys to a warm place and, little by little, work the flour paste into the sauce.

Lightly grease a mould and shape the rice in it. Turn the rice out into the centre of a warmed serving dish and surround it by the kidneys over which the sauce has been poured.

Elle says the flour paste must be incorporated into the sauce with the pan off the heat. When it is all blended in, return the pan to a low heat and cook for a few minutes, whisking all the time.

BROCHETTES DE ROGNONS AU BEURRE VERT
Lambs' kidneys with herb butter

PREPARATION TIME: 30 minutes
COOKING TIME: 20 minutes
FOR SIX

12 lambs' kidneys
50 g (scant 2 oz) butter
1 handful of watercress

For the herb butter:
150 g (5 oz) butter
3 sprigs of tarragon
1 small bunch of parsley
1 small bunch of chives
salt, pepper
3 tablespoons mayonnaise

Halve the kidneys and trim in the usual way. Put two opened kidneys onto each kebab skewer. Grill them on both sides for a total of 18–20 minutes. Remove from the heat, put kidneys on to a warmed serving dish and put a knob of butter in the centre of each kidney. Garnish with a few watercress leaves.

To make the herb butter, plunge all the fresh herbs into boiling water for 1 minute. Drain and dry them, then chop them as finely as possible. Work the herbs into the butter, which should have been removed from the refrigerator well in advance, season, then mix in the mayonnaise. Serve in a separate bowl with the kidneys.

Elle warns that the kidneys should not be overcooked. They should be pink in the centre when served.

RIS DE VEAU AUX RAISINS
Sweetbreads in grape sauce

PREPARATION TIME: 25 minutes (plus 2 hours soaking)
COOKING TIME: 35 minutes
FOR SIX

calves' sweetbreads weighing
*   800–900 g (1¾–2 lb)*
15 white grapes
15 black grapes
250 ml (scant 9 fl oz) Sauternes
salt, pepper

flour
50 g (scant 2 oz) butter
10 green olives (pitted)
10 black olives (pitted)
125 g (4½ oz) crème fraîche

Leave the sweetbreads to soak in cold water for at least 2 hours. During that time, peel the grapes and put them to soak in the Sauternes.

Drain the sweetbreads, put in a saucepan and cover with fresh water. Bring slowly to the boil and boil for 5 minutes. Drain once more and rinse the sweetbreads in cold water. Remove skin and membrane and fatty parts, then slice and season.

Dredge the slices with flour on both sides, shaking to remove any surplus. Gently melt the butter in a sauté pan and fry each slice on both sides until golden-brown. Pour in the Sauternes from the grapes, cover the pan and cook over a low heat for 25 minutes. Five minutes before the end of this time, add the grapes and the olives.

Arrange the sweetbread slices on a warmed serving dish and keep in a warm place. Stir the crème fraîche into the juices in the pan, reduce the sauce by about one-third and pour over the sweetbreads. Serve at once.

<u>Elle says</u> that a Sauternes as used in the cooking should accompany the dish, well chilled.

RIS DE VEAU À MA FAÇON
Sweetbreads in pastry

PREPARATION TIME: 1 hour
COOKING TIME: 1 hour 20 minutes
FOR SIX

3 calves' sweetbreads each
*   weighing about 450 g (1 lb)*
75 g (2½ oz) butter
2 onions
2 carrots
bouquet garni
salt, pepper

300 g (10½ oz) button mushrooms
1 lemon
100 ml (3½ fl oz) port
250 g (scant 9 oz) crème fraîche
500 g (generous 1 lb) frozen puff
*   pastry*
1 egg yolk

Leave the sweetbreads to soak in cold water for at least 1 hour, with frequent rinsings under running water. Drain and put them into boiling water and let them just bubble for 2–3 minutes. Drain and wipe the sweetbreads and cut them in half.

Melt 50 g (scant 2 oz) butter in a casserole. Peel and slice the onions and the carrots and cook them gently in the butter. When the onions are transparent, add the pieces of sweetbread and the bouquet garni. Season, cover the casserole and simmer over a low heat for about 1 hour.

During this time, trim and wipe the mushrooms, cut them into small pieces and cook them in remaining butter, 50 ml (1¾ fl oz) water and the juice of the lemon. Drain and reserve the liquid.

When the sweetbreads are cooked, remove them from the casserole and leave to cool. Deglaze the casserole with the port, the crème fraîche and the liquid given off by the cooking mushrooms. Bubble the sauce until it has reduced by half, strain it, add the cooked mushrooms and put to one side in a warm place.

Fold the pastry over twice, roll it out and cut it into six oblong pieces. Put a piece of sweetbread on each, seal the pastry into a neat packet, brush each with beaten egg yolk and cook in a very hot oven (230°C/450°F/Gas Mark 8) for 5 minutes. Reduce to a moderate heat (180°C/350°F/Gas Mark 4) and continue cooking for a further 15 minutes. Serve hot, with the sauce separate.

CERVELAS FOURRÉ
Stuffed sausages

PREPARATION TIME: 10 minutes
COOKING TIME: 10 minutes
FOR SIX

6 cervelas sausages　　　*1 pot strong mustard*
400 g (14 oz) Emmenthal cheese　*12 thin slices streaky bacon*

Skin the sausages and split them lengthways without completely dividing them in half. Slice up the cheese, spread the insides of sausages with plenty of mustard and then put one slice of cheese into each one. Wrap the sausages in bacon, two slices side by side for each one, held in place by a toothpick.

Put the sausages in a baking tin and cook them for 10 minutes in a pre-heated very hot oven (240°C/475°F/Gas Mark 9). Serve at once.

<u>Elle says</u> that, served with French-fried potatoes and a green salad, this inexpensive dish makes a satisfying and simple meal.

CHOUCROUTE AU SAUCISSON
Sauerkraut and sausage

PREPARATION TIME: 15 minutes
COOKING TIME: 20 minutes
FOR SIX

1 kg (2¼ lb) prepared　　*salt, pepper*
* sauerkraut*　　　　　　*walnut oil*
1 large saveloy　　　　　*sherry vinegar*
bouquet garni　　　　　*handful of shelled walnuts*

Rinse the sauerkraut in cold running water, drain it and plunge it into boiling salted water for 2 minutes. Drain thoroughly and put to one side.

Prick the sausage-skin to prevent it from bursting during cooking. Put it, with the bouquet garni, into boiling water which has been salted and peppered, and cook for 20 minutes with the water just on the boil. Remove, allow to cool, cut off 6 round slices and cut the remainder of the sausage into dice.

Make a dressing with the walnut oil, the sherry vinegar and seasoning. Mix the sauerkraut, the dressing, the cubes of sausage and some of the walnut kernels together, and decorate with the round slices of sausage topped with half a shelled walnut.

<u>Elle says</u> that 500 g (a good 1 lb) of sausage will be enough for six servings of a starter or supper dish.

RILLETTES DE POULE
Terrine of chicken

PREPARATION TIME: 15 minutes
COOKING TIME: 4 hours
FOR A LARGE TERRINE

2 chickens each weighing about 2 kg (4½ lb)	1 bay leaf
	salt, pepper
1 kg (scant 2¼ lb) bacon	150 g (5 oz) goose fat
1 bottle white Mâcon	100 g (3½ oz) lard
4 sprigs fresh thyme	

Joint each chicken into 8 pieces. Cut the fat from the bacon, put it to one side and cut the flesh into large dice. Put the pieces of chicken into a large saucepan together with the bacon, the bacon fat, the white wine, 750 ml (1¼ pints) water, the thyme and the bay leaf. Season lightly. Check that the chicken pieces are completely immersed in liquid. If necessary, add more water. Cover the pan, bring to the boil and cook at a slow boil for 4 hours. Thirty minutes before the end of cooking time, add the goose fat.

Remove the bacon and the chicken pieces with a perforated spoon. Skin the chicken and take the meat from the bones. Bring the cooking liquids back to the boil and reduce the volume by half, remove from the heat, put the chicken meat into the stock and break up the flesh in the liquid with a fork or an electric hand-whisk. The purpose is to obtain a textured and not a smooth mixture.

When the mixture has cooled a little, turn it into a mould. Cover it with a layer of melted lard when it is quite cold.

Elle notes that this terrine will keep better if made in a number of smaller moulds. Lard may be substituted for goose fat if the latter is unobtainable.

POULET SAINT-LAGER
Chicken pie

PREPARATION TIME: 30 minutes
COOKING TIME: 30–35 minutes
FOR SIX

1 young chicken weighing about 1 kg (scant 2¼ lb)	salt, pepper
	1 teaspoon sugar
125 g (4½ oz) butter	1 packet frozen puff pastry (400 g/14 oz)
4–6 spring onions	
1 large tin petits pois	1 egg

Joint the chicken and strip all the meat from the bones. Season it liberally and leave to stand for 10 minutes.

Melt a good tablespoon of butter in a pan and, over a very moderate heat, lightly cook the chicken until it is about half-cooked. Put to one side to keep warm.

Cut the white part of the spring onions into slices about 12 mm (½ inch) thick and gently cook them in the same fats used for the chicken. When they are transparent, turn them into a pie dish together with the peas, thoroughly drained of any liquid. Season, sprinkle with sugar and dot with the rest of the butter, cut into knobs. Next add all the pieces of chicken. Do not press them down into the dish, just lay them lightly on top of each other.

Roll out the pastry to a size sufficient to cover the dish. Make patterns with the tines of a fork, then lay the pastry over the dish. Trim off the outer edges inside the pie dish and down the sides. Again, do not press the pastry down onto the contents of the dish. Brush with beaten egg.

Cook in a very hot oven (230°C/450°F/Gas Mark 8) for 15 minutes, then lower the heat to a hot oven (200°C/400°F/Gas Mark 6) until the pastry is quite cooked. Serve at once.

POULET COCOTTE GRAND-MÈRE
Chicken grand-mère

PREPARATION TIME: 25 minutes
COOKING TIME: 1 hour 20 minutes
FOR SIX

1 chicken weighing about 2 kg
  (4½ lb)
2 cloves of garlic
salt, pepper
3 tablespoons butter
250 g (scant 9 oz) salt pork

bouquet garni
300 g (10 oz) small onions
6 carrots
600 g (generous 1¼ lb) potatoes
olive oil

Prepare the chicken as if for roasting. Work the peeled and crushed cloves of garlic, a pinch of salt and a pinch of pepper into a tablespoon of butter. Put this inside the chicken.

Cut the salt pork into strips and blanch it in boiling water for 5 minutes. Put the chicken and 2 tablespoons of butter into a casserole. Over a very moderate heat, lightly brown the chicken on all sides. This operation will take at least 20 minutes and the butter must not be allowed to blacken.

Fry the pork-strips until crisp, remove them with a perforated spoon and add them to the chicken together with the bouquet garni. Cover the casserole.

Peel the onions and leave them whole. Peel the carrots and potatoes and cut them up into small dice. Heat 3 tablespoons of oil in a pan and quickly cook all the vegetables to a golden-brown. Remove with a perforated spoon to drain off surplus liquid and add them to the casserole. Moisten with a small glass (3½ fl oz) of water, season and put the casserole in a fairly hot oven (200°C/400°F/Gas Mark 6) for 20 minutes per 450 g (1 lb). Stir the vegetables and turn the chicken twice during the cooking.

Remove and carve the chicken and serve it with its vegetables. Drain off the cooking juices and serve them as a sauce.

POULET AU GINGEMBRE
Chicken with ginger

PREPARATION TIME: 25 minutes
COOKING TIME: 50–60 minutes
FOR SIX

1 large chicken
2 preserved lemons (see p.16)
1 tablespoon grated fresh ginger
6 tablespoons olive oil
60 g (2 oz) butter
500 g (generous 1 lb) chopped
  onion

2 cloves of garlic
1 chicken stock cube
salt
4 cloves
good pinch of powdered saffron
pinch cayenne pepper

Stuff the chicken with a lemon cut into quarters and the grated ginger. Heat 3 tablespoons of oil in a casserole and seal the chicken to a golden-brown on all sides. Remove and put to one side.

Pour off the oil from the casserole and replace it with the butter. Gently cook the onion and the peeled and sliced garlic until transparent, then replace the chicken in the casserole. Moisten with 200 ml (7 fl oz) of stock made from the chicken cube. Lightly season with salt, add the crushed cloves, the saffron and the cayenne, the remainder of the oil and the second lemon, cut into quarters. Stir, cover the casserole, bring to the boil and cook for 50–60 minutes.

Elle warns that salt should be used sparingly because of the saltiness of the chicken cube.

COQUELETS AUX CÈPES
Chicken with cèpes

PREPARATION TIME: 5 minutes
COOKING TIME: 30 minutes
FOR SIX

2 young cockerels, each
   weighing about 750 g (1½ lb)
500 g (generous 1 lb) cèpes
1 tablespoon goose fat or lard
salt, pepper

wine vinegar
2 tablespoons olive oil
2 cloves of garlic
1 bunch parsley
100 ml (3½ fl oz) dry white wine

Heat the fat in a pan and seal the chickens to a golden-brown. Season, cover the pan and cook for 25 minutes over a moderate heat.

During this time, trim the fungi, wipe them in a mixture of vinegar and water, slice them and cook them gently in the oil. Towards the end of cooking, season and sprinkle with peeled and chopped garlic and chopped parsley.

Take the chickens from the pan and split each one in half. Put them onto a warmed serving dish. Deglaze the cooking pan with the white wine, let it boil for a few moments then pour it over the chickens. Serve surrounded by cèpes.

Elle says that if fresh cèpes are not available, use dried cèpes and reconstitute according to the packet instructions.

POULET AU BEAUFORT
Chicken with melted cheese

PREPARATION TIME: 15 minutes
COOKING TIME: 45 minutes
FOR SIX

1 chicken weighing 1½ kg (3 lb
   5 oz)
12 small onions
50 g (scant 2 oz) butter

200 ml (7 fl oz) dry white wine
salt, pepper
250 g (scant 9 oz) Beaufort or
   Gruyère cheese

Joint the chicken. Peel the small onions and lightly brown them in butter. Remove from the casserole and replace them with the pieces of chicken which should also be cooked to a light golden-brown on all sides. Put the onions back into the casserole, pour in half the white wine, season and cover the casserole. Cook for 40 minutes over a low heat, remove and arrange the pieces in an ovenproof dish.

Cut the cheese into thin strips, put them into a small saucepan and pour in the rest of the white wine. Season, and melt the cheese over a very low heat, stirring constantly with a wooden spoon. Pour the melted cheese over the chicken and put the whole dish under the grill for 5 minutes.

Elle states that the cheese must be melted just before the chicken is served. Done in advance, it becomes stiff and rubbery and quite unusable.

COQUELETS À LA CIBOULETTE
Chicken with chives

PREPARATION TIME: 20 minutes
COOKING TIME: 35 minutes
FOR SIX

2 young cockerels, each
    weighing about 750 g (1½ lb)
1 bunch of chives
50 g (scant 2 oz) butter (at room
    temperature)

salt, pepper
6 tablespoons thick crème
    fraîche

Split each chicken in half. Finely chop the chives and work them into the butter with salt and pepper. Spread this mixture onto the chicken halves. Put each piece of chicken on a large square of kitchen foil and seal it completely into an envelope. Cook in a hot oven (220°C/425°F/ Gas Mark 7) for 35 minutes.

Five minutes before the end of cooking, partly open the envelopes and put a tablespoon of crème fraîche into each. Complete the cooking with the envelopes still partly open so that the chicken halves get a little more colour.

Serve in their envelopes with a selection of fresh vegetables.

Elle warns that the envelopes should be opened carefully so that the juices do not escape.

POULET AU CITRON
Chicken with lemon

PREPARATION TIME: 10 minutes (plus 10 minutes the previous day)
COOKING TIME: 30 minutes
FOR SIX

1 large or 2 small chickens
6 tablespoons olive oil
2 lemons
1 teaspoon paprika

1 clove of garlic
1 onion
mixed herbs
salt, pepper

Joint the chicken(s). Prepare the marinade on the day before by mixing together the olive oil, the juice of 2 lemons, the paprika, the peeled and crushed garlic, the peeled and sliced onion, a tablespoon of mixed fresh herbs and seasoning. Put the pieces of chicken in the mixture and let them marinate in it overnight.

Drain the pieces of chicken and put each one on a large piece of greaseproof paper, or kitchen foil. Sprinkle a tablespoon of the marinade onto each, close up the envelope and cook for 30 minutes in a very hot oven (240°C/475°F/Gas Mark 9).

Serve with boiled rice and grilled tomatoes.

Elle notes that if two small chickens are used, 20 minutes will be a sufficient cooking time.

POULET AU BLÉ CONCASSÉ
Chicken with cracked wheat

PREPARATION TIME: 15 minutes
COOKING TIME: 55 minutes
FOR SIX

2 small chickens	olive oil
750 g (generous 1½ lb) cracked wheat	1 pinch of powdered saffron
	salt, pepper
3 onions	12 small potatoes
4 cloves of garlic	6 hard-boiled eggs

Put the cracked wheat in a bowl, pour on 1½ litres (generous 2½ pints) of hot water, cover the bowl and leave the wheat to swell.

Peel and separately chop both the onions and the garlic. Heat 4 tablespoons of oil in a casserole and seal the chickens to a light golden-brown on all sides. Remove from the casserole and replace them by the chopped onions and half of the garlic. Put the chickens back, sprinkle on the saffron and the remainder of the chopped garlic. Season. Cover the pot and cook over a moderate heat for 45 minutes.

Fifteen minutes before the end of the cooking, put in the peeled potatoes and 5 minutes before the end, add the cracked wheat and the halved boiled eggs.

Serve the chicken on a bed of cracked wheat, surrounded by potatoes and hard-boiled eggs.

Elle advises that the whole of the hot water should not be poured onto the cracked wheat at one time. Start with 1 litre (1¾ pints), keep an eye on the process of absorption and pour in small quantities as required.

FRICASSÉE DE POULET À L'AIL
Chicken with garlic

PREPARATION TIME: 20 minutes
COOKING TIME: 30 minutes
FOR SIX

2 corn-fed chickens each weighing 1 kg (scant 2¼ lb)	bouquet garni
	150 g (5 oz) streaky bacon
salt, pepper	8 slices of bread, fried in butter
200 g (7 oz) butter	200 ml (7 fl oz) dry white wine
15 cloves of garlic (unpeeled)	chopped parsley

Divide each chicken into 4 pieces, putting the livers to one side. Season.

Melt 75 g (generous 2½ oz) butter in a pan and cook the chicken pieces to a light golden-brown. Do not heat the butter so much that it blackens. Reduce the heat and add the cloves of garlic and the bouquet garni: cover the pan and cook over a low heat for 20–25 minutes.

In the meantime, slice the bacon into strips across the grain, cut up the chicken livers and cook them in a little butter. When cooked, pass them together through a blender and put the mixture to one side.

Arrange the pieces of chicken on a warmed serving dish. Remove the bouquet garni and push the garlic cloves through a fine sieve. Add this garlic purée to the bacon–liver mixture and spread it on the newly fried pieces of bread. Arrange them around the chicken pieces.

Deglaze the casserole with the white wine, let it boil for a few moments and pour the sauce over the chicken. Serve sprinkled with chopped parsley.

From the 'Hôtel de France' in Nantua: the chef recommends a red wine with this dish, either a claret from St. Emilion or a Beaujolais.

POULET VALLÉE D'AUGE
Chicken with Calvados

PREPARATION TIME: 20 minutes
COOKING TIME: 40 minutes
FOR SIX

2 corn-fed chickens, each
   weighing 1 kg (scant 2¼ lb)
130 g (generous 4½ oz) butter
100 ml (3½ fl oz) Calvados
5 shallots
2 carrots

2 leeks (white parts)
2 glasses (10 fl oz) dry cider
salt, pepper
2 egg yolks
250 g (scant 9 oz) crème fraîche

Divide each chicken into 4 pieces. Melt 50 g (scant 2 oz) butter in a casserole and cook the chicken pieces to a light golden-brown on all sides. Remove the chicken temporarily while the cooking fats are poured off, replace the pieces in the casserole and flame them in Calvados.

Peel and slice the shallots, trim the other vegetables and cut them into thin strips. Cook them lightly in 30 g (1 oz) butter, then add them to the casserole. Pour in the cider, season, cover the casserole and simmer for about 35 minutes. Arrange the chicken pieces on their serving dish and keep in a warm place.

Slightly reduce the juices in the casserole over a brisk heat. Beat the egg yolks into the crème fraîche, remove the casserole from the heat and whisk the egg/cream mixture into the juices to make a sauce. Return to the heat to warm it through, withdraw it once more and finally whisk in remaining butter, knob by knob. Check the seasoning and pour the sauce over the chicken just before serving.

<u>Elle suggests</u> that either apple slices cooked in butter or a selection of vegetables will go well with this dish which should be accompanied either by a good still cider, or a white wine from the Loire.

POULET AU PAPRIKA
Chicken with paprika

PREPARATION TIME: 20 minutes
COOKING TIME: 40 minutes
FOR SIX

2 young chickens
salt
2 tablespoons of lard
2 onions
1 clove of garlic

1½ tablespoons paprika
250 ml (scant 9 fl oz) chicken
   stock
20 g (¾ oz) flour
300 g (10½ oz) crème fraîche

Joint the chickens and sprinkle the pieces with plenty of salt. Melt the lard in a casserole and, when it is hot, seal the chicken pieces all over. Remove the chicken, lower the heat and cook the peeled and chopped onions and garlic until transparent. Put the cooked onion and garlic to one side and pour off the cooking fats. Away from the heat put the paprika into the casserole and, using the back of a fork, mix it vigorously with the scrapings of the dish.

Put the chicken, onion and garlic back into the casserole, moisten it with the chicken stock, cover the dish and bring slowly to the boil. Simmer for 25–30 minutes.

Arrange the chicken on a warmed serving dish. Skim the fat from the cooking juices and bring them to a slow boil. Mix the flour into a paste with a teaspoon of water and stir it into the sauce to thicken it. Stir in the crème fraîche and simmer the sauce for 6–8 minutes. Just before serving, pour the sauce through a sieve onto the chicken.

POUSSINS AU CORBIÈRES
Baby chicken in white wine

PREPARATION TIME: 25 minutes
COOKING TIME: 1 hour 15 minutes (part the day before)
FOR SIX

6 poussins, each weighing about 300 g (10½ oz)	salt, pepper
	4 gherkins
300 g (10½ oz) carrots	
150 g (5 oz) baby turnips	For the stock:
300 g (10½ oz) leeks	2 carrots
150 g (5 oz) button mushrooms	1 leek, 1 onion
500 g (generous 1 lb) crème fraîche	1 handful fresh basil
	1 bottle white wine
1 tablespoon curry powder	salt, pepper

Prepare the stock the day before, cooking the ingredients listed in 2 litres (3½ pints) water for 1 hour.

To make the dish, begin by trimming and washing the vegetables. Cut up carrots and baby turnips into dice, the leeks into round slices and the mushrooms into thin slices.

Arrange the trussed birds in a large casserole and pour in the cold stock through a sieve. Slowly bring the casserole to a simmer. Continue cooking at this temperature for about 12 minutes, then remove the dish from the heat.

Put all the vegetables into a pan and stir in the crème fraîche and the curry powder. Season, bring to the boil, then allow to cook over a low heat for 5 minutes (or longer if the vegetables are not extremely young). At this point add the gherkins, divided in half lengthways.

Remove the birds from the hot stock, split them in half and arrange them on a warmed serving dish. Cover with the vegetable sauce.

From 'La Peupleraie' restaurant in Carcassonne in the south-west of France: the chef recommends a local white Corbières, both in the cooking and to drink with the dish.

COQ AUX CHAMPIGNONS
Chicken and mushrooms

PREPARATION TIME: 15 minutes
COOKING TIME: 1 hour
FOR SIX

1 large chicken	1 bottle Loire rosé wine
2 onions	salt, pepper
2 tablespoons olive oil	500 g (generous 1 lb) button mushrooms
80 g (scant 3 oz) butter	
1 tablespoon flour	1 lemon

Joint the chicken, peel and chop and onions. Heat the oil in a pan and seal the chicken pieces to a light golden-brown all over. Remove from the pan and replace them by the chopped onion. Lower the heat and cook them gently until transparent.

Melt 50 g (scant 2 oz) butter in a large casserole, and arrange the chicken pieces in it. Add the onions, raise the heat, sprinkle the meat with flour and stir around. Pour in the rosé wine, season, cover the casserole and continue to cook over a moderate heat for 45 minutes.

Trim the mushrooms, wipe them in a mixture of lemon juice and water and cut them in halves or quarters according to size. Fifteen minutes before the end of cooking, add them to the casserole.

Serve with fresh pasta, preferably tagliatelle.

SAUTÉ DE POULET AU CONCOMBRE
Chicken with cucumber

PREPARATION TIME: 35 minutes
COOKING TIME: 25 minutes
FOR SIX

1 large chicken	40 g (scant 1½ oz) butter
2 cucumbers	2 cloves of garlic
350 g (scant 12½ oz) button	2 tablespoons soy sauce
mushrooms	1 chicken stock cube
1 lemon	1 teaspoon flour

Skin the chicken, take the flesh off the bones and cut it into small pieces. Trim the mushroom stalks, wipe the mushrooms in a mixture of water and lemon juice and cut them into halves or quarters, according to size. Leave any really small ones whole. Peel the cucumbers, divide them in half lengthways, scoop out the seeds and cut them into 5-cm (2-inch) lengths. Trim each piece into a rough oval shape.

Melt the butter in a casserole and cook the chicken pieces to a light golden-brown on all sides. Add the mushrooms and continue cooking until all the liquid given off has evaporated. Sprinkle on the peeled and crushed cloves of garlic, add the cucumber pieces, the soy sauce and 300 ml (10½ fl oz) of stock made by dissolving the chicken cube according to the instructions on the packet. Mix everything together, bring to the boil and simmer for 5 minutes.

Make the flour into a paste with a little water, stir it into the cooking juices and bring it momentarily to the boil. The sauce should be smooth.

Serve direct from the cooking pot, accompanied by boiled rice.

Elle says that those with time to spare may prefer to make their own stock from the chicken carcass, by cooking it for 2 hours over a low heat in 1 litre (1¾ pints) of water, together with a carrot, an onion and a leek.

COQ À LA BIÈRE
Chicken in beer

PREPARATION TIME: 25 minutes
COOKING TIME: 2 hours 20 minutes
FOR SIX TO EIGHT

1 large chicken weighing 3 kg	75 g (generous 2½ oz) flour
(6½ lb)	1 litre (1¾ pints) brown ale
250 g (8 oz) button mushrooms	salt, pepper
1 lemon	bouquet garni
200 g (7 oz) shallots	100 g (3½ oz) crème fraîche
100 ml (3½ fl oz) oil	50 ml (1¾ fl oz) gin

Joint the chicken. Trim the stalks of the mushrooms and wipe them all over with a mixture of water and the juice of half a lemon. Cut them in half and sprinkle with the remaining lemon juice. Peel and chop the shallots.

Heat the oil in a large casserole and seal each piece of chicken to a light golden-brown on all sides. Remove them and replace with the shallots and mushrooms; lower the heat and cook gently until the shallots are transparent.

Roll the chicken pieces in flour and put them back into the casserole. Stir. Put aside 200 ml (7 fl oz) of beer and pour the rest over the chicken. Season, add the bouquet garni, cover the casserole and cook over a moderate heat for 2 hours. Remove the chicken and mushrooms and keep warm. Pour the juices through a sieve into a saucepan and reduce over a brisk heat until the sauce coats the back of a spoon. Skim it and stir in the crème fraîche, the gin and the beer set aside. Bring it to the boil, skim again and let it cook for 10 minutes.

Arrange the chicken and mushrooms on a warmed serving dish and cover it with sauce.

Elle suggests that if you are fond of the flavour of juniper, put 3–4 crushed berries into the casserole when the beer is added.

POULET MARENGO
Chicken Marengo

PREPARATION TIME: 25 minutes
COOKING TIME: 1 hour
FOR SIX

1 chicken weighing 1½ kg
  (generous 3¼ lb)
24 green olives
4 tablespoons olive oil
6 small white onions
salt, pepper
1 tablespoon chopped parsley

For the sauce Marengo:
3 ripe tomatoes
1 clove of garlic
250 ml (scant 9 fl oz) dry white
  wine
200 g (7 oz) button mushrooms
1 tablespoon tomato purée
salt, pepper

Chicken Marengo is *not* a stew but is made in two parts which come together at the end.

Stone the olives and if they have been preserved in brine soak them in warm water to reduce their saltiness.

Joint the chicken, heat the oil in a pan and slowly cook the pieces of chicken completely, together with the peeled and sliced onions. Season and keep in a warm place.

To make the sauce, pour off excess fat from the pan and put it to one side. Return the pan to the heat and add the chopped tomatoes and the crushed garlic. Cook gently, scraping the bottom of the pan vigorously with the back of a fork. Add the white wine, the trimmed and sliced mushrooms and the tomato purée. Season, cover the pan and simmer the sauce until it reaches a creamy consistency. (Should it be too thin, bind it with a teaspoon of flour worked into a paste with 30 g (1 oz) butter.)

Add the chicken pieces and the olives and cover the pan to heat the dish through thoroughly, without allowing the sauce to boil. Serve from the pan, sprinkled with chopped parsley.

<u>Elle says</u> this classic dish is sometimes served with fried eggs on fried rounds of bread cooked in the fat left after cooking the chicken. This addition is entirely optional.

POT-AU-FEU DE VOLAILLE
Chicken and rabbit casserole

PREPARATION TIME: 40 minutes
COOKING TIME: 1½ hours
FOR SIX TO EIGHT

1 chicken weighing about 1¼ kg
  (scant 2¾ lb)
1 head of celery
600 g (1 lb 5 oz) carrots
4 leeks
6 courgettes
heart of 1 small cabbage
400 g (14 oz) French beans (or
  mange-tout peas)
2 onions stuck with cloves
bouquet garni

1 rabbit or rabbit pieces weighing
  about 900 g (2 lb)
6 turkey wings or pieces
salt, pepper

For the sauce:
1 tablespoon cornflour
200 g (7 oz) cream
3 egg yolks
½ lemon

Trim or peel and slice all the vegetables as appropriate and cook them in a large saucepan in plenty of boiling salted water, together with the onion stuck with cloves and the bouquet garni. When they are about three-quarters cooked, add the chicken, trussed as for roasting, the rabbit jointed into pieces and the turkey pieces. Check seasoning and continue to cook slowly so that the meat does not break up; in all, it will take about 1½ hours.

Strain and reserve 1 litre (1¾ pints) of the stock and reduce over a brisk heat to half its volume. Make a paste with the cornflour and a little water and stir this into the reduced sauce, boil it once or twice, then remove from the heat and stir in the cream and egg yolks, beaten together. The sauce should be smooth and velvety and should be cooked further if too thin, but without boiling.

Strain the vegetables, carve the chicken and arrange meat and vegetables together on a warmed serving dish. Serve the sauce separately, at the last moment stirring in the lemon juice.

GRATIN DE POULET
Chicken with apple

PREPARATION TIME: 20 minutes
COOKING TIME: 15 minutes
FOR SIX

1 cold roasted or boiled chicken
1 onion
100 g (3½ oz) butter
1 tablespoon flour
2 glasses (10 fl oz) dry cider

100 ml (3½ fl oz) chicken stock
salt, pepper
6–8 firm eating apples
150 g (5 oz) crème fraîche

Take all the meat from the carcass, removing skin and gristle, and cut the meat into small pieces. Peel and finely chop the onion and cook it gently in 40 g (scant 1½ oz) butter until it is transparent. Add the pieces of chicken, stir and cook for a few moments longer. Sprinkle the flour into the pan and stir once more. Pour in the cider and the chicken stock, season, and continue cooking for 5 more minutes over a low heat.

Peel and core the apples and cut them into slices. Fry them in the rest of the butter until golden-brown.

Stir the crème fraîche into the chicken and cook with the pan uncovered at a slow boil for 10 minutes. Check the seasoning.

Butter a gratin dish and cover the bottom with a layer of half of the apples. Next spread out the chicken in its sauce in a single layer and finish with a second layer of apples. Put the dish quickly under a hot grill to brown it. Serve at once.

Elle says that stock made from a chicken cube may be substituted if fresh chicken stock is not available, but less salt should be used in the seasoning.

GRATIN AUX CHAMPIGNONS
Gratin of chicken

PREPARATION TIME: 10 minutes
COOKING TIME: 25 minutes
FOR SIX

1 cooked chicken (cold)
750 g (generous 1½ lb) button
    mushrooms
1 lemon
150 g (5 oz) butter
40 g (scant 1½ oz) flour

300 ml (10½ fl oz) milk
salt, pepper
150 g (5 oz) grated Gruyère
    cheese
3 slices cooked ham

Trim the mushrooms, wipe them in a mixture of lemon juice and water, slice them and cook gently for 5 minutes in 50 g (scant 2 oz) of butter. Put to one side.

Prepare a béchamel sauce: melt 50 g (scant 2 oz) of butter in a pan, add all the flour and cook it for 2–3 minutes. Remove the pan from the heat and slowly whisk in the cold milk. Bring it gently to the boil, keep it there for 5 minutes, season.

Take all the meat off the cold chicken and cut it into small pieces. When the béchamel is ready, add the chicken, the strained mushrooms and half the grated cheese to it. Stir. Cut the ham into dice and line the bottom of a gratin dish with it. Pour the chicken and sauce mixture into the dish, sprinkle the rest of the grated cheese over the surface and dot it with the rest of the butter in knobs. Put to brown in a very hot oven (230°C/450°F/Gas Mark 8) for 15 minutes.

Elle advises you to be sure that all the mushroom liquid has evaporated before the mushrooms are added to the sauce.

PINTADES À L'ESTRAGON
Guinea-fowl with tarragon

PREPARATION TIME: 30 minutes
COOKING TIME: 50 minutes
FOR SIX

2 guinea-fowl
1 large bunch of tarragon
100 g (3½ oz) butter
salt, pepper
2 strips of larding fat

600 ml (generous 1 pint) Chablis
1 chicken stock cube
1 tablespoon of cornflour
150 g (5 oz) crème fraîche

Stuff the guinea-fowl with a few leaves of tarragon and the butter into which salt and pepper has been worked. Tie larding fat onto the breasts and quickly brown the fowl on all sides in a hot open casserole. Remove the fowl temporarily, pour off the fats in the casserole and deglaze it with the white wine, scraping the bottom of the pan vigorously with the back of a fork. Crumble the chicken cube into the liquid, return the guinea-fowl to the casserole and add about half the remaining tarragon. Cover the dish and cook over a moderate heat for 50 minutes. Take out the fowl, remove the larding fat, and put them in a warm place.

Reduce the liquids left in the casserole by half and bind the sauce with the cornflour, made into a paste with a little water. Stir in the crème fraîche and let the sauce bubble once or twice. Check the seasoning. Remove the tarragon and replace it by the rest of the tarragon, finely chopped.

Carve the guinea-fowl into large pieces and arrange them on a warm serving dish. Serve the sauce separately together with a dish of buttered wild rice.

Elle advises that the cornflour paste should be incorporated into the sauce a little at a time, and over a low heat. Add only enough to give a smooth and velvety consistency.

PINTADES AUX FIGUES
Guinea-fowl with figs

PREPARATION TIME: 20 minutes
COOKING TIME: 1 hour
FOR SIX

2 good guinea-fowl
1 kg (scant 2¼ lb) ripe figs
60 g (2 oz) butter

salt, pepper
250 ml (scant 9 fl oz) dry white
wine

Truss the guinea-fowl. Wash the figs, divide them into two equal parts and cut all the figs in one part in half.

Heat the butter in a large casserole (or two smaller casseroles if preferred) and seal the fowl to a golden-brown on all sides. Pour off the cooking butter and return the guinea-fowl to the casserole, together with the fig-halves arranged around them. Season, pour in the wine and the same amount of water, cover the dish and cook over a moderate heat for 45 minutes. Add the whole figs at this point and continue the cooking for a further 15 minutes.

Take out the guinea-fowl and the whole figs and keep them in a warm place. Purée the remaining contents of the casserole in a blender, put into a saucepan and warm through over a low heat.

Carve the guinea-fowl into large pieces and arrange them on a warmed serving dish. Surround them with whole figs and cover them with fig sauce. Serve at once with boiled rice.

Elle says that to those who like sweet and sour flavours, the taste of cooked figs will come as a revelation.

DINDONNEAU AU CHAMPAGNE
Turkey in Champagne

PREPARATION TIME: 30 minutes (excluding time taken to peel chestnuts)
COOKING TIME: 2 hours
FOR SIX

1 young turkey weighing about
 2½ kg (5½ lb)
1 bottle champagne
1 black truffle
1½ kg (generous 3¼ lb)
 chestnuts
250 g (scant 9 oz) forcemeat
1 egg
1 small glass of brandy

250 g (scant 9 oz) onions
2 carrots
1 stick of celery
175 g (generous 6 oz) butter
salt, pepper
250 g (scant 9 oz) crème fraîche
300 g (10½ oz) cranberry sauce
3 tablespoons redcurrant jelly

Cut 5 thin slices from the truffle and chop up the rest. Peel the chestnuts in the usual way and cook for 15 minutes in salted boiling water. Make a stuffing with the forcemeat, one-quarter of the chestnuts, the chopped truffle, the egg and the brandy. Insert the slices of truffle under the skin of the breast. Stuff the bird with the prepared stuffing and re-seal the opening.

Trim, peel and chop the vegetables into small dice. Melt 50 g (scant 2 oz) of butter in a large casserole and gently cook the vegetables. Put in the turkey and lightly brown it on all sides. Pour in the champagne, season, cover and cook over a moderate heat for 1¾ hours.

During this time, fry the remaining chestnuts in the rest of the butter, season, and put to one side.

When the bird is cooked, put it on its carving dish in a warm place. Pass the cooking liquids through a sieve, skim off the fat and reduce the remainder to a volume of 250 ml (scant 9 fl oz). Stir in the cream and bring to a slow boil for 5 minutes. Slice one or two pieces of truffle retrieved during the carving, and add to the sauce. Serve separately.

Carve the turkey and arrange the pieces on a serving dish with the stuffing in the centre and the whole chestnuts around them. Mix the cranberry sauce and the redcurrant jelly together and this too is served separately.

DINDONNEAU À LA LANDAISE
Escalopes of turkey

PREPARATION TIME: 20 minutes
COOKING TIME: 45 minutes
FOR SIX

1¼ kg (scant 2¾ lb) turkey
 escalopes
24 prunes
100 ml (3½ fl oz) Armagnac
750 g (generous 1½ lb) carrots
3 large onions
1 stick of celery

200 g (7 oz) sliced ham
150 g (5 oz) butter
2 tablespoons olive oil
1 tablespoon flour
½ bottle sweet white wine
bouquet garni
salt, pepper

Put the prunes into a dish, sprinkle them with Armagnac and let them soak, stirring from time to time.

Peel and slice the carrots and the onions into round slices and the celery into dice. Cut the ham into small pieces.

Melt the butter in a pan with the oil and when it is hot put in the vegetables and the ham and cook for 15 minutes. Roll the turkey escalopes in flour, put them into the pan and turn once or twice. Pour in the white wine, add the bouquet garni and season. Then add the prunes and the Armagnac in which they soaked. Stir, bring to the boil then simmer over a low heat for 20 minutes.

Remove the turkey and vegetables to a warm dish, and serve the strained cooking juices separately as a sauce.

Elle advises that if the cooking juices are too thin for a sauce, either reduce them over a brisk heat or thicken them by stirring in a paste made by working a little flour and butter together.

CANARDS SAUVAGES
Wild duck with green noodles

PREPARATION TIME: 25 minutes
COOKING TIME: 35–40 minutes
FOR SIX

3 mallard	*300 g (10½ oz) crème fraîche*
salt, pepper	*2 tablespoons brown meat glaze*
olive oil	*(optional)*
2 shallots	*120 g (scant 4½ oz) butter*
300 ml (10½ fl oz) wine vinegar	*450 g (1 lb) green tagliatelle*

Buy the duck dressed and trussed. Season the cavity of each bird, brush all over with oil, put them in a roasting tin and cook them in a very hot oven (230°C/450°F/Gas Mark 8) for 35 minutes. Baste from time to time.

Peel and finely chop the shallots and put them in a pan with the vinegar. Reduce over a moderate heat until all the liquid has evaporated. Stir in the crème fraîche and the meat glaze, bring to the boil and simmer for 10 minutes. Remove from the heat and, whisking constantly, incorporate the butter little by little. Check seasoning.

Carve the duck and arrange the pieces on a warmed serving dish. Surround with freshly-cooked green tagliatelle and serve the sauce separately.

From the 'Hôtellerie du Bas-Bréau' in Barbizon near Fontainebleau: the chef recommends that you drink a good red Burgundy with this dish.

CANARD FARCI AUX PRUNEAUX
Duck stuffed with prunes

PREPARATION TIME: 15 minutes
COOKING TIME: 2¼ hours
FOR SIX

1 large duck	*3 firm eating apples*
salt	*10 prunes*

Make sure that you get the neck and the giblets with the duck. Put them in a saucepan with 500 ml (17½ fl oz) of water and a pinch of salt, bring to the boil and simmer for 1 hour.

Peel and core the apples and cut them into small slices. Take the stones out of the prunes and mix apple and prunes together. Season with salt. Stuff the duck with this mixture then add the duck's liver, whole. Close up the opening.

Rub the skin of the duck with salt and put it in a baking pan containing 3 tablespoons of water. Cook in a moderate oven (180°C/ 350°F/Gas Mark 4) for 1 hour. Baste the duck from time to time with the giblet stock. Finish the cooking with 15 minutes under the grill to make the skin crisp and golden, but be careful not to let it burn. Serve with braised chopped red cabbage, and the remainder of the giblet stock as a sauce.

Elle notes that, in the original recipe, the purpose of the stuffing was to flavour the duck, and it was not eaten. However, it is a delicious stuffing and may be served as an accompaniment.

CANETON FARCI FLAMBÉ AU CALVADOS
Stuffed duckling with Calvados

PREPARATION TIME: 20 minutes
COOKING TIME: 40 minutes
FOR SIX

1 large duckling	2 eggs
100 ml (3½ fl oz) Calvados	7 firm eating apples
80 g (scant 3 oz) butter	salt, pepper
200 g (7 oz) chicken livers	300 ml (10½ fl oz) dry cider
150 g (5 oz) sausage-meat	

Melt 20 g (¾ oz) butter in a pan and, when it is hot, seal the chicken livers and cook until they are firm but pink inside. Remove and replace with the sausage-meat rolled into balls: cook for 5–6 minutes, shaking the pan frequently so that the sausage cooks evenly. Chop the livers and the sausage-meat and mix them thoroughly together with the two eggs and the finely-chopped flesh of one apple. Season, and work in 1 tablespoon of Calvados with a fork. Stuff the duck with the mixture and truss it as for roasting.

Heat a good knob of butter in a heavy casserole and seal the duck on all sides to a golden-brown. Pour off the cooking fats, pour the rest of the Calvados over the duck and flame it. Pour in the cider, cover the casserole and cook for about 35 minutes over a moderate heat.

Peel and core the apples and cut them in half across. Put them into an ovenproof dish, dot them with knobs of butter and cook in a very hot oven (240°C/475°F/Gas Mark 9) for 5–7 minutes.

Remove the cooked duck to a carving dish. Skim the fat from the cooking juices and whisk in the remaining butter, knob by knob. Carve the duck, arrange the pieces on a warmed serving dish and pour the sauce over them. Arrange the cooked apples and spoonfuls of stuffing around the meat and serve at once.

Elle says that the liver and sausage-meat must be pre-cooked as described, or the stuffing will be raw.

CANTETONS À LA VERDURE
Duckling with spinach

PREPARATION TIME: 30 minutes
COOKING TIME: 1 hour
FOR SIX

2 young ducklings	2 leeks
100 g (3½ oz) shallots	500 g (generous 1 lb) fresh
30 g (1 oz) butter	spinach
350 ml (scant 12½ fl oz) dry cider	salt, pepper
500 ml (17½ fl oz) chicken stock	1 jar tarragon mustard
1 lettuce	breadcrumbs

Peel and finely chop the shallots and cook them gently in a good knob of butter until transparent. Pour the cider into the pan, raise the heat and cook without the lid until the liquid has evaporated. Add the chicken stock and simmer, skimming frequently, until the volume is reduced by half. Keep in a warm place.

Trim and wash the vegetables in the usual way, and chop them very finely. Melt the rest of the butter and put the vegetables in to cook gently until again the liquids have evaporated. Season. Stir in the chicken stock and keep the mixture warm.

Season the trussed ducks and cook them in a very hot oven (230°C/450°F/Gas Mark 8) for 25 minutes. Retaining the skin, remove the breasts from the duck and put on a serving dish in a warm place. Cut off the thighs, spread them all over with tarragon mustard and roll them in breadcrumbs. Grill the thighs and put them onto the serving dish with the breasts. Surround with vegetable mixture and serve at once.

MAGRETS DE CANARD AU CORBIÈRES
Breast of duck in red wine

PREPARATION TIME: 5 minutes
COOKING TIME: 2 hours
FOR SIX

6 boned duck breasts	bouquet garni
1 bottle red wine	3 juniper berries
100 g (3½ oz) butter	2 cloves
2 carrots	salt, pepper
1 onion	nutmeg
1 clove of garlic	blood from the duck (if available)
1 tablespoon tomato purée	

Trim each duck breast so they are all about the same size and shape. Keep the trimmings.

Heat 50 g (2 oz) butter in a large pan and, when it bubbles, put in the duck trimmings, the sliced carrot, the peeled and chopped onion and garlic. Lower the heat and cook gently, stirring frequently. Stir in the tomato purée and pour in the wine: bring to the boil and add the bouquet garni, the juniper berries and the cloves. Cook for 1¾ hours.

Strain out the vegetables and spices from the liquid, pass them through a blender, return them to the liquid, stir and then press through a fine sieve. Reduce the sauce to a volume of 300 ml (generous ½ pint), season liberally, add grated nutmeg, and put on one side in a warm place.

In a heavy iron pan, cook the duck breasts skin side downwards, without using any additional fats. When the skins are golden, reduce the heat and continue cooking on both sides for 12–15 minutes. They should spend longer on the skin side.

Cut the duck breasts into crossways slices from below, without piercing the skin, arrange them on a serving dish and keep them warm.

Stir the blood (if available) into the sauce and bring it *very briefly* to the boil. Lower the heat and whisk in the rest of the butter, knob by knob. When the sauce is bound, pour it over the duck breasts and serve at once, with a dish of leeks.

MIGNONNETES DE CANARD
Breast of duck with orange

PREPARATION TIME: 20 minutes
COOKING TIME: 20 minutes
FOR SIX

6 boned duck breasts	wine vinegar
5 oranges	salt, pepper
100 ml (3½ fl oz) Grand-Marnier	100 g (3½ oz) butter
100 g (3½ oz) caster sugar	

Peel the oranges, and divide into skinned segments, being sure to catch the juices spilled. Put the orange segments, the orange juice and the Grand-Marnier together into a pan and gently warm them through. Keep warm over a very low heat.

Put the sugar into a small saucepan, just cover it with water and heat to a syrup, stirring constantly. When it boils, remove from the heat and stir in 3 tablespoons of wine vinegar. Put to one side.

Cook the duck breasts in a heavy iron pan, skin side downwards, without any added fats. When the skin is golden-brown, turn the breasts and brown the other side. Put them all in a roasting tin, season and continue the cooking for a further 8–10 minutes in a hot oven (220°C/425°F/Gas Mark 7).

Pour the fats from the iron pan and deglaze it with the liquid from the oranges and with the vinegar-syrup. Bring the sauce to the boil, reduce it by a quarter, remove from the heat and whisk in the butter, knob by knob.

Arrange the duck breasts on a warmed serving dish, cover them with the sauce and serve at once, surrounded by the orange slices and individual Yorkshire puddings.

From 'Le Gambetta' restaurant in Houilles near Paris: the chef says that a good claret should be drunk with this dish.

CAILLES EN COCOTTE
Casserole of quail

PREPARATION TIME: 25 minutes
COOKING TIME: 20 minutes
FOR SIX

9 quail	2 tablespoons olive oil
100 g (3½ oz) sultanas	30 g (1 oz) butter
100 ml (3½ fl oz) Armagnac	2 shallots
salt, pepper	200 ml (7 fl oz) dry white wine
9 thin slices streaky bacon	1 bunch of Muscat grapes

Remove the stalks from the sultanas, cover them with Armagnac and leave to soak for 20 minutes. Drain and divide them into nine equal parts: stuff each quail with one part, season and close up the opening. Wrap a rasher of bacon around each bird and tie it on with culinary thread.

Heat the oil and the butter in a casserole and seal the quail to a golden-brown on all sides. Peel and chop the shallots and add them to the dish together with the Armagnac from the raisins, the white wine and the peeled and de-pipped grapes. Cover the casserole and cook over a moderate heat for 15 minutes.

Arrange the quail on a warmed serving dish and serve surrounded by the Muscat grapes.

CAILLES EN FRICASSÉE
Quails in brandy

PREPARATION TIME: 20 minutes
COOKING TIME: 50 minutes
FOR SIX

6 quail	salt, pepper
200 g (7 oz) fat ham	nutmeg
40 g (scant 1½ oz) butter	1 sprig of thyme
6–8 small onions	3 slices white bread
100 ml (3½ fl oz) brandy	

Taste the ham and if it is salty, soak it in hot (not boiling) water for 10 minutes.

Melt the butter in a pan and put in the ham and the small onions. When the fat takes colour and the onions are a light golden-brown, remove them to one side.

Put the quail in the pan in their place. Continuing with a moderate heat, seal the birds on all sides: do not let the cooking butter blacken.

Return the ham and onion mixture to the pan. Add the brandy and warm it through. Cover the pan, remove it from the heat and leave to stand for 10 minutes.

Return the pan to a low heat once more, season with salt, pepper and a little nutmeg, and add the sprig of thyme. Let the birds just simmer over a very low heat for 40–45 minutes. Serve the birds on small pieces of bread fried in extra butter, and accompanied by the contents of the cooking pan.

Elle says that very slow cooking is essential for quail or they will dry out. For this reason, it would be wise to wrap the birds in larding fat which should be removed halfway through the cooking.

PIGEONS FARCIS AUX PISTACHES
Pigeons stuffed with pistachios

PREPARATION TIME: 40 minutes
COOKING TIME: 40 minutes
FOR SIX

3 pigeons each weighing about
   450 g (1 lb)
2 tablespoons oil
200 g (7 oz) button mushrooms
1 lemon
150 g (5 oz) cooked long grain
   rice

75 g (generous 2½ oz) shelled
   pistachios
salt, pepper
1 tin of vine leaves
6 strips of larding fat
100 ml (3½ fl oz) white wine
50 g (scant 2 oz) butter

When the pigeons are drawn, retain their livers; if not available, chicken livers may be substituted. Quickly cook the livers in the oil until they are firm and then coarsely chop them.

Trim the mushrooms of their stalk ends, wipe them in a mixture of lemon juice and water, chop them up and mix them with the liver, the cooked rice and the whole pistachios. Season, and stuff the pigeons with the mixture. Close up the opening, cover the breasts with vine leaves (two to each pigeon), then with two lengths of larding fat. Tie leaves and larding fat to the birds with culinary thread.

Put the pigeons in a hot oven (220°C/425°F/Gas Mark 7) and cook for 15 minutes. Lower to a moderate oven (180°C/350°F/Gas Mark 4) and cook for 20–25 minutes longer. Remove the pigeons to a warm place and deglaze the roasting tin with the white wine and 50 ml (1¾ fl oz) water. Boil, and reduce the sauce somewhat; remove from the heat and whisk in the butter, little by little, to obtain a smooth sauce.

Garnish the pigeons with French beans and sauté potatoes: the sauce should be served separately.

From the 'Hostellerie de la Caillère' in Candé-sur-Beuvron in the Loire valley: the chef recommends either a red Chinon from the middle Loire or a Brouilly from Beaujolais to go with this dish.

PIGEONS EN PIE
Pigeon pie

PREPARATION TIME: 45 minutes–1 hour
COOKING TIME: 35–40 minutes
FOR SIX

2 fat pigeons
60 g (2 oz) butter
200 g (7 oz) chicken livers
200 g (7 oz) streaky bacon
12–15 small onions
200 g (7 oz) button mushrooms
salt, pepper
3 leaves of sage
1 pinch of chopped thyme

100 ml (3½ fl oz) Madeira
2 tablespoons brandy
1 egg

For the pastry:
250 g (scant 9 oz) flour
125 g (4½ oz) butter
chilled water
1 pinch of salt

Make a pastry in the usual way, roll it into a ball and let it stand in a cool place for at least 30 minutes.

Melt the butter in a pan and seal the birds on all sides, but do not let the butter blacken. Remove, replace with the chicken livers and cook them until they are firm. Put these aside also. Cut the bacon across the grain into thin slices and put these in their turn into the same pan with the onions. Fry them until they just begin to colour: put aside. Trim and slice the mushrooms and cook them in the same butter until only a small part of their liquid has been given off.

Divide each pigeon into four pieces and arrange them in a pie dish. Chop up the chicken livers and add them, the mushrooms, the bacon and the onions to the dish. Season with very little salt, with pepper and with crumbled herbs. Pour on the Madeira and the brandy.

Roll the pastry out to a thickness of about 5 mm (bare ¼ inch) and cover the dish, including a firm bond by pressing between finger and thumb. Brush the surface with beaten egg and make an air escape hole in the centre of the crust. Cook in a fairly hot oven (200°C/400°F/Gas Mark 6) for 40 minutes. Halfway through the cooking time, brush with more egg. Serve the pie as soon as the crust is completely cooked.

LAPIN AUX OLIVES VERTES
Rabbit with green olives

PREPARATION TIME: 20 minutes
COOKING TIME: 1 hour
FOR SIX

2 saddles of rabbit	4 tablespoons tomato purée
200 g (7 oz) green olives	6 cloves of garlic
2 onions	bouquet garni
100 ml (3½ fl oz) olive oil	salt, pepper
400 ml (14 fl oz) white wine	2 sprigs of fresh basil

Plunge the olives into a saucepan of boiling water; return to the boil for a moment or two, drain and rinse under a cold tap. Drain them thoroughly and remove their stones.

Divide up the saddles of rabbit. To avoid small bone splinters, pull apart, rather than cut, the spine joints. Peel and slice the onions. Heat the oil in a heavy casserole and seal the pieces of meat to a light golden-brown. Remove the meat and replace it by the sliced onions; cook them gently until they become transparent. Remove and put to one side.

Pour off the fat and deglaze the casserole with the white wine. Return rabbit and onions to the casserole, add the tomato purée, half of the olives, the peeled cloves of garlic and the bouquet garni. Season, using salt sparingly, cover the casserole and simmer gently for 1 hour.

Fifteen minutes before the end of cooking time, add the remainder of the olives. Serve sprinkled with chopped basil.

Elle suggests that if the sauce becomes too thick, add a few tablespoons of hot water during the course of the cooking.

LAPIN À L'AÏOLI
Rabbit in garlic sauce

PREPARATION TIME: 20 minutes
COOKING TIME: 30 minutes
FOR SIX

	For the garlic sauce:
2 saddles of rabbit	5 cloves of garlic
2 tablespoons olive oil	1 egg yolk
salt, pepper	salt, pepper
1 small sprig of thyme	250 ml (scant 9 fl oz) olive oil

Divide up the saddles of rabbit as described in the previous recipe.

Cut as many squares of greaseproof paper or kitchen foil as there are pieces of meat. Brush each one with oil, put a piece of rabbit in the centre of each, season, using salt sparingly, and crumble on a little thyme. Close up the envelopes and cook in a very hot oven (240°C/475°F/Gas Mark 9) for 30 minutes.

During this time, peel and crush the garlic with a pestle and mortar. Mix in the beaten egg yolk, season. Prepare the garlic sauce by whisking in the oil, drop by drop, as if making a mayonnaise.

Present the rabbit on its opened paper, with the garlic sauce served separately, and a dish of small sauté potatoes.

LIÈVRE AUX PIGNONS
Hare with pine kernels

PREPARATION TIME: 20 minutes (12 hours in advance)
COOKING TIME: 2 hours
FOR SIX

1 hare weighing about 2 kg
  (scant 4½ lb)
1 bottle of red wine
2 onions
3 cloves of garlic
thyme, bay leaf
rosemary, sage
200 ml (7 fl oz) olive oil
2 tablespoons flour
salt, pepper

For the sauce:
2 tablespoons sugar
100 ml (3½ fl oz) sherry vinegar
50 g (scant 2 oz) grated chocolate
50 g (scant 2 oz) pine kernels

Divide the hare into pieces. Put them into a large dish with the wine, the sliced onions, the chopped garlic and the herbs of Provence. Cover the dish, put in a cool place and leave to marinate overnight.

The following day, remove and drain the pieces of hare, put them in a heavy casserole and seal them in olive oil over a brisk heat. When all the pieces have been browned, roll them in flour, return them to the casserole, and season. Pour in all the marinade, cover and simmer over a low flame for 2 hours.

During this time, prepare the sweet-and-sour sauce. Melt the sugar in the vinegar, stir in little by little the grated chocolate, then add the pine kernels.

When the hare is cooked, arrange the pieces on a serving dish and keep in a warm place. Strain the cooking juices through a sieve into the chocolate sauce, stir everything together thoroughly and pour over the hare just before serving.

Elle repeats that, in order to avoid sharp bone splinters getting into the meat, the backbone should not be cut. If the spinal joints have to be cut, however, carefully remove all splinters before marinating the meat.

LIÈVRE À LA BIÈRE
Hare in beer

PREPARATION TIME: 30 minutes (12 hours in advance)
COOKING TIME: 1½ hours
FOR SIX TO EIGHT

1 hare of 2½–3 kg (5½–6½ lb)
flour
quatre-épices (see p.16)
goose fat or lard
200 g (7 oz) sliced ham
150 g (5 oz) crème fraîche

For the marinade:
3 small bottles brown ale

200 ml (7 fl oz) wine vinegar
12 small onions
6 juniper berries
12 peppercorns
6 cloves
1 sprig of rosemary
1 teaspoon chopped thyme
2 bay leaves
salt

Divide the hare into pieces (as described in the preceding recipe) and put them into a dish. Put all the marinade ingredients into a saucepan and cook them together over a brisk heat for 25 minutes: pour the marinade directly over the hare. Allow to cool, cover the dish and leave in a cool place for 12 hours.

Drain and wipe the pieces of hare: keep the marinade. Spread a wooden board with a mixture of 3 tablespoons of flour and one teaspoon of quatre-épices and lightly roll each piece of meat in it.

Melt 4 tablespoons of goose fat or lard in a heavy casserole and over a brisk heat, seal each piece of hare. Strain off the liquid from the marinade and bring to the boil. Add to the casserole, stirring and scraping the bottom with the back of a fork. Cover and simmer over a very low heat for 1½ hours. Stir from time to time and be sure that the bottom of the casserole does not catch.

Fry the ham together with the onions from the marinade, without any cooking fat being added. Add them to the hare when it is cooked.

Just before serving the hare, check the seasoning and stir the crème fraîche into the sauce. If, before the cream is added, the sauce appears to be too thin, mix a level tablespoon of flour into the crème fraîche, add to the sauce and boil for 1 minute.

NOISETTES DE CHEVREUIL SAINT-HUBERT
Venison with apples

PREPARATION TIME: 20 minutes (the day before)
COOKING TIME: 1 hour 50 minutes
FOR SIX

1 boned saddle of venison
   weighing 1¼ kg (scant 2¾ lb)
3 firm eating apples
50 g (scant 2 oz) butter
salt, pepper
50 ml (1¾ fl oz) brandy
150 g (5 oz) crème fraîche
125 g (4½ oz) redcurrant jelly
1 lemon
125 g (4½ oz) cranberry sauce

For the marinade:
½ bottle Riesling wine
2 onions
2 carrots
3 sprigs thyme
1 bay leaf
10 juniper berries

game stock (see p.15) using
   ½ bottle Riesling wine

Ask your game-dealer to divide the saddle into 12 boneless steaks (see opposite). Peel the onions and carrots and both cut into rounds, then add to rest of marinade ingredients. Put in the venison steaks, turning them occasionally, and leave for up to 24 hours. Make the game stock as indicated. The marinating and the preparation of the stock can all be done the previous day.

On the day of cooking, remove the venison steaks from the marinade, drain and wipe them with kitchen paper. Cook them in butter over a brisk heat, on both sides: when done, they should still be pink in the middle. Season and arrange on a warmed serving dish.

Pour off the fat and deglaze the pan with the brandy and a ladle of stock. Reduce to half its volume, then stir in the crème fraîche and the redcurrant jelly. Check the seasoning and pour the sauce over the venison.

Core the apples, cut them in half and gently poach them in water seasoned with lemon juice. Fill the centres with cranberry sauce, and arrange on the serving dish with the venison steaks.

FILETS DE CHEVREUIL AUX POIRES
Venison steaks with pears

PREPARATION TIME: 30 minutes (the day before)
COOKING TIME: 1½ hours
FOR SIX

1 boned saddle of venison
   weighing 1¼ kg (scant 2¾ lb)
6 pears
flour
150 g (5 oz) butter
salt, pepper
1 small glass of brandy
100 ml (3½ fl oz) red wine
100 ml (3½ fl oz) double cream

For the marinade:
200 ml (7 fl oz) red Burgundy
6 juniper berries
thyme
bay leaf

game stock (see p.15) using ½
   bottle red Burgundy

Ask your game-dealer to bone the saddle, to cut and trim 12 steaks from it, and to give you the bones and the trimmings.

Put the steaks in a dish, and marinate them as described in the previous recipe. Next make a game stock, again in the same way as indicated. Both marinade and stock can be prepared the day before.

Wrap the pears in oiled greaseproof paper or kitchen foil and bake them in a very hot oven (240°C/475°F/Gas Mark 9) for 25 minutes.

Take the venison steaks out of the marinade, drain them and wipe with kitchen paper. Then roll them in flour. Heat 100 g (3½ oz) butter in a pan and cook the steaks on both sides, long enough to leave them still pink in the centre. Season and arrange them on a serving dish: keep in a warm place. Pour off the cooking fat from the pan and deglaze it with the brandy, the red wine, the strained marinade and 200 ml (7 fl oz) of strained stock.

Reduce the volume by half, lower the heat and stir the cream into the sauce, bring it momentarily to the boil and check the seasoning. Remove from the heat and whisk in the rest of the butter, knob by knob.

The cooked pears are presented with the venison steaks and the sauce served separately.

RAGOÛT PRINTANIER
Spring casserole

PREPARATION TIME: 20 minutes
COOKING TIME: 30 minutes
FOR SIX

1½ kg (generous 3¼ lb) young
  asparagus
2 kg (generous 4¼ lb) young
  peas (weight in pod)

150 g (5 oz) small onions
200 g (7 oz) ham in a single slice
50 g (scant 2 oz) butter
salt, pepper

Trim the asparagus, keeping only the green spears. Blanch them for 5 minutes in boiling salted water, remove and drain. Shell the peas and peel the onions. Cut the ham into large dice.

  Melt the butter in a heavy pan and add the onions and peas. Cook them in the butter for a few minutes, then moisten with 100 ml (3½ fl oz) water. Season (use very little salt), cover the pan and cook slowly over a low heat for 20 minutes. At this point, add the ham and asparagus and continue cooking for a further 10 minutes.

Elle advises that if this dish has to be prepared in advance, it must be re-heated very gently. The unused stalks of the asparagus should not be discarded, but used as the main ingredient of a delicious soup.

TOPINAMBOURS AU CERFEUIL
Jerusalem artichokes with chervil

PREPARATION TIME: 10 minutes
COOKING TIME: 25 minutes
FOR SIX

1 kg (2¼ lb) Jerusalem
  artichokes
2 tablespoons chopped chervil
1 lemon

1 large onion
30 g (1 oz) butter
200 g (7 oz) crème fraîche
salt, pepper

Peel the artichokes and rinse them in a mixture of water and lemon juice. Blanch them for 5 minutes in a large pan of boiling salted water. Remove and drain them.

  Peel and chop the onion and cook it in the butter over a gentle heat until transparent. Remove from the pan and replace it by the artichokes which should be cooked until golden brown. Return the onion to the pan, cover it and continue cooking for a further 15 minutes, then stir in the crème fraîche and the chopped chervil. Season, and cook uncovered for 5 more minutes.

  Serve as an accompaniment to grilled or pan-fried white meats.

Elle says that cooking time can be shortened if the artichokes are sliced after blanching. Test the progress of their cooking by inserting a sharp-pointed knife; it should penetrate easily.

AUBERGINES À LA BORDELAISE
Golden aubergines

PREPARATION TIME: 15 minutes (1 hour in advance)
COOKING TIME: 15 minutes
FOR SIX

1200 kg (scant 2¾ lb) aubergines	2 cloves of garlic
sea salt	sprig of parsley
350 ml (12½ fl oz) olive oil	75 g (generous 2½ oz) stale breadcrumbs
150 g (5 oz) shallots	salt, pepper

Trim the aubergines and cut them into round slices. Lay them out in a shallow dish, sprinkle them with a good handful of sea salt and leave them to sweat for an hour, turning them from time to time. Drain them and dry on kitchen paper.

Heat the oil in a pan and over a brisk heat brown the aubergines for about 2–3 minutes each side. Sprinkle on a mixture of chopped shallots, chopped garlic, chopped parsley and breadcrumbs. Season and continue cooking for 10 minutes.

Elle advises that it may be more practical to cook the aubergine slices in small batches in order to achieve a nice golden colour. In this case, bring them all together in the same pan before sprinkling on the breadcrumb and herb mixture.

JARDINIÈRE FANTAISIE
Carrot and cauliflower casserole

PREPARATION TIME: 25 minutes
COOKING TIME: 45 minutes
FOR SIX

500 g (generous 1 lb) carrots	3 cloves of garlic
500 g (generous 1 lb) cauliflower	3 sprigs savory
500 g (generous 1 lb) radishes	salt, pepper

Trim and wash the vegetables. Leave the radishes whole, cut the carrots into strips and break off the flower-heads of the cauliflower.

Put the carrots into a saucepan with three times their volume of salted water, add the chopped garlic, and the savory. Season and bring the pan, uncovered, to a slow boil. After 10 minutes, add the radishes and, following a further 10 minutes' cooking, the cauliflower. Continue to cook everything together for 20 minutes more, always over a low heat. The dish will be ready when all the water has evaporated.

Elle notes that this cooking method preserves the essential minerals in the vegetables.

CAROTTES PRINTANIÈRES
Spring carrots

PREPARATION TIME: 15 minutes
COOKING TIME: 1 hour
FOR SIX

2½ kg (5½ lb) large carrots
2 tablespoons lard
12 small onions
bouquet garni

4 small leaves of sage
2 sugar lumps
salt, pepper

Peel the carrots, cut them in half lengthways, then into smaller lengths. Trim them to look like small young carrots.

Melt the lard in a heavy iron casserole, then add the carrots. When lightly cooked, remove and replace with the onions which should be cooked until golden brown. Replace the carrots and add the bouquet garni, the sage leaves and the sugar lumps. Season, moisten with 1 glass (5 fl oz) water and cook covered over a low heat for 50–60 minutes.

Elle says that if goose fat is used in place of lard, this delicious dish will be even better. Take care when stirring during cooking not to break up the onions.

CAROTTES À LA GRECQUE
Coriander carrots

PREPARATION TIME: 10 minutes
COOKING TIME: 1 hour 30 minutes
FOR SIX

1 kg (2¼ lb) small carrots
400 ml (14 fl oz) olive oil
1 bottle white wine
48 peppercorns
72 coriander seeds

3 stalks of celery
2 sprigs of thyme
1 bay leaf
salt

Into a heavy iron casserole put oil, wine, peppercorns, coriander seeds, the trimmed, washed and sliced celery, the herbs and a good pinch of salt. Let it all simmer over a low heat for 1 hour.

Wash and trim the carrots, add them to the casserole, cover it and continue cooking for 30 minutes more. Allow to cool and serve chilled.

Elle says this dish should be made with young, small carrots left whole. If these cannot be found, cut and trim larger carrots to size.

ENDIVES AU PORTO
Chicory in port wine

PREPARATION TIME: 15 minutes
COOKING TIME: 1 hour
FOR SIX

1½ kg (generous 3¼ lb) chicory	salt, pepper
150 g (5 oz) butter	300 ml (½ pint) port wine
100 g (3½ oz) smoked bacon	

Remove any damaged outer leaves from the chicory, trim the bases and make a crossways slit with a sharp knife. Melt 100 g (3½ oz) butter in a heavy iron casserole and gently brown the chicory, cooking a small batch at a time. Keep warm while cooking the rest.

Plunge the bacon into boiling water for 2 minutes, then run it under a cold tap. Cut into strips across the grain and in a pan gently fry it in 10 g (a good knob) of butter.

When all the chicory is golden-brown, put the rest back into the casserole and add the bacon and any fat given off during the frying. Season with pepper and very little salt, and cook half-covered for about 30 minutes until most of the liquid from the chicory has evaporated.

Pour in the port and add the rest of the butter, divided into knobs. Cover the casserole and continue cooking for 30 minutes.

Serve hot as an accompaniment to white meat.

<u>Elle notes</u> that since the sweetness of the port will overcome the natural bitterness of chicory, it will not be necessary to use sugar in the cooking.

COURGETTES À LA TOMATE
Courgettes in tomato sauce

PREPARATION TIME: 15 minutes
COOKING TIME: 20 minutes
FOR SIX

1 kg (2¼ lb) courgettes	salt, pepper
2 large onions	cinnamon
150 ml (5 fl oz) olive oil	2 tablespoons tomato purée
2 cloves of garlic	2 tablespoons chopped parsley

Peel the onions and cut them into rings. Wipe and trim the courgettes and cut them into round slices.

Heat the oil in a heavy pan and gently cook the onions until transparent. Add the courgettes and the crushed garlic. Season and add a pinch of powdered cinnamon. Just cover the vegetables with hot water and stir in the tomato purée. Cook for 20 minutes over a low heat.

Sprinkle on the chopped parsley 5 minutes before the end of the cooking time. Serve either hot or cold.

<u>Elle suggests</u> that, when preparing the courgettes, alternate strips be removed from the peel with a potato peeler.

FENOUILS GLACÉS
Fennel with mayonnaise

PREPARATION TIME: 10 minutes
COOKING TIME: 20 minutes
FOR SIX

6–8 young bulbs of fennel
2 egg yolks
1 tablespoon mustard
500 ml (17½ fl oz) peanut oil
3 tablespoons milk

1 dessertspoon of tomato purée
a pinch of chilli paste
½ lemon
salt, pepper
chives, parsley

Trim the bases of the fennel and cut back stalks and leaves. Split each bulb in half and cook them in boiling salted water for 20 minutes. Drain thoroughly, allow to cool and set them out on a serving dish.

Make a mayonnaise in the usual way with the egg yolks, the mustard and the peanut oil. Extend it with the milk and mix in the tomato purée, the chilli paste and the juice of half a lemon. Season.

Pour this sauce over the fennel and sprinkle with chopped chives and parsley. Serve chilled.

Elle advises that the fennel should be tested with a sharp-pointed knife during cooking and each one removed as it is sufficiently cooked.

FENOUIL AU XÉRÈS
Fennel in sherry

PREPARATION TIME: 5 minutes
COOKING TIME: 30 minutes
FOR SIX

9 medium-sized bulbs of fennel
salt, pepper
40 g (scant 1½ oz) butter

50 ml (1¾ fl oz) sherry
100 g (3½ oz) crème fraîche

Trim and wash the fennel and cut them in half lengthways. Arrange them close together in a large pan, season, add the butter in knobs. Just cover with water and cook covered over a gentle heat for 30 minutes. Remove the fennel to a warmed serving dish and put to one side.

Raise the heat to reduce the cooking liquid, pour in the sherry and deglaze the pan by vigorously scraping with the back of a fork. Mix in the crème fraîche, let the sauce bubble up twice and then pour it over the fennel. Serve at once.

HARICOTS À LA TOMATE
French beans and tomato

PREPARATION TIME: 15 minutes
COOKING TIME: 50 minutes
FOR SIX

1¼ kg (2¾ lb) French beans
3 large tomatoes
2 onions

½ glass (2½ fl oz) olive oil
bunch of parsley
salt, pepper

Peel and chop the onions and cook them gently in oil until transparent. Add the French beans, washed and trimmed, and half a glass of water. Cover the pan and cook for 20 minutes.

Peel the tomatoes, remove the seeds and chop them up. Add them to the pan together with the chopped parsley and a small amount of water. Season and continue to cook covered for another 30 minutes.

Allow the dish to cool before refrigerating. Serve chilled.

PURÉE DE HARICOTS À L'AIL
Purée of beans and garlic

PREPARATION TIME: 5 minutes
COOKING TIME: 2½ hours
FOR SIX

300 g (10½ oz) dried haricot
 beans
3 medium cloves of garlic
bouquet garni
1 onion
4 cloves

salt, pepper
40 g (scant 1½ oz) ground
 walnuts
120 ml (generous 4 fl oz) olive oil
2 tablespoons sherry vinegar

Sort and wash the beans and put them in a pan with a large quantity of cold water. Bring very slowly to the boil over a period of 45 minutes. As soon as the water bubbles, drain off the water and cover the beans with more boiling water. Add the bouquet garni and the peeled onion stuck with the cloves. Continue cooking slowly for another 1¾ hours. Season with salt halfway through this time.

Drain the beans thoroughly, reserving about a glass (5 fl oz) of the cooking liquid. Put the beans through a blender, but watch the process carefully so as to retain a texture in the final purée. Mix in crushed garlic and ground walnuts, extending the purée with the olive oil and as much of the cooking liquid as is needed. Season and add sherry vinegar to taste.

Serve warm with any grilled or roasted meat.

Elle advises that the cooking time of the beans will vary according to the quality being used. Make sure the beans are well cooked.

POIREAUX EN GRATIN
Gratin of leeks

PREPARATION TIME: 15 minutes
COOKING TIME: 30 minutes
FOR SIX

2½ kg (5½ lb) leeks
60 g (2 oz) butter
50 g (scant 2 oz) flour
250 ml (9 fl oz) milk
250 ml (9 fl oz) double cream

salt, pepper
grated nutmeg
2 eggs
50 g (scant 2 oz) grated
    Emmenthal cheese

Trim the leeks to remove all except the white part. Wash them in several changes of water, tie them in bundles and cook them for 10 minutes in plenty of boiling salted water. Drain thoroughly and dry with kitchen paper. Cut them into short 2·5-cm (1-inch) lengths.

Make a roux with the melted butter and flour and cook it briefly. Mix in first the milk, then the cream, season with salt, pepper and nutmeg. Remove the sauce from the heat and incorporate the beaten eggs and the grated cheese.

Arrange the leeks in a buttered fireproof dish, pour over the sauce and brown in a very hot oven (230°C/450°F/Gas Mark 8) for 20 minutes.

Elle recommends that the green part of the leeks are not discarded but used as part of a vegetable soup.

SEGRESSE
Leeks and potatoes

PREPARATION TIME: 15 minutes
COOKING TIME: 1 hour
FOR SIX

1 kg (2¼ lb) leeks
1 kg (2¼ lb) potatoes

100 g (3½ oz) butter
salt, pepper

Wash the vegetables, peel the potatoes and trim the leeks to leave only the white part. Cut the potatoes into round slices and the leeks into small pieces.

Melt the butter in a heavy iron casserole: put in a layer of potatoes, then a layer of leek and continue alternately, ending with a layer of potatoes. Season between each layer.

Cover the casserole and simmer over a moderate heat for 1 hour. Serve hot, with a roast of beef.

CHAMPIGNONS AU RHUM
Mushrooms in rum

PREPARATION TIME: 10 minutes
COOKING TIME: 30 minutes
FOR SIX

500 g (generous 1 lb) button mushrooms	*2 limes*
3 tomatoes	*1 tablespoon green peppercorns*
3 tablespoons olive oil	*salt*
bouquet garni	*50 ml (1¾ fl oz) white rum*
	1 tablespoon tomato ketchup

Trim the stalks of the mushrooms and wipe them with a damp cloth. Cut the larger ones into halves or quarters. Peel the tomatoes, remove the seeds and chop them up.

Heat 2 tablespoons of oil in a small pan, put in the chopped tomatoes and the bouquet garni and cook uncovered for 5–6 minutes. Add the mushrooms, the juice of 1 lime, and the green peppercorns. Season with salt, cover the pan and cook over a moderate heat for about 20 minutes.

Remove the pan from the heat, and the lid from the pan. Thoroughly mix in the rum, the juice of the second lime, the tomato ketchup and the remaining tablespoon of olive oil. Allow to cool and refrigerate. Serve chilled.

GIROLLES À LA CIBOULETTE
Girolles and chives

PREPARATION TIME: 15 minutes
COOKING TIME: 10 minutes
FOR SIX

750 g (generous 1½ lb) girolles	*salt, pepper*
wine vinegar	*30 ml (1 fl oz) walnut oil*
50 g (scant 2 oz) chives	*30 g (1 oz) crème fraîche*
3 limes	

Trim the stalks of the fungi (note: since fresh girolles may be hard to find, dried fungi, soaked in water for 1 hour may be substituted) and wash them in a mixture of water and wine vinegar. Clean and chop the chives and squeeze the juice from the limes.

Drain the fungi and put them in a pan with the chopped chives and the juice and the pulp of the limes. Season, cover the pan and cook over a moderate heat for 10 minutes.

Beat the walnut oil and the crème fraîche together into a sauce and serve it with the hot fungi.

COMPÔTE D'OIGNONS
Onion compôte

PREPARATION TIME: 20 minutes
COOKING TIME: 1¼ hours
FOR SIX

1½ kg (generous 3¼ lb) onions
150 g (5 oz) butter
100 g (3½ oz) raisins

150 ml (5 fl oz) white wine
salt, pepper

Peel and slice the onions. Melt the butter in a heavy pan: when it begins to foam, add the onions, the raisins and the white wine. Season, cover the pan and cook over a very low heat for 1¼ hours.

Serve very hot as an accompaniment to a roast duck, breast of duck or loin of pork.

Elle says that the progress of cooking must be carefully watched to prevent the onions taking on any colour.

MARRONS AUX OIGNONS
Chestnuts with onions

PREPARATION TIME: 20 minutes
COOKING TIME: 45 minutes
FOR SIX

1½ kg (generous 3¼ lb)
  chestnuts
3 good onions
75 g (generous 2½ oz) butter

250 ml (9 fl oz) dry white wine
1 chicken stock cube
salt, pepper

Make a slit in the rounded face of each chestnut, taking care not to pierce the flesh. Arrange them in a shallow pan in 1 cm (½ inch) of water and put the pan for 10 minutes under the grill turned up to its maximum. At the end of this time, they should be easy to peel but if not leave them under the grill longer, covered with a damp cloth to prevent the chestnuts burning.

Peel and slice the onions. Melt the butter in a heavy pan and gently cook the onions until transparent. Add the peeled chestnuts, the white wine and 250 ml (9 fl oz) of stock made from the stock cube. Season, cover the pan and cook for about 45 minutes.

Serve this Limousin dish as an accompaniment to roast meat or poultry.

PANCAKES AUX POMMES DE TERRE
Potato pancakes

PREPARATION TIME: 20 minutes
COOKING TIME: 6 minutes per pancake
FOR SIX

350 g (scant 12½ oz) grated raw
  potatoes
2 eggs, separated
1 teaspoon salt
500 ml (17½ fl oz) milk

200 g (7 oz) flour
1 tablespoon melted butter
oil
butter
chopped mixed herbs

In a bowl, beat together the egg yolks, the salt and the milk. Slowly sift in the flour, beating continuously to prevent it getting lumpy. Then mix in the melted butter. Press the grated potatoes in a cloth to remove as much moisture as possible, then stir them into the batter.

Whip the whites of the eggs until they are stiff and, with a spatula, fold them carefully into the batter.

Heat a little oil and butter together on a griddle and pour on sufficient batter to make a pancake. Cook for 3 minutes each side and repeat until sufficient have been made, or the batter used up. As each pancake is made, keep it in a warm place.

Serve, sprinkled with chopped mixed herbs, as an accompaniment to roast meat.

Elle advises that a floury variety of potato should be used. Cook the pancakes on two griddles if possible.

PAILLASSON DE POMMES
Potato cake

PREPARATION TIME: 15 minutes
COOKING TIME: 30 minutes
FOR SIX

5 large potatoes
3 leeks
30 g (1 oz) butter

2 tablespoons goose fat
salt, pepper

Peel and wash the potatoes, cut them into matchsticks and press out the moisture with a dry cloth.

Wash and trim the leeks, retaining only the white parts. Slice them and cook them very gently in the butter. Put to one side.

Heat the goose fat in a large frying pan and put in half of the potato. Season, cover with a layer of the cooked leeks and finish with the remainder of the potato. Season again, reduce the heat and cook for 10–15 minutes until the cake is evenly browned. Turn it over and cook the other side for the same length of time.

POMMES DE TERRE FORESTIÈRE
Potatoes with mushroom and bacon

PREPARATION TIME: 20 minutes
COOKING TIME: 1 hour
FOR SIX

1 kg (2¼ lb) potatoes
500 g (generous 1 lb) button
 mushrooms
300 g (10½ oz) smoked bacon

100 ml (3½ fl oz) oil
100 g (3½ oz) butter
salt, pepper

Cut the bacon into thick strips across the grain. Blanch them for 5 minutes in boiling water, let them cool in their cooking water, then drain them and dry them with kitchen paper. Peel the potatoes and cut them into dice: trim the stalks of the mushrooms and quarter them.

In a thick-bottomed pan, heat together the oil and half the butter. Add the potato and the bacon, season with pepper but with very little salt and cook over a very low heat to a light golden brown. This should take about an hour.

Heat the rest of the butter in a second pan, add the mushrooms and cook them gently for about 10 minutes until they have given up all their liquid. Season lightly, drain and put to one side.

Ten minutes before the end of cooking time for the potatoes, put the mushrooms in with them, mix them carefully together and check the seasoning.

Serve very hot, either as an accompaniment to grilled or roast meat or poultry, or by itself with a green salad.

Elle advises that if the potatoes are well washed and dried after being cut into dice, they will remain separate during the cooking.

FARÇON SAVOYARD
Savoy potato cake

PREPARATION TIME: 30 minutes (3 hours in advance)
COOKING TIME: 45 minutes
FOR SIX

1½ kg (generous 3¼ lb)
 potatoes
150 g (5 oz) raisins
750 ml (generous 1¼ pints) milk
4 eggs

3 tablespoons flour
75 g (generous 2½ oz) butter
salt, pepper
nutmeg

Soak the raisins in milk for 3 hours to allow them to swell.

Peel, wash and drain the potatoes, grate them coarsely and press out as much water as possible with dry cloths. Put them into a bowl and mix in the beaten eggs. Incorporate the flour by sieving it onto the potatoes while stirring constantly.

Add the raisins, the milk and the butter cut into knobs and season with salt, pepper and nutmeg. Mix everything well together.

Butter an ovenproof earthenware dish and fill it with the potato mixture. Cook in a very hot oven (240°C/475°F/Gas Mark 9) for 45 minutes.

FRICASSÉE DE RADIS ROSES
Glazed radishes

PREPARATION TIME: 5 minutes
COOKING TIME: 25 minutes
FOR SIX

4 bunches of radishes
125 g (4½ oz) butter
salt, pepper

1 tablespoon wine vinegar
2 tablespoons caster sugar

Trim the radishes top and bottom and wash them in running water. Drain and dry them in a cloth.

Melt the butter in a pan and, as it begins to foam, put in the radishes. Lower the heat, season and continue cooking for 15 minutes. Add the wine vinegar, sprinkle with the sugar and continue cooking for 8–10 minutes more, stirring constantly. When ready, the radishes should be evenly covered with a glaze.

Elle says this vegetable goes well with all roast meat and particularly with pork.

SALADE AU PIMENT DOUX
Cold ratatouille

PREPARATION TIME: 20 minutes
COOKING TIME: 40 minutes
FOR SIX

4 green peppers
2 aubergines
3 medium-sized courgettes
4 tomatoes
1 fresh green chilli

150 ml (5 fl oz) peanut oil
2 cloves garlic
1 teaspoon sweet chilli powder
salt

Wipe and trim the aubergines and courgettes and, without peeling them, cut them into dice. Peel the tomatoes, remove the seeds and chop them up. Put all these vegetables in a casserole with the chilli, the oil, the crushed garlic and the sweet chilli powder. Season with salt and add water until the contents of the casserole are covered. Cook uncovered over a moderate heat for about 15 minutes, stirring from time to time.

Peel the green peppers by first grilling them until the skin blisters. Wrap them in damp paper and the skin should then be easily peeled off. Remove stalks, membranes and seeds and cut the flesh into dice. Add the peppers to the casserole and continue cooking for the allotted time until all the liquid has evaporated. Serve cold.

Elle advises that this delicious vegetable dish will keep for three days in a refrigerator.

RATATOUILLE À L'ÉTOUFFÉE
Slow-cooked ratatouille

PREPARATION TIME: 15 minutes
COOKING TIME: 1½ hours
FOR SIX

200 g (7 oz) green peppers
500 g (generous 1 lb) aubergines
1 kg (2¼ lb) tomatoes
1 kg (2¼ lb) courgettes
25 g (scant 1 oz) garlic
salt, pepper
thyme

Wipe and drain all the vegetables. Remove stalks, membranes and seeds from the peppers and cut the flesh into strips. Cut the aubergines into dice. Peel the tomatoes, remove the seeds and chop flesh up. Peel alternate strips lengthways from the courgettes, then cut them into round slices about 2 cm (¾ inch) thick. Finely chop the garlic.

Put all the vegetables into a heavy iron casserole, season generously and sprinkle with crumbled thyme. Cover the pan and cook over a low heat for 1½ hours. The vegetables will cook in their own juices without any additional fats; in this way, all the flavours will blend together slowly. If too much liquid is given off, complete the cooking with the lid of the casserole removed.

Serve either hot as an accompanying vegetable or as a cold hors d'oeuvre.

(CONTINUED)

10 minutes, stirring frequently. Season with salt, pepper and nutmeg, stir in the rest of the tomato–pepper mixture and pour into the gratin dish. Sprinkle the surface with grated cheese and put to brown for 20 minutes in a very hot oven (230°C/450°F/Gas Mark 8).

Elle advises that the béchamel sauce should be made reasonably thick as liquid from the vegetables is likely to thin it in the oven.

GRATIN PROVENÇAL
Mediterranean gratin

PREPARATION TIME: 30 minutes
COOKING TIME: 30 minutes
FOR SIX

1½ kg (generous 3¼ lb) courgettes
1 kg (2¼ lb) aubergines
flour
oil
4 onions
2 green peppers
1 kg (2¼ lb) tomatoes
50 g (scant 2 oz) butter
30 g (1 oz) grated Emmenthal cheese

For the béchamel sauce:
50 g (scant 2 oz) butter
30 g (1 oz) flour
330 ml (11½ fl oz) milk
250 g (scant 9 oz) crème fraîche
salt, pepper
nutmeg

Trim the courgettes and the aubergines, cut them into large dice and roll them in flour, shaking them in a sieve to remove any excess. Plunge them into a saucepan of very hot oil for 5 minutes, remove with a perforated spoon and put to one side.

Peel and slice the onions. Remove stalks, membranes and seeds from the peppers and cut the flesh into strips. Peel the tomatoes and remove their seeds.

Melt 40 g (scant 1½ oz) butter in a pan and gently cook the onions until transparent. Add next the strips of pepper then the tomatoes and cook everything together for 10 minutes.

Butter a gratin dish and put in the courgettes and aubergines. Cover with a layer of one-half of the tomato and pepper mixture.

Proceed to the preparation of the béchamel sauce. Melt the butter in a saucepan and whisk in the flour. Cook for 2–3 minutes, still continuing to whisk. Remove the pan from the heat and, still whisking, slowly add the cold milk. Return to the heat and bring the sauce to the boil gently, then add the crème fraîche and continue at a slow boil for
(CONTINUED OPPOSITE)

RIZ AUX COURGETTES
Courgettes and rice

PREPARATION TIME: 5 minutes
COOKING TIME: 25 minutes
FOR SIX

4 courgettes
400 g (14 oz) long grain rice
salt, pepper
nutmeg

75 g (generous 2½ oz) butter
75 g (generous 2½ oz) grated
  Emmenthal cheese

Measure the volume of the rice, then wash it under running water. Drain. Put it into a pan with twice its volume of water and bring slowly to the boil.

During this time, wipe and trim the courgettes and cut them into round slices. Add them to the cooking rice, reduce the heat, season with salt, pepper and nutmeg and cover the pan. Continue cooking slowly for 20 minutes.

Remove from the heat, carefully fold in the butter and the grated cheese and turn out on to a warmed serving dish.

Elle says that, served with a chilled rosé wine, this dish goes admirably with grilled lamb or pork chops, or with fried eggs.

RIZ BRUN AUX ANCHOIS
Anchovy rice

PREPARATION TIME: 5 minutes
COOKING TIME: 20 minutes
FOR SIX

400 g (14 oz) brown rice
200 g (7 oz) crème fraîche
2 tablespoons anchovy paste
1 tablespoon brandy
grated peel of ½ lemon

pinch of grated nutmeg
mixed herbs (chervil, parsley
  basil)
salt, pepper

Wash the rice thoroughly under running water, drain. Cook it in plenty of boiling salted water for 18–20 minutes.

During this time, heat up the crème fraîche in a double-boiler. Stir in the anchovy paste, the brandy, the lemon peel, the nutmeg and the chopped herbs. Season.

When the rice is cooked, drain and mix the sauce into it. Serve hot.

Elle says this rice goes splendidly with grilled fish.

SALSIFIS AU LARD
Salsify and bacon

PREPARATION TIME: 15 minutes
COOKING TIME: 1 hour
FOR SIX

1½ kg (3 lb 5 oz) salsify
300 g (10½ oz) thick streaky
  bacon
50 g (scant 2 oz) flour

30 g (1 oz) butter
125 g (4½ oz) chopped shallots
200 ml (7 fl oz) white wine
salt, pepper

Trim and peel the salsify and cut into lengths of about 3 cm (1¼ inches).

Make a soft paste with the flour and sufficient water and add it to the pan containing 2 litres (3½ pints) boiling water. Return the water to the boil and stir to incorporate the flour completely. Add the salsify and cook for 40–45 minutes. Remove and drain.

In the meantime, put the slices of bacon in a pan and cover them with cold water. Bring to the boil and continue boiling for 5 minutes. Remove the bacon, dry it on kitchen paper and cut into dice.

Melt the butter in a saucepan and gently cook the shallots and the diced bacon together. Add the white wine, season and cook covered over a low heat for 20 minutes.

Add the salsify to the pan and simmer gently together for another 10 minutes.

Elle says that it is important to add flour to the cooking water as this preserves the colour of the vegetable.

NAVETS BRAISÉS AU CIDRE
Young turnips in cider

PREPARATION TIME: 15 minutes
COOKING TIME: 30 minutes
FOR SIX

1½ kg (generous 3¼ lb) small
  young turnips
750 ml (generous 1¼ pints) dry
  cider

75 g (generous 2½ oz) butter
150 ml (5 fl oz) chicken stock
bouquet garni
salt, pepper

The vegetables required for this dish are the small young turnips known in France as navets. Trim them, wash in running water, then plunge them into boiling salted water for 5 minutes. Drain and dry with kitchen paper.

Boil the cider in an open saucepan until its volume is reduced by half.

Melt the butter in a pan and gently sauté the turnips. When they are a good golden-brown, add the cider, the chicken stock and the bouquet garni. Season, cover the pan and simmer for 30 minutes.

Serve very hot with roast meat or poultry.

TERRINE VERTE
Spinach terrine

PREPARATION TIME: 30 minutes
COOKING TIME: 1 hour
FOR SIX

2 kg (4½ lb) fresh spinach　　　100 g (3½ oz) pesto (basil sauce)
150 g (5 oz) Swiss cheese　　　salt, pepper
6 eggs

Strip the spinach leaves from their stalks and cook them for 5 minutes in boiling salted water. Drain and squeeze out all surplus liquid. Cut the cheese into small dice.

Put the spinach into a bowl. Break in the eggs, and add the cheese, together with the pesto. Season, stir together.

Butter a shallow terrine, pour in the spinach mixture and cook in a pan of water in a very hot oven (240°C/475°F/Gas Mark 9) for 1 hour. Serve hot.

Elle says this terrine is very good when cold. Serve it with a sauce made by stirring chopped *fines herbes* (chervil, chives, parsley and tarragon) into crème fraîche.

TOMATES À LA PROVENÇALE
Provençal tomatoes

PREPARATION TIME: 5 minutes
COOKING TIME: 25 minutes
FOR SIX

1½ kg (3 lb 5 oz) tomatoes　　　3 tablespoons olive oil
salt, pepper　　　　　　　　　　4 cloves of garlic
2 teaspoons chopped thyme　　　parsley
1 teaspoon chopped rosemary　　2 tablespoons dried breadcrumbs

Wash the tomatoes and cut each one in half. Arrange them cut-side upwards in an ovenproof dish. Season each half and sprinkle with a pinch of mixed thyme and rosemary. Pour on the olive oil and cook in a pre-heated hot oven (220°C/425°F/Gas Mark 7).

Finely chop the garlic and the parsley and mix them well with the dried breadcrumbs.

After 15–20 minutes in the oven, remove the tomatoes and cover each half with a good teaspoon of breadcrumb and herb mixture. Put under the grill for 5 minutes until the surfaces are golden brown. Serve either hot or cold.

SAUCE À LA CRÈME D'ANCHOIS
Cream of anchovy sauce

SAUCE À L'AVOCAT
An avocado sauce

PREPARATION TIME: 10 minutes
COOKING TIME: 10 minutes (excluding preparation of stock)
FOR SIX

1 teaspoon anchovy paste
100 g (3½ oz) butter
50 g (scant 2 oz) flour
salt, pepper
2 egg yolks

For the fish stock:
1 fish stock cube if available (see p.15)
½ bottle dry white wine

Mix the crumbled fish stock cube and wine in a casserole. Add the fish which this sauce is to accompany and pour in sufficient water to cover. Bring to the simmer and when the fish is cooked, pour off the stock and strain it through a sieve. There should be about 1 litre (1¾ pints) of fish stock.

Gently melt 50 g (scant 2 oz) butter in a saucepan, add the flour. Stirring vigorously, first blend the butter and flour together, then slowly add fish stock in sufficient quantity for a smooth and creamy sauce. Stir briskly while adding the stock. Season, and let the sauce continue to cook for 10 minutes, skimming as necessary.

Remove the sauce from the heat and whisk in a mixture of the beaten yolks and the anchovy paste. Follow this with the rest of the butter, whisked in knob by knob.

Check the seasoning and serve the sauce with the cooked fish.

Elle advises that while the butter is being added, the sauce should be gently reheated from time to time, but not allowed to boil.

PREPARATION TIME: 5 minutes
COOKING TIME: nil
FOR SIX

1 large avocado pear
200 g (7 oz) fromage blanc
1 lemon

2 cloves of garlic
salt, pepper
tabasco sauce

Cut the avocado in half, remove the stone and scoop out the flesh. Put it in a bowl with the fromage blanc, the juice of the lemon and the peeled and crushed garlic. Mix it thoroughly together, season and add a few drops of tabasco sauce to taste. Stir once more.

Serve in a bowl with a dish of crudités (trimmed and sliced raw vegetables).

Elle advises that because of the blandness of the avocado, the finished sauce should be quite spicy.

BEURRE AU BASILIC
Basil butter

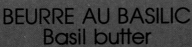

PREPARATION TIME: 15 minutes
COOKING TIME: nil
FOR SIX

250 g (scant 9 oz) butter   *salt, pepper*
1 large bunch of basil   *1 lemon*

Bring the butter out of the refrigerator well in advance so that it can soften at room temperature. Wash the basil, trim off the stalks and dry the leaves with kitchen paper. Either pound the leaves in a mortar or chop them as finely as possible. Cut the butter into pieces and put them into a double-boiler in which the water is hot, but not boiling. Maintain the temperature over a very low heat. Work the butter into a smooth cream, season with salt and plenty of pepper.

Thoroughly mix in the chopped basil and the lemon juice and serve hot as an accompaniment to grilled or poached fish, scallops or shellfish.

Elle advises that it is important to maintain the temperature in the double-boiler at the correct level. The success of the sauce rests in achieving a creamy texture to the butter.

BEURRE D'OLIVE
Olive butter

PREPARATION TIME: 15 minutes
COOKING TIME: nil
FOR SIX TO EIGHT

300 g (10½ oz) black olives   *200 g (7 oz) butter*
2 shallots   *salt, pepper*

Stone the olives. Put them in a blender with the peeled shallots and the butter cut into knobs. Season with pepper and mix thoroughly. Taste the mixture and check the seasoning.

Serve either on small rounds of toast or as an accompaniment to poached fillets of white fish.

Elle says that, stored in an airtight pot, this savoury butter will keep for several days in the refrigerator.

SAUCE AU CHILLI
Chilli sauce

PREPARATION TIME: 10 minutes
COOKING TIME: 20 minutes
FOR SIX

1½ kg (generous 3¼ lb) tomatoes	1 lemon
2 large onions	bouquet garni
5 tablespoons peanut oil	1 teaspoon chilli powder
	salt, pepper

Peel the tomatoes in the usual way, remove the seeds and cut them up. Peel and slice the onions.

Heat the oil in a pan, add the onions and the tomatoes and cook together for a few moments. Then add the juice of the lemon, the bouquet garni and the chilli powder. Season and stir the mixture.

Lower the heat and, with the pan uncovered, simmer for about 20 minutes. Finally, pass the sauce through a blender or a sieve.

Serve with grilled meat.

<u>Elle says</u> that this sauce keeps well when deep-frozen.

SAUCE CUMBERLAND
Cumberland sauce

PREPARATION TIME: 15 minutes
COOKING TIME: 25 minutes
FOR SIX

4 oranges	500 g (generous 1 lb) redcurrant jelly
2 lemons	2 shallots
2 teaspoons English powdered mustard	½ teaspoon salt
3 tablespoons cider vinegar	black pepper
100 ml (3½ fl oz) port	

Carefully remove the peel from the oranges and the lemons, taking care to leave the pith behind, and cut it into very fine julienne strips. Blanch them for 5 minutes in boiling water. Drain through a sieve, rinse under cold running water, and put to one side.

Squeeze the oranges and the lemons and put the juice into a small saucepan. Mix the powdered mustard and the vinegar together and add it to the contents of the saucepan, together with the port, the redcurrant jelly, the peeled and finely-chopped shallots, the salt, freshly ground pepper and the strips of peel. Bring to the boil over a brisk heat and continue to stir until the redcurrant jelly is completely dissolved. Lower the heat and simmer the sauce, with the pan uncovered, for 20 minutes.

When all the ingredients are well melded together, allow to cool and refrigerate. The sauce will thicken as it cools. Serve with game, or roast mutton; it goes equally well with hot or cold dishes.

PEURE
Coriander sauce

PREPARATION TIME: 15 minutes
COOKING TIME: nil
FOR SIX

1 bunch of fresh coriander	1 green chilli
3 medium-sized onions	2½ tablespoons of olive oil
2 cloves of garlic	1 lemon
1 green pepper	salt, pepper
1 tomato	

Peel the onions and the garlic. Put the pepper under the grill and heat it until it can be easily peeled (*see* p.15). Also remove stalk and seeds. Peel the tomato and remove its seeds. Chop up all these vegetables very fine, or better still, chop them in a food processor together with the chilli and the coriander.

Put the chopped herbs and vegetables into a bowl and pour in the oil, the juice of the lemon and 50 ml (1¾ fl oz) water. Mix everything together, and serve with braised pork dishes.

Elle says that water should be added sparingly as the sauce should be quite thick.

SAUCE À L'AIL
A garlic sauce

PREPARATION TIME: 10 minutes
COOKING TIME: 10 minutes
FOR SIX TO EIGHT

20 cloves of garlic	wine vinegar
6 anchovy fillets	tabasco sauce
1 tablespoon of capers	salt, pepper
400 ml (14 fl oz) olive oil	

Put the unpeeled cloves of garlic in a saucepan, cover them in cold water, bring to the boil and cook for 10 minutes. Drain and peel them.

When they are cold, put them into a mortar with the anchovy fillets and the capers and crush everything together well. Then proceed as if making a mayonnaise: drip the oil into the mixture while whisking constantly. Finally, stir in a few drops of wine vinegar and tabasco, and season to taste. Serve with hard-boiled eggs and crudités (trimmed and sliced raw vegetables).

Elle advises that if the sauce should separate while it is being made, bring it back by putting a little chilled water into a mixing-bowl, then very slowly pouring in the separated sauce, whisking all the time.

SAUCE MOUSSELINE AU CITRON
Smooth lemon sauce

PREPARATION TIME: 15 minutes
COOKING TIME: nil
FOR FOUR

juice of ½ lemon
1 egg
200 g (7 oz) fromage blanc

1 teaspoon olive oil
pepper

Separate the egg and beat the yolk into the fromage blanc to make a smooth sauce. Stir in the olive oil and the lemon juice.

Whisk the egg white until stiff and carefully fold it into the sauce. Season with pepper.

Serve with either hot or cold fish.

SAUCE AUX OIGNONS
An onion sauce

PREPARATION TIME: 10 minutes
COOKING TIME: 25 minutes
FOR SIX

6 onions
50 g (scant 2 oz) butter
2 tablespoons strong mustard

125 g (4½ oz) crème fraîche
salt, pepper

Peel the onions and cut them into thin slices. Melt the butter in a pan, add the sliced onions and cook very gently, stirring often until they are transparent. At this point mix in the mustard, then add the crème fraîche and mix once more. Season, and warm the sauce through.

If it seems too thick, it may be lightened with the addition of a little hot water.

Serve with grilled beef or grilled pork.

SAUCE CRÉOSA
A vegetable sauce

PREPARATION TIME: 45 minutes (24 hours in advance)
COOKING TIME: nil
FOR EIGHT TO TEN

150 g (5 oz) onions	1 teaspoon chopped tarragon
200 g (7 oz) cucumber	50 g (scant 2 oz) chopped parsley
150 g (5 oz) sweet red pepper	4 tablespoons strong mustard
400 g (14 oz) firm tomatoes	200 ml (7 fl oz) olive oil
100 g (3½ oz) gherkins	50 ml (1¾ fl oz) wine vinegar
100 g (3½ oz) capers	salt, pepper

Peel the onions and the cucumber. Split the cucumber in half lengthways and scoop out the seeds. Remove stalk, membranes and seeds from the pepper: cut the tomatoes in half, and scoop out the seeds. Cut all these vegetables into small pieces about the size of a pea, and put them into an earthenware dish.

Chop up the gherkins similarly and put them and the capers into the dish with the tarragon, the parsley, the mustard, the oil and the wine vinegar. Season generously and mix everything thoroughly with a wooden spoon. Cover the dish and leave in a cool place (but *not* in a refrigerator) for 24 hours.

The sauce will keep for several days and, indeed, improves with keeping.

Sauce Créosa may be eaten by itself, with grilled or roast beef or with grilled fish.

SAUCE AUX ARACHIDES
Peanut sauce

PREPARATION TIME: 10 minutes
COOKING TIME: 25 minutes
FOR 500 ML (17½ FL OZ) OF SAUCE

200 g (7 oz) salted peanuts	1 lemon
4 tablespoons of peanut oil	1 teaspoon sugar
2 onions	salt, pepper
2 teaspoons curry powder	1 tablespoon unsalted peanuts
500 ml (17½ fl oz) apple juice	

Finely crush the salted peanuts, either with a pestle and mortar or in a blender.

Heat the oil in a pan and mix together the finely-chopped onions and the curry powder. Cook gently until the onions become transparent. Transfer the onions to a saucepan and add the crushed salted peanuts, the apple juice, the lemon juice and the sugar. Season, stir, bring to the boil and cook for 10 minutes.

Pass the sauce through a sieve and, just before serving, sprinkle the surface with chopped unsalted peanuts.

Elle says that this sauce goes equally well with grilled meat or grilled fish.

SAUCE À L'OSEILLE
Sorrel sauce

PREPARATION TIME: 15 minutes
COOKING TIME: 10 minutes
FOR SIX

400 g (14 oz) sorrel (leaves only)	*4 egg yolks*
60 g (2 oz) butter	*300 g (10½ oz) crème fraîche*
4 cloves of garlic	*salt, pepper*

Make sure all the stalks have been stripped from the sorrel: wash the leaves in plenty of water, drain thoroughly. Heat the butter until it just bubbles, add the sorrel leaves and cook them gently. Peel and crush the garlic and add it to the sorrel.

Continue cooking until all the liquid given off has evaporated. Remove from the heat and put to one side.

Mix the beaten egg yolks and the crème fraîche together, season and pour them onto the sorrel. Return to a very low heat, stirring constantly until the mixture thickens.

Serve with grilled or poached fish.

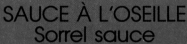 the temperature must be carefully controlled after the egg–cream mixture is added. The sauce should not be allowed even to approach the boil.

SAUCE TOMATÉE
Creamy tomato sauce

PREPARATION TIME: 20 minutes
COOKING TIME: 10 minutes
FOR SIX

600 g (generous 1¼ lb) tomatoes	*300 g (10½ oz) crème fraîche*
2 cloves of garlic	*salt, pepper*
3 good shallots	*100 g (3½ oz) butter*
small bunch of parsley	*1 good bunch of chives*

Peel the garlic and the shallots and chop them and the parsley up very finely. Peel, de-seed and chop up the tomatoes.

Put garlic, shallots, parsley and tomatoes into a saucepan together with the crème fraîche. Season, stir and bring to the boil. Lower the heat so that the mixture just bubbles occasionally and stir until a creamy sauce is obtained.

Remove the pan from the heat and whisk in the butter, knob by knob. Finally stir in chopped chives.

Serve with grilled or poached fish.

VINAIGRETTE À LA TOMATE
Tomato vinaigrette

PREPARATION TIME: 10 minutes
COOKING TIME: nil
FOR SIX

450 g (1 lb) tomatoes
9 tablespoons of olive oil
3 tablespoons of sherry vinegar

3 tablespoons of lemon juice
1½ teaspoons strong mustard
salt, pepper

Peel and de-seed the tomatoes and put them through a blender with the oil, the vinegar, the lemon juice, the mustard and seasoning. Continue blending until a smooth and homogeneous mixture results. Turn it into a bowl and chill in a refrigerator.

Serve with cold poached fish.

PURÉE DE TOMATES À LA MENTHE
Tomato and mint purée

PREPARATION TIME: 10 minutes
COOKING TIME: 15 minutes
FOR SIX

1¾ kg (scant 4 lb) tomatoes
30 leaves of fresh mint
3 cloves of garlic

4 limes
1 teaspoon celery salt
pepper

Peel the tomatoes in the usual way and remove the seeds. Put the flesh into a blender with the peeled and chopped garlic, the chopped mint, juice of 3 limes, the celery salt and freshly ground pepper. Mix to a smooth purée, turn it out into a saucepan and cook, just on the boil, for 15 minutes.

Decorate the sauce dish with a few leaves of mint set aside for the purpose, and a slice of lime.

Elle says this purée is equally good hot or cold. It goes well with hard-boiled eggs or fish, or it can be eaten on its own.

COULIS DE TOMATES
Tomato purée

PREPARATION TIME: 15 minutes
COOKING TIME: 50 minutes
FOR SIX

500 g (generous 1 lb) tomatoes
salt, pepper
1 bay leaf

4 sprigs of thyme
50 g (scant 2 oz) onions

Wash the tomatoes and cut them into quarters. Cook in an open saucepan over a moderate heat for 30 minutes, together with ½ teaspoon of salt, four turns of a black pepper mill, the bay leaf, chopped thyme and the peeled and chopped onion.

Press the tomato mixture through a fine sieve back into the saucepan and cook for a further 20 minutes. There should remain about 10 tablespoons of rich tomato purée at the end of the cooking.

 says that the coulis is delicious both with poached fish or cold meat.

SAUCE AUX NOIX ET AU ROQUEFORT
Walnut and cheese sauce

PREPARATION TIME: 10 minutes
COOKING TIME: nil
FOR SIX

75 g (generous 2½ oz) Roquefort
  cheese
30 g (1 oz) walnut kernels

4 tablespoons of olive oil
salt, pepper
paprika

Crush the cheese with a fork. Put the shelled walnuts into a grinder and reduce to a fine powder. Transfer the walnuts to a blender, add the cheese and mix them together. Pour the oil, in very slowly, as if making a mayonnaise, until a thick sauce is achieved. Season and finally stir in the paprika.

This sauce goes well with all grilled or roast meat.

Elle advises that only fresh walnuts should be used. Discard any that show signs of having been kept too long.

THOÏONNADE
Tunny pâté

PREPARATION TIME: 15 minutes
COOKING TIME: 20 minutes
FOR SIX

200 g (7 oz) tunny fish in oil   50 g (scant 2 oz) capers
100 g (3½ oz) black olives   olive oil
1 egg yolk   salt
1 clove of garlic   cayenne pepper

Drain the tunny fish and stone the olives. Put olives and tunny into a blender with the egg yolk, the peeled garlic and the capers. Blend together, adding just sufficient oil to give a smooth paste. Season with salt if necessary and sprinkle lightly with a little cayenne pepper.

Serve as an appetiser, surrounded by black olives, slices of lemon and rounds of toast.

Elle says that this delicious mixture can also be used as a garnish for raw tomatoes or for artichoke bottoms. Also, if mixed thoroughly with the yolks, as a stuffing for hard-boiled eggs.

ANCHOÏADE AUX POIVRONS
Anchovy and pepper appetiser

PREPARATION TIME: 20 minutes
COOKING TIME: 10 minutes
FOR SIX

2 small tins anchovy fillets   150 g (5 oz) stoned green olives
2 sweet red peppers   200 ml (7 fl oz) olive oil

Put the peppers under a hot grill until they can be peeled easily (see p.15). Remove stalks, seeds and membranes and cut up the flesh into strips.

Put the olives, the drained anchovies and the peppers into a blender and mix together. With the blender still turning, incorporate the oil, drop by drop, as if making mayonnaise.

Serve as an appetiser on hot toast.

Elle notes that this purée will be more liquid than the classical anchoïade.

MELON SURPRISE
Melon with ice cream

PREPARATION TIME: 15 minutes
COOKING TIME: 5 minutes
FOR SIX

2 good-sized melons
500 g (generous 1 lb) cherries
150 g (5 oz) caster sugar

500 ml (generous ¾ pint) vanilla
   ice cream
500 ml (generous ¾ pint)
   pistachio ice cream

Stone the cherries and put them in a saucepan with the sugar and a glass (5 fl oz) of water. Bring to the boil and poach them gently for 5 minutes, drain.

Cut the cap (stalk-end) from each melon and scoop out the seeds. Then make melon-balls of the flesh with a small scoop, put them into a bowl and mix them with the cherries. Keep in a cool place, with the shells of the melons.

Just before serving, divide the ice cream into scoops and fill each melon with a mixture of the two sorts of ice cream and the fruit. Serve at once.

Elle suggests as an alternative, buying six small individual melons.

SOUPE DE MELON
Melon with kirsch

PREPARATION TIME: 10 minutes
COOKING TIME: 15 minutes
FOR SIX

6 small melons (not over-ripe)
225 g (8 oz) thick crème fraîche

120 g (scant 4½ oz) caster sugar
4 tablespoons kirsch

Cut the top-third from the stalk-end of each melon and take out the seeds. Discard the seeds but retain the caps.

Scoop out all the flesh of each melon taking care not to pierce the shells. Cut it up into small pieces and mix them with the crème fraîche, the sugar and the kirsch. Divide the mixture between the melon shells and replace the caps. Securely wrap each melon in kitchen foil and, being careful to keep them upright, heat them in a very hot oven (230°C/450°F/Gas Mark 8) for 15 minutes.

Serve either very hot, or warm.

Elle says that this dish may be prepared in advance up to the stage of wrapping in foil, and heated just before serving.

SALADE DE FRUITS D'ÉTÉ
Summer salad

PREPARATION TIME: 45 minutes (2 hours in advance)
COOKING TIME: 10 minutes (syrup)
FOR SIX

1 medium-sized melon	*250 g (scant 9 oz) strawberries*
3 apricots	*200 g (7 oz) sugar*
3 peaches	*150 g (5 oz) raspberries*
150 g (5 oz) wild strawberries	

Halve the melon, remove the seeds and divide the flesh into balls with a small scoop. Stone the apricots and peaches and cut them into quarters. Put these and both sorts of strawberries into a large bowl, well spread out to reduce the risk of the berries being crushed.

Boil the sugar for 10 minutes in 250 ml (scant 9 fl oz) of water. Leave to cool and, while it is still warm, pour it over the fruit. Leave the salad in a cool place for 2 hours.

Just before serving, divide the fruit among individual serving bowls. Add the raspberries at this point and pour in the syrup.

Serve cool (not refrigerated) with double cream and caster sugar separately.

PÊCHES AUX FRAMBOISES
Peaches and raspberries

PREPARATION TIME: 15 minutes
COOKING TIME: 15 minutes
FOR SIX

6 good, firm peaches	*½ vanilla pod*
250 g (scant 9 oz) raspberries	*1 tablespoon of kirsch*
100 g (3½ oz) sugar	

Cut the peaches in half, peel them and remove the stones. Put the sugar, vanilla and 200 ml (7 fl oz) of water into a saucepan and make a syrup, stirring frequently as it comes to the boil. Simmer the peach halves in the syrup for about 10 minutes; remove the peaches, drain them, arrange them in the serving bowl and put into a cool place.

Raise the heat under the syrup and reduce it, briskly, until only a small cup remains. In a blender, make a purée of 150 g (5 oz) of the raspberries and thoroughly mix it into the syrup. Remove from the heat and stir in the kirsch. Leave to cool.

Pour the raspberry syrup over the peaches and decorate with the rest of the raspberries.

Elle says that unsweetened frozen or preserved raspberries may be used to make the purée.

FRAMBOISES AU VIN
Raspberries in wine

PREPARATION TIME: 15 minutes (well in advance)
COOKING TIME: nil
FOR SIX

750 g (generous 1½ lb)
  raspberries
225 g (8 oz) caster sugar
¾ bottle good red wine

200 ml (7 fl oz) double cream
60 g (2 oz) vanilla sugar (see
  p.16)

Put the raspberries either into individual bowls or into a serving bowl. Sprinkle with caster sugar and pour the red wine over them. Cover with kitchen foil and leave to soak in a refrigerator for 5–6 hours.

A few minutes before serving, whip up the well-chilled double cream into a light and frothy Chantilly cream, mixed with the vanilla sugar. Serve the raspberries and the cream separately.

Elle advises that when whipping the cream it is better to use a pre-chilled bowl.

SAUCE MELBA
Melba sauce

PREPARATION TIME: 1 hour 20 minutes
COOKING TIME: nil

1½ kg (generous 3¼ lb) either
  strawberries or raspberries

1½ kg (generous 3¼ lb) caster
  sugar (for a given amount of
  fruit the same weight of sugar
  is used)

The fruit should be weighed after the stalks have been removed. Wash the fruit if necessary.

Purée the fruit, then force it through a fine-meshed sieve into a mixing bowl. Add the sugar, one-third at a time, stirring so that each batch is thoroughly absorbed into the fruit pulp. Leave to stand for 1 hour to complete the dissolving of the sugar.

This sauce keeps well: a week in a refrigerator, six months in a freezer or it may be stored in Kilner jars after sterilising in boiling water.

Elle says this sauce is an indispensable accompaniment to ice cream of any fruit flavour and to puddings made with rice, semolina, etc.

BRUGNONS AU VIN BLANC
Nectarines in white wine

PREPARATION TIME: 15 minutes (plus 2 hours of soaking)
COOKING TIME: nil
FOR SIX

1 kg (scant 2¼ lb) nectarines   *1 bottle sweet white wine*
75 g (generous 2½ oz) caster
  sugar

Wash and stone the nectarines and cut them into thin, even slices. Arrange them in the serving bowl, sprinkle them with sugar and pour in the white wine.

Leave to stand for at least 2 hours. Serve chilled.

<u>Elle advises</u> that the real success of this simple dish is in choosing a wine of quality.

FRUITS EN GRATIN
Fruit gratin

PREPARATION TIME: 15 minutes
COOKING TIME: 10 minutes
FOR SIX

250 g (scant 9 oz) strawberries   *200 ml (7 fl oz) Grand-Marnier*
1 small melon   *6 dessertspoons caster sugar*
3 good white peaches   *6 egg yolks*
250 g (scant 9 oz) raspberries   *3 dessertspoons double cream*

Wash and hull the strawberries, and cut them lengthways into 2 or 3 pieces. Remove the seeds from the melon and divide the flesh into chunks. Peel and cut up the peaches. Leave the raspberries whole.

Put all the fruit into a bowl, sprinkle with Grand-Marnier and shake on half the sugar. Leave to stand for 30 minutes, then drain off the juices through a sieve.

Put the egg yolks into a bowl together with 6 teaspoons of cold water, the cream and the rest of the sugar. Put the bowl into a dish of hot water and vigorously beat the mixture into a cream. Add the fruit juice little by little, whisking all the time.

Just before serving, arrange the fruit in a buttered fireproof dish, pour the fruit-cream over it and put momentarily under a hot grill to brown the surface.

<u>From 'La Diligence' restaurant in Saint-Julien-en-Genevois on the France/Switzerland border:</u> the chef suggests that all is needed to go with this delicious pudding is a small glass of Grand-Marnier.

CRÈME BRÛLÉE
Baked custard with figs

PREPARATION TIME: 10 minutes
COOKING TIME: 15 minutes
FOR SIX

24 figs	*2 vanilla pods*
500 g (generous 1 lb) granulated sugar	*6 egg yolks*
	300 g (10½ oz) caster sugar
500 ml (17½ fl oz) red wine	*1 litre (1¾ pints) whipping cream*

Make a syrup by melting the granulated sugar in the wine plus 500 ml (17½ fl oz) of water, add one vanilla pod. Poach the figs in batches in the boiling syrup, allowing 2 minutes per batch. Drain and keep warm.

Beat the egg yolks and caster sugar together until stiff enough to flow in an unbroken ribbon when poured from a spoon. Bring the cream to the boil and stir it into the egg-mixture. Add a vanilla pod and put over a very low heat, stirring constantly, until a smooth cream results. Do *not* let the mixture boil. Allow to cool.

Arrange 4 figs in each of 6 individual ovenproof dishes. Remove the vanilla pod from the cream, pour it over the figs and brown quickly under a hot grill. Serve at once.

<u>From the restaurant 'Chez Marie' in Paris-6^e</u>: the chef says that a well-chilled demi-sec champagne is quite delicious with this dish.

CRUMBLE AUX FRUITS ROUGES
Summer crumble

PREPARATION TIME: 30 minutes
COOKING TIME: 30 minutes
FOR SIX

500 g (generous 1 lb) mixed red fruits (currants, raspberries and cherries)	For the crumble:
	125 g (4½ oz) butter
	200 g (7 oz) flour
150 g (5 oz) granulated sugar	*125 g (4½ oz) granulated sugar*

First make the crumble topping. Cut the butter into small pieces and, in a dish, work it into the flour and sugar. Mix thoroughly.

Wash the fruit, remove the stalks and stone the cherries. Stir the sugar into the mixed fruit and arrange it in an ovenproof dish about 23 cm (9 inches) in diameter. Spread the crumble topping over the fruit and cook in a hot oven (220°C/425°F/Gas Mark 7) for 30–40 minutes. The dish will be cooked when the crumble topping has browned.

Serve warm, straight from the dish, with a bowl of cream.

<u>Elle says</u> that, if preferred, this pudding may be eaten cold, when it may be easily turned out of its dish. It is, however, nicer eaten warm.

CERISES EN CLAFOUTIS
Cherries in batter

PREPARATION TIME: 15 minutes
COOKING TIME: 30 minutes
FOR SIX

500 g (generous 1 lb) fresh
cherries
500 ml (17½ fl oz) full-cream milk
4 eggs

100 ml (3½ fl oz) of the liqueur in
which the cherries below have
been preserved
6 cherries preserved in liqueur

Wash and dry the cherries and remove the stalks. Boil the milk.

Beat the eggs in a bowl, whisk in the boiling milk and stir in the liqueur.

Divide the fresh cherries between 6 small ramekin dishes. Top each one with a single preserved cherry and pour in the beaten eggs and milk. Arrange the ramekin dishes in a pan of water and cook in a cool oven (150°C/300°F/Gas Mark 2) for 30 minutes. Check that the mixture is not boiling. Serve warm.

Elle says that if preserved cherries are not available, soak 6 of the best cherries in 100 ml (3½ fl oz) Armagnac overnight.

MOUSSE À LA MANDARINE
Mandarin mousse

PREPARATION TIME: 15 minutes (3 hours in advance)
COOKING TIME: 5 minutes
FOR SIX

375 g (13 oz) caster sugar
12 egg yolks
500 ml (17½ fl oz) milk
350 g (scant 12½ oz) crème
fraîche

100 ml (3½ fl oz) mandarin
liqueur (or Cointreau)
100 g (3½ oz) preserved
mandarin or orange peel

Work the sugar into the yolks while beating them. Bring the milk to the boil and pour it slowly onto the beaten yolks, whisking constantly.

Pour the mixture into a saucepan and thicken it over a low heat, beating constantly and not allowing it to boil. As soon as it is thick enough to coat a spoon, pour it into a bowl and leave to cool.

Whip the crème fraîche and when the custard is quite cool, carefully fold in the cream and the mandarin liqueur. Pour the mousse into 6 individual serving bowls and chill them in the freezer compartment for 3 hours. It should be thoroughly chilled but still creamy. Decorate just before serving with strips of preserved peel.

Elle advises that to lighten the whipped cream, 100 ml (3½ fl oz) of very cold water should be added before whipping, which should be done in a bowl pre-chilled for 10 minutes in the freezer.

CRÈME DE MANGUE AU COULIS DE FRAMBOISE
Mango cream with raspberry purée

PREPARATION TIME: 10 minutes (12 hours in advance)
COOKING TIME: nil
FOR SIX

4 mangoes
500 g (17½ oz) whipping cream
200 g (7 oz) icing sugar

For the purée:
500 g (generous 1 lb) raspberries
100 g (3½ oz) icing sugar

Cut the mangoes in half, remove the large stones and scoop out the flesh. Pass it through a blender.

Whip the cream and fold the mango pulp and the icing sugar into it. Pour the mixture into its serving bowl and leave it overnight in the freezer.

Just before serving, blend the raspberries and the icing sugar together to make a purée. Serve mango cream and raspberry purée from separate dishes.

Elle advises that the mango cream should be taken out of the freezer at least 30 minutes before serving.

ORANGES GIVRÉES
Frosted oranges

PREPARATION TIME: 1 hour
COOKING TIME: nil
FOR SIX

6 large oranges
1 tablespoon best apricot jam
500 g (generous 1 lb) caster sugar

1 lemon
1 egg white
100 g (3½ oz) icing sugar

These delicious sorbets cannot be prepared without an ice cream maker (sorbetière).

Cut the cap off each orange a little above the half-way point, and remove all the flesh. Be careful not to cut through the skin.

Dissolve the apricot jam in a tablespoon of hot water. Brush a thin layer over the outsides of both parts of each orange, roll each piece in caster sugar and put them all into the freezer.

Chop up the flesh of the oranges and the lemon and squeeze them to remove all the juice. Measure the volume of juice and add double its quantity of water: mix in caster sugar in the proportion of 300 g per litre of mixture (6 oz per pint). Stir until the sugar is dissolved and pour the syrup into the ice cream maker.

When the syrup has stiffened, mix the egg white and icing sugar and whip to a stiff foam. Fold it into the sorbet mixture and return it to the ice cream maker to complete the freezing.

To serve, fill each orange skin, which will be stiff and frosted, with sorbet. Handle the oranges as carefully as possible in order to retain the frosted look. Serve at once, or return to the freezer to wait.

POMMES SURPRISES AU CIDRE
Baked apples in cider

PREPARATION TIME: 15 minutes
COOKING TIME: 25 minutes
FOR SIX

6 good firm eating apples	*50 g (scant 2 oz) butter*
500 ml (17½ fl oz) cider	*200 g (7 oz) chopped walnuts*
400 g (14 oz) sugar	

Peel and core the apples. Put the cider and an equal volume of water in a saucepan and stir in 300 g (10½ oz) sugar. Bring to the boil: when the sugar has melted, plunge in the apples and poach them for about 15 minutes. Remove, drain and arrange on an ovenproof dish.

Thoroughly mix together the butter and the remaining sugar, then stir in the chopped walnuts. Stuff the apples and let any remaining butter mixture spill over the tops. Cook in a very hot oven (230°C/450°F/Gas Mark 8) until the butter mixture becomes caramelised.

<u>Elle advises</u> that a firm variety of apple which will not disintegrate during cooking should be chosen.

POMMES SOUFFLÉES
Fluffy apples

PREPARATION TIME: 20 minutes (2 hours in advance)
COOKING TIME: 10 minutes
FOR SIX

6 firm eating apples	*3 liqueur glasses of Calvados*
250 g (scant 9 oz) granulated sugar	*6 egg whites*

Prepare a syrup by melting 200 g (7 oz) sugar in 1 litre (1¾ pints) of water. Bring to the boil and keep at a slow boil for 10 minutes. Allow to cool and stir in half the Calvados.

Halve the apples horizontally and remove core and pips from each half. Put them to soak in the syrup for 2 hours.

Scoop out part of the flesh from the stalk-halves of each of the apples to make a hollow. Peel all the other halves and put the flesh, together with the apple scooped from the stalk-halves, into a blender and make a purée with the rest of the sugar.

Whip the egg whites until stiff and with a spatula carefully fold in the rest of the Calvados and the raw apple purée. Arrange the apple halves on a baking-sheet, hollowed size upward and, with the aid of an icing-bag, divide the mixture between the apple halves. Bake in a moderate oven (180°C/350°F/Gas Mark 4) for 10–15 minutes. Serve very hot.

<u>Elle advises</u> that the apple purée and Calvados should be folded into with whipped egg whites with the greatest care to prevent the mixture collapsing and becoming liquid.

POMMES FLAMBÉES
Apples flambé

PREPARATION TIME: 15 minutes
COOKING TIME: 15 minutes
FOR SIX

6 firm eating apples   100 g (3½ oz) caster sugar
1 lemon   1 liqueur glass Grand-Marnier
25 g (scant 1 oz) butter

Peel the apples, cut them in half lengthways, remove cores and pips and sprinkle them with lemon juice.

Butter an ovenproof dish and arrange the apple halves in it, cut side downwards. Take a sharp knife and make parallel incisions in each fruit.

Melt the rest of the butter and brush the fruit with it. Sprinkle with the caster sugar and cook in a pre-heated fairly hot oven (200°C/400°F/Gas Mark 6) for 15 minutes. Remove and place under the grill to brown the surface of the apples. Bring to the table, pour flaming Grand-Marnier over the apples and serve at once.

POMMES RÔTIES À L'ORANGE
Baked apples in orange sauce

PREPARATION TIME: 10 minutes
COOKING TIME: 40 minutes
FOR SIX

6 firm eating apples   3 tablespoons caster sugar
3 oranges

Make a slit in the skin, all round the apples, at a line about two-thirds from the stalk end. Otherwise, leave the apples whole. Cut two horizontal slices from the centre of each orange and put one in each of 6 individual ovenproof dishes. Place an apple on top of each orange slice and put them all into a moderate oven (180°C/350°F/Gas Mark 4).

Squeeze the juice from the remaining orange halves and stir in the sugar until it is dissolved. As soon as the slits in the apples open, baste them from time to time with the orange syrup. The apples will be cooked when a sharp pointed knife pierces them easily.

Serve warm, with caster sugar on the table.

PÈCHES PÂTISSIÈRE
Peach meringue

PREPARATION TIME: 35 minutes
COOKING TIME: 30 minutes
FOR SIX

1 kg (scant 2¼ lb) peaches	1 litre (1¾ pints) milk
350 g (scant 12½ oz) caster sugar	6 eggs
	100 g (3½ oz) flour
1 tablespoon kirsch	30 g (1 oz) butter
1 vanilla pod	50 g (scant 2 oz) flaked almonds

Peel and stone the peaches and cut them into pieces. Put them into a saucepan with 100 g (3½ oz) sugar and cook for 10 minutes to reduce them to a purée. Add the kirsch.

In the meantime, split the vanilla pod in two and boil it in the milk.

Take 2 whole eggs and 4 egg yolks and work them together with the flour, the softened butter and 150 g (5 oz) sugar. When a smooth and even mixture has been achieved, slowly extend it with the hot milk from which the vanilla pod has been removed, stirring continuously. Transfer the mixture to a saucepan and, still stirring constantly, bring slowly to the boil. Remove from the heat after a few seconds.

Pour the mixture into an ovenproof dish and spread the purée of peaches over the surface. Whisk the 4 egg whites until stiff with the remaining sugar, adding it little by little, as the egg whites stiffen. Fold in the flaked almonds and, using an icing-bag, pipe the meringue mixture over the peach purée, as illustrated.

Put into a pre-heated very hot oven (230°C/450°F/Gas Mark 8) for 5 minutes. Allow to cool, then refrigerate. Serve chilled.

CHARLOTTE AUX FRAMBOISES
Raspberry charlotte

PREPARATION TIME: 10 minutes (plus 30 minutes the day before)
COOKING TIME: nil
FOR SIX TO EIGHT

750 g (generous 1½ lb) raspberries	350 g (scant 12½ oz) sponge fingers
250 g (scant 9 oz) ground almonds	100 g (3½ oz) flaked almonds
250 g (scant 9 oz) caster sugar	For the sauce:
250 g (scant 9 oz) butter	750 g (generous 1½ lb) raspberries
200 ml (7 fl oz) orange liqueur	350 g (scant 12½ oz) icing sugar

Begin with the almond filling. Gently brown the ground almonds under the grill, leave to cool. With an electric beater, thoroughly work the sugar and softened butter together, then add the ground almonds. The object is to achieve a light mousse, twice its original volume.

Butter a 23-cm (9-inch) soufflé dish. Mix the orange liqueur in a flat dish with an equal volume of water and one by one dip the sponge fingers into the mixture. Line the bottom and sides of the soufflé dish with sponge fingers, flat sides outwards and downwards. Fill the inside with successive layers of almond filling, broken sponge fingers and raspberries, beginning with almond filling and ending with broken biscuit. Be sure there is enough almond filling left to ice the whole cake. Break off any part of the lining-fingers sticking up above the rim, adding the pieces to the top layer. Press down lightly with the palm of the hand and put the charlotte overnight in the refrigerator, together with the remaining almond filling.

The following day, take the charlotte out of its dish and, with the help of a spatula, spread it all over with the rest of the almond-filling. Grill the flaked almonds, allow to cool and cover the top and sides of the charlotte with them.

To make the sauce, put raspberries and sugar through the blender together, pass through a sieve into a serving bowl. Decorate the cake with a few raspberries kept aside, and serve with its raspberry sauce.

FRAISES EN COURONNE
Crown of strawberries

PREPARATION TIME: 45 minutes
COOKING TIME: 40 minutes
FOR SIX

500 g (generous 1 lb)
  strawberries
200 g (7 oz) redcurrant jelly

For the cream:
250 ml (scant 9 fl oz) double
  cream
2 tablespoons vanilla sugar
2 tablespoons icing sugar

For the choux pastry:
1 small pinch of salt
50 g (scant 2 oz) butter
75 g (generous 2½ oz) sifted flour
3 eggs
50 g (scant 2 oz) flaked almonds

First make the pastry. Salt 125 ml (4½ fl oz) water, put in the butter, bring to the boil and when the butter has melted, remove the saucepan from the heat. Put all the flour in at once and beat the mixture vigorously with a wooden spoon. Return to a moderate heat for 2 minutes, still beating until the mixture comes away from the sides of the pan easily. Take pan off the heat and break an egg into the centre of mixture. Beat in thoroughly before adding the second egg. Beat thoroughly again. Lightly whisk the third egg separately in a bowl, add half to the mixture and keep the rest aside. Continue to beat the pastry mixture vigorously as it thickens.

Using an icing-bag with a 1-cm (½-in) nozzle, pipe a pastry ring 21 cm (8½ in) in diameter onto a buttered baking sheet. Brush it with the rest of the beaten egg and sprinkle it with flaked almonds. Bake it in a moderate oven (180°C/350°F/Gas Mark 4) with the oven door ajar for the first 5 minutes, then closed for a further 35 minutes. Check the colour occasionally to see that the pastry is not over-cooking. Remove, allow to cool and split the ring into halves.

Whip the cream with the vanilla sugar and 1 tablespoon icing sugar. Spread the bottom pastry half generously with whipped cream, place the other half on top, sprinkle with the remaining icing sugar and
(CONTINUED OPPOSITE)

ABRICOTS À LA CRÈME
Apricots with crème pâtissière

PREPARATION TIME: 20 minutes
COOKING TIME: 10 minutes
FOR SIX

750 g (generous 1½ lb) apricots
3 egg yolks
40 g (scant 1½ oz) flour
150 g (5 oz) caster sugar
500 ml (17½ fl oz) milk

100 ml (3½ fl oz) rum or brandy
100 g (3½ oz) lump sugar
50 g (scant 2 oz) flaked almonds
  icing sugar

Begin by making the crème pâtissière. Work egg yolks, flour and caster sugar together thoroughly. Warm the milk and blend it in: pour the mixture into a saucepan, put it over a low heat and stir as it thickens. Add a tablespoon of rum and transfer the cream to an ovenproof dish.

Halve the apricots and remove the stones. Make a syrup with the lump sugar and 200 ml (7 fl oz) of water, bring it to the boil and poach the apricot halves in it for 3 minutes. Remove, drain and reduce the syrup to half its volume.

Arrange the apricot halves, cut sides downwards, on top of the cream. Sprinkle with flaked almonds and icing sugar, pour on the syrup and put the dish quickly under a hot grill. At the moment of serving, pour flaming rum over the dish. Serve at once.

(CONTINUED)

carefully transfer the ring to its serving dish.

Wash, dry and hull the strawberries, and pile them inside the centre of the pastry ring. Warm the redcurrant jelly in a saucepan to liquefy it and serve separately.

Elle advises that the firmness of the pastry should be checked before adding the half of beaten egg to it. The pastry must not be allowed to become so floppy that it spreads itself out on the baking sheet.

TARTE AUX FRAISES ET AUX ABRICOTS
Apricot and strawberry tart

PREPARATION TIME: 15 minutes (2 hours beforehand)
COOKING TIME: about 20 minutes
FOR SIX TO EIGHT

6 ripe apricots
500 g (generous 1 lb)
  strawberries
200 g (7 oz) flour
1 pinch of salt

1 teaspoon sugar
100 g (3½ oz) butter
1 glass (5 fl oz) water
2 tablespoons icing sugar

Sift the flour into a mixing bowl and, using the fingers, work it together with the salt, the sugar, the softened butter (divided into small pieces), and half of the water. Work quickly to make a firm but supple dough, using only as much as necessary of the remaining water. Roll into a ball and leave to stand for 2 hours in a cool place.

Roll out the pastry and line a buttered 25-cm (10-inch) flan tin with it. Blind-bake it: prick the bottom all over with a fork, cover first with greaseproof paper, then a layer of dried beans. Cook for 10–12 minutes in a very hot oven (230°C/450°F/Gas Mark 8). Take it out of the oven, remove beans and paper and leave to cool.

Wash and hull the strawberries; keep them whole. Stone the apricots and cut them into slices. Fill the pastry-case with a mixture of the two fruits and sprinkle the surface with icing sugar. Put into a very hot oven (240°C/475°F/Gas Mark 9) for 10 minutes.

Elle advises that to prevent the pastry becoming soggy from the juices given out by the fruit during cooking, four sponge fingers should be arranged on the bottom of the pastry case before the fruit is put in.

TARTE MOUSSEUSE AUX ABRICOTS
Apricot cream tart

PREPARATION TIME: 50 minutes (2 hours in advance)
COOKING TIME: 50 minutes
FOR SIX TO EIGHT

500 g (generous 1 lb) apricots
50 g (scant 2 oz) icing sugar

For the pastry:
250 g (scant 9 oz) flour
125 g (4½ oz) butter
1 egg yolk
1 pinch of salt
1 teaspoon sugar
200 ml (7 fl oz) water

For the cream:
330 ml (scant 12 fl oz) milk
½ vanilla pod
3 eggs
100 g (3½ oz) caster sugar
50 g (scant 2 oz) flour

Begin by making the pastry in the usual way with the ingredients listed. Roll out the pastry, line a 25-cm (10-inch) flan tin and blind-bake it by covering the pastry with greaseproof paper and a layer of dried beans. The pastry will require 10 minutes in a moderate oven (180°C/350°F/Gas Mark 4).

The cream is prepared by first boiling the milk with the vanilla pod. Separate the egg yolks from the whites and mix the beaten yolks and sugar together. Sift on the flour and mix in thoroughly. Remove the vanilla pod and add the milk, little by little, to the pan and let the mixture thicken over a low heat while stirring continuously. At the first bubble, remove from the heat.

Beat the egg whites stiffly and carefully fold in the hot cream mixture. Pour it all into the pastry case and spread it evenly.

Cut the apricots in half and remove their stones. Arrange them in the cream, cut-side upwards. Crack the stones, remove the kernels and use them to decorate the apricot halves. Cook in a cool oven (150°C/300°F/Gas Mark 2) for about 40 minutes.

Sprinkle with icing sugar and serve either warm or cold.

TARTE LONGUE AUX FRAISES
Long thin strawberry tart

PREPARATION TIME: 20 minutes (during the morning if the tart is to be served the same evening)
COOKING TIME: 25 minutes
FOR SIX

750 g (generous 1½ lb)   1 egg
    strawberries   100 g (3½ oz) redcurrant jelly
400 g (14 oz) frozen puff pastry

Before starting to cook, make sure the pastry is thoroughly defrosted.

Roll out the pastry on a floured board to a thickness of 5 mm (bare ¼ inch). Cut one strip 10 cm (4 inches) wide and the length of your baking sheet. With beaten egg, stick a narrow strip about 12-mm (½-inch) wide along the top of each long outside edge of the pastry. Slash the edges diagonally with a sharp knife every 12 mm (½ inch) to the full depth of both layers of pastry: this will help the pastry to puff up properly.

Place the pastry on a greased baking sheet and lightly brush all over with beaten egg. Cook in a very hot oven (240°C/475°F/Gas Mark 9) for 20 minutes, then reduce the heat to a moderate oven (180°C/350°F/Gas Mark 4). Continue to cook until the surface is a golden-brown and the base of the pastry thoroughly cooked.

Hull the strawberries and quickly wash and dry the fruit. Arrange the whole berries on the pastry. Put the redcurrant jelly into a saucepan with 4 tablespoons of water. Mix and let it simmer for 10 minutes over a low heat. Stir into a rich syrup, let it cool, then pour it over the strawberries just before serving.

Elle advises that the pastry should be rolled out in advance and made up and left to rest in a refrigerator. Just before cooking, the pastry should be lightly brushed with beaten egg. The egg must not be given time to soak into the pastry.

If the redcurrant syrup is also prepared beforehand, very little will be left to do at the last moment.

POMMÉ
Apple puffs

PREPARATION TIME: 30 minutes (from rolling out the pastry)
COOKING TIME: 1 hour 10 minutes
FOR SIX

1½ kg (3¼ lb) firm eating apples   30 g (1 oz) vanilla sugar (see
250 g (scant 9 oz) best apricot   p.16)
    jam   500 g (generous 1 lb) puff pastry
150 g (5 oz) caster sugar   1 egg

Peel and core the apples and cut them into pieces. Mix the apple with the apricot jam, and the two sugars.

Roll out half the pastry to a thickness of 4 mm (⅛ inch) and lay it out on a lightly-floured baking sheet. Brush the surface with beaten egg.

Arrange the apple mixture in an even layer in the centre of the pastry, leaving a border about 2½-cm (1-inch) wide all the way round. Roll out the second half of the pastry and cover the tart; press down the edges, then slash the edges diagonally all round at regular intervals. Brush the top with beaten egg, making sure that none drips down into the slashed cuts since this will prevent the puff pastry from rising completely.

Score the surface of the pastry to indicate 12 equal portions and decorate at will. Cook for about 1 hour 10 minutes, beginning with a very hot oven (230°C/450°F/Gas Mark 8). Check the progress of cooking and reduce the heat to 200°C/400°F/Gas Mark 6 and cover with greaseproof paper as the pastry browns.

Allow to cool a little before dividing the tart.

EL MÉNÉNAS
Date and nut pastries

PREPARATION TIME: 30 minutes
COOKING TIME: 30 minutes
FOR SIX

*250 g (scant 9 oz) preserved
   dates*
50 g (scant 2 oz) almonds
50 g (scant 2 oz) hazelnuts
50 g (scant 2 oz) pistachio nuts
500 g (generous 1 lb) flour

300 g (10½ oz) butter
2 teaspoons orange essence
100 g (3½ oz) caster sugar
½ teaspoon powdered cinnamon
1 egg

First make the pastry by working together the flour and 250 g (scant 9 oz) butter, cut into small pieces. Moisten with about 50 ml (1¾ fl oz) water and the orange essence. When the dough is firm but supple, form it into a sausage shape about 30 cm (12 inches) long.

   Cut the pastry into 20 round slices, roll each into a ball and, with the fingers, open into a pocket.

   Finely chop up the dates and the nuts and thoroughly mix in the rest of the butter, the caster sugar and the powdered cinnamon, making a paste. Divide into 20 parts, roll each one into a ball and put it into a pastry case. Close up the entrance to make a smooth ball of pastry, and brush with beaten egg.

   Arrange the pastries on a buttered baking-sheet and cook for 30 minutes in a hot oven (220°C/425°F/Gas Mark 7).

<u>Elle advises</u> that puff pastry can equally well be used.

FEUILLETÉS DE POIRES
Pear puffs

PREPARATION TIME: 1 hour
COOKING TIME: 25 minutes
FOR SIX

400 g (14 oz) puff pastry
1 egg
flour
icing sugar

For the filling:
400 g (14 oz) granulated sugar
1 vanilla pod
3 good pears

For the almond cream:
100 g (3½ oz) butter
100 g (3½ oz) caster sugar
100 g (3½ oz) ground almonds
10 g (⅓ oz) flour
1 egg

Roll out the pastry to a thickness of 3 mm (⅛ inch) and cut it into 6 oblong pieces about 10×5 cm (4×2 inches). Dust a baking sheet lightly with flour, lay out the pastries, brush them with beaten egg and cook in a very hot oven (230°C/450°F/Gas Mark 8) for 15 minutes.

   Proceed to make the almond cream. Work butter and sugar together, add the ground almonds, sift on the flour, and finally incorporate the beaten egg. Mix to a smooth paste; put to one side.

   For the filling, first make a syrup with the sugar, 1 litre (1¾ pints) of water and the vanilla pod. Bring it to the boil. Peel the pears, cut them in half lengthways and core. Poach them in the syrup, at a slow boil, for 8–10 minutes. Remove and drain.

   Split the pastries in half and spread the bottom halves with almond cream. Slice the pear halves and arrange them in layers on top of the cream. Cover with the top halves of the pastries, sprinkle with icing sugar and serve while they are warm.

TARTELETTES AUX AMANDES
Almond tartlets

PREPARATION TIME: 10 minutes
COOKING TIME: 20 minutes
FOR SIX

300 g (10½ oz) flaked almonds　　*6 tablespoons crème fraîche*
3 tablespoons honey　　*1 packet of frozen puff pastry*
2 tablespoons caster sugar

Put honey, caster sugar and crème fraîche into a bowl and thoroughly mix them together. Stir in the flaked almonds.

Roll out the puff pastry to a thickness of about 5 mm (bare ¼ inch) and cut 6 rounds of pastry. Line individual patty tins with the pastry and fill each one with a good spoonful of almond mixture.

Cook in a fairly hot oven (200°C/400°F/Gas Mark 6) for 15–20 minutes. The tartlets will be done when the pastry is a light golden-brown and the almonds browned: if they seem to be cooking too quickly, cover the tin with a sheet of greaseproof paper. Serve while still warm.

Elle says that if the honey is hard and crystallised, gently heat it in a double boiler until it is liquid.

(CONTINUED)

Mix the peel strips into the cream and pour into the pastry case (having removed paper and dried beans). Spread evenly.

Wash the rest of the oranges and, without peeling them, cut them into thin slices. Arrange these in layers on top of the cream. Sprinkle the remaining sugar over the top and put the tart under a hot grill until the surface is caramelised.

TART À L'ORANGE
Orange tart

PREPARATION TIME: 20 minutes
COOKING TIME: 30 minutes
FOR SIX TO EIGHT

6 good oranges
3 eggs
175 g (6¼ oz) sugar
15 g (½ oz) vanilla sugar (see p.16)
50 g (scant 2 oz) flour
500 ml (17½ fl oz) milk
salt
Grand-Marnier

For the pastry:
125 g (4½ oz) butter
75 g (generous 2½ oz) sugar
250 g (scant 9 oz) flour
1 egg
salt

First make the pastry in the usual way from the ingredients given. When the dough is made, divide it into four pieces, place them on top of one another and press together with the fingertips. Repeat this operation three times, roll the dough into a ball and leave to rest for 1 hour.

Roll out the pastry to a thickness of 5 mm (bare ¼ inch). Line a lightly-buttered 25-cm (10-inch) flan dish with the pastry. Blind-bake it by covering the bottom first with greaseproof paper, then with a layer of dried beans. Cook for 25 minutes in a very hot oven (230°C/450°F/Gas Mark 8).

To make the filling, beat together 2 egg yolks, 100 g (3½ oz) sugar and the vanilla sugar. Sift in the flour and mix thoroughly. Add 1 whole egg and continue to beat until a smooth and even mixture results.

Boil the milk with a little salt and pour it slowly into the egg mixture, beating the whole time. Return the pan to the heat and, still beating, bring to the boil. Allow to bubble 2 or 3 times, remove from the heat, stir in a small glass of Grand-Marnier.

Peel one orange and cut the skin into thin strips. Blanch them for 1 minute in boiling water. Remove and rinse under cold running water.
(CONTINUED OPPOSITE)

FLAN DOURLAISIEN
Apple and almond pie

PREPARATION TIME: 40 minutes
COOKING TIME: 55 minutes
FOR SIX TO EIGHT

2 kg (scant 4½ lb) firm eating apples
300 g (10½ oz) puff pastry
100 g (3½ oz) ground almonds
2 eggs
200 g (7 oz) butter
100 g (3½ oz) caster sugar
vanilla essence
icing sugar

For the crème pâtissière:
6 eggs
200 g (7 oz) caster sugar
100 g (3½ oz) flour
salt
30 g (1 oz) vanilla sugar (see p.16)
1 litre (1¾ pints) milk
10 g (⅓ oz) butter

First make the crème pâtissière. Beat 5 egg yolks with the caster sugar until the sugar is completely absorbed. Sift in the flour, mix, add 1 whole egg and continue beating until a smooth creamy mixture is achieved.

Put a pinch of salt and the vanilla sugar into the milk and bring it to the boil. Add it slowly to the egg mixture, whisking constantly. Put the pan on the heat, still whisking, until the mixture has begun to bubble. Remove from the heat, cover with greaseproof paper and leave to cool.

Peel and core the apples and cut them into quarters. Roll out the puff pastry on a lightly-floured board and line a high-sided flan dish about 25 cm (10 inches) in diameter. Pour in half the crème pâtissière, add the quartered apples and cover with the remainder of the cream.

In a bowl, mix together the ground almonds, 2 beaten eggs, 100 g (3½ oz) melted butter, the caster sugar and 1 or 2 drops of vanilla essence. Pour this over the surface of the pie and finish off with a good layer of icing sugar. Dot the surface with the rest of the butter divided into knobs and cook in a very hot oven (240°C/475°F/Gas Mark 9) for 45 minutes.

GÂTEAUX AUX ABRICOTS
Apricot flan

PREPARATION TIME: 20 minutes (1 hour in advance)
COOKING TIME: 50 minutes
FOR EIGHT TO TEN

750 g (generous 1½ lb) apricots
100 g (3½ oz) flour
100 g (3½ oz) butter
200 g (7 oz) caster sugar
30 g (1 oz) vanilla sugar (see p.16)
75 g (generous 2½ oz) ground almonds
250 g (scant 9 oz) crème fraîche

For the pastry:
½ glass (2½ fl oz) milk
5 g (⅙ oz) fresh yeast
250 g (scant 9 oz) flour
60 ml (2 fl oz) peanut oil
60 g (2 oz) butter
1 egg
1 tablespoon sugar
1 pinch salt

To make the pastry, begin by warming the milk and stirring the yeast into it. Pile the flour onto the working surface, make a well in its centre and pour in the oil, the melted butter, the yeast and milk, the egg, the sugar and a pinch of salt. Knead everything together with the fingertips to make a firm and supple dough. Roll it into a ball and leave it to rest in a warm place for 1 hour.

During this time, prepare the filling. Wash the apricots, cut them in half and remove their stones. On a pastry board, mix together the flour, the softened butter divided into pieces, the caster and vanilla sugars and the ground almonds into a crumbly mixture.

Take the ball of dough and spread it out with the hands until it is large enough to line a 25-cm (10-inch) flan tin. Arrange the apricots on the pastry, cut-side downwards, in a layer and cover them evenly with the ground-almond mixture. Cook in a moderate oven (180°C/350°F/Gas Mark 4) for 50 minutes.

Serve warm with a bowl of cream.

Elle says that if fresh apricots are not available, well-drained tinned ones may be used instead.

TARTE AUX CERISES NOIRES
Black cherry tart

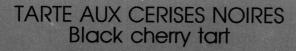

PREPARATION TIME: 30 minutes
COOKING TIME: 30 minutes
FOR SIX

750 g (generous 1 ½ lb) black cherries	
20 g (¾ oz) flour	*For the pastry:*
100 g (3½ oz) caster sugar	*250 g (scant 9 oz) flour*
30 g (1 oz) butter	*125 g (4½ oz) butter*
50 g (scant 2 oz) icing sugar	*½ glass (2½ fl oz) water*
	salt

Begin with the pastry. On a pastry board, work together with the fingers, the flour and the softened butter divided into pieces. Add the salted water, roll the dough into a ball and leave in a cool place to rest for 15 minutes.

Roll out the pastry. Butter and lightly flour a 25-cm (10-inch) flan tin and line it with the pastry. Wash the cherries carefully and remove their stones.

Proceed to the filling. Mix flour and caster sugar together and spread it evenly over the bottom of the pastry case. Arrange the cherries in a layer on top and dot them with knobs of butter. Cook in a very hot oven (240°C/475°F/Gas Mark 9) for 25–30 minutes. Remove from oven, sprinkle with icing sugar and serve warm.

FROMAGÉ AUX FRUITS DE LA PASSION
Passion fruit cheesecake

PREPARATION TIME: 40 minutes (1 hour in advance)
COOKING TIME: 35 minutes
FOR SIX

750 g (generous 1 ½ lb) passion fruit	*1 large ripe pear*
	extra sugar
100 ml (3½ fl oz) milk	
15 g (½ oz) butter	*For the pastry:*
50 g (scant 2 oz) sugar	*125 g (4½ oz) butter*
salt	*75 g (generous 2½ oz) sugar*
1 lemon	*salt*
100 g (3½ oz) fromage blanc	*1 egg*
2 eggs	*250 g (scant 9 oz) flour*
20 g (¾ oz) flour	

Begin by making the pastry and blind-baking it in a 23-cm (9-inch) flan dish in the usual way (*see* p.173).

To make the filling, bring the milk to the boil, remove from heat and stir in the butter, sugar and a pinch of salt, grated peel of ½ lemon and the fromage blanc. Beat the eggs and work them into the flour: mix this paste also into the warm milk. Return to the heat and bring momentarily to the boil.

Remove beans and paper from the pastry case and add a layer made up of the peeled and cored pear cut into thin slices. Sprinkle with a little lemon juice and then pour in the filling. Put in a very hot oven (240°C/475°F/Gas Mark 9) for 10 minutes.

Make a sauce by putting the flesh of the passion fruit through a blender with an equal weight of sugar. Serve the tart either hot or cold, with the passion fruit sauce separately.

From the restaurant 'Le Pré Catelan' in the Bois de Boulogne in Paris: the chef recommends a chilled Sauternes to accompany this dish.

TARTE AU FROMAGE BLANC
Savoury cheese flan

PREPARATION TIME: 20 minutes (1 hour in advance)
COOKING TIME: 50 minutes
FOR SIX

300 g (10½ oz) fromage blanc
4 eggs, separated
salt, pepper
1 pinch of grated nutmeg
1 small bunch of chives
1 small sprig of chervil
1 small bunch of parsley

For the pastry:
60 g (2 oz) margarine
120 g (scant 4½ fl oz) flour
salt

Divide the margarine into small pieces and, using the fingertips, work it completely into the flour. Moisten it with a little salted water and roll the dough into a ball. Let it rest for 1 hour.

Roll out the pastry and line a flan tin 23 cm (9 inches) in diameter.

Hand-beat the egg yolks and the fromage blanc together, season with salt, pepper and nutmeg. Using an electric beater, whisk the egg whites into a stiff foam. Carefully fold the cheese–egg mixture into the stiffened whites, together with all the herbs, finely chopped.

Cook in a very hot pre-heated oven (230°C/450°F/Gas Mark 8) for 45–50 minutes. Serve either hot or cold.

<u>Elle says</u> this herby dish is as much a savoury as a pudding.

TARTE AU MIEL ET AUX NOIX
Honey and walnut tart

PREPARATION TIME: 10 minutes (2 hours in advance)
COOKING TIME: 30 minutes
FOR SIX TO EIGHT

250 g (scant 9 oz) shelled walnuts
500 g (generous 1 lb) honey

For the pastry:
200 g (7 oz) flour
1 teaspoon sugar
1 pinch of salt
100 g (3½ oz) butter
1 glass (5 fl oz) water

First make the pastry. Sift the flour and work it together with the sugar, the pinch of salt, the butter, slightly softened, and about half the water. Moisten only sufficiently to ensure a firm but supple dough. Roll into a ball and leave to stand for 2 hours in a cool place.

Roll out the pastry on a lightly-floured board and line a 25-cm (10-inch) flan tin. Blind-bake it for 20 minutes in a very hot oven (230°C/450°F/Gas Mark 8) having lined the bottom with a sheet of greaseproof paper and a layer of dried beans.

Roughly chop the walnuts and stir them into the honey. Remove paper and beans from the pastry case and fill it with the honey–walnut mixture. Return the tart to the oven for 10 minutes.

Serve hot or cold.

SOUFFLÉ AU FROMAGE BLANC
Fromage blanc soufflé

PREPARATION TIME: 15 minutes
COOKING TIME: 1 hour
FOR SIX

700 g (generous 1½ lb) fromage
  blanc
160 g (generous 5½ oz) butter
6 eggs, separated

250 g (scant 9 oz) caster sugar
60 g (2 oz) fine semolina
1 lemon

Put the butter in a bowl and work it into a paste. Add the egg yolks and beat with an electric whisk until a light mousse results.

In a separate bowl, whisk the egg whites into a stiff foam, adding the caster sugar towards the end.

Take the butter-mousse and quickly mix in, all at the same time, the semolina, the fromage blanc and the grated peel of 1 lemon. Carefully fold in the egg whites with a spatula and fill a buttered soufflé dish with the mixture. Cook in a moderate oven (160°C/325°F/Gas Mark 3) for up to 1 hour.

SOUFFLÉ GLACÉ AUX ABRICOTS
Iced apricot soufflé

PREPARATION TIME: 25 minutes (5 hours in advance)
COOKING TIME: 10 minutes
FOR EIGHT

750 g (generous 1½ lb) apricots
100 g (3½ oz) lump sugar
4 eggs, separated
1 small glass apricot brandy

100 ml (3½ fl oz) milk
500 ml (generous 17½ fl oz)
  double cream

Halve the apricots and remove their stones. Make a syrup with the lump sugar and 200 ml (7 fl oz) water. Bring it to the boil: plunge in the halved apricots and bring the syrup back to the boil. Gently poach the apricots in syrup for about 8 minutes. Remove from the heat, drain the apricots and put to one side.

Boil up the syrup until it thickens. Whisk the whites of the eggs into a stiff foam, and, beating continuously, pour the boiling syrup into the egg white mixture. The beating should go on while the mixture cools. Put to one side in the refrigerator.

Make a fruit purée by putting the poached apricots through a blender. Stir in the apricot brandy and put in a cool place. Beat the milk and double cream together to make a light cream.

Surround a 16-cm (6½-inch) soufflé dish with buttered greaseproof paper as described on page 178. Using a spatula, carefully fold together the apricot purée, the cream mixture and the beaten egg whites. Fill the soufflé dish with the mixture up to the level of the top of the paper ring and put into a freezer for a minimum of 5 hours. Remove the paper just before serving.

<u>Elle reminds</u> that the soufflé should be transferred from freezer to refrigerator about 30 minutes before it is to be served.

SOUFFLÉ GLACÉ AU CAFÉ
Iced coffee soufflé

PREPARATION TIME: 40 minutes (3 hours beforehand)
COOKING TIME: nil
FOR SIX TO EIGHT

1 tablespoon coffee essence	200 g (7 oz) crème fraîche
200 g (7 oz) sugar lumps	100 g (3½ oz) icing sugar
6 egg whites	chocolate coffee beans

Soak the sugar lumps in about 100 ml (3½ fl oz) water and prepare a caramel with them. Whisk the egg whites into a stiff foam and pour the boiling caramel in a thin stream around the inner edges of the bowl while continuing to whisk vigorously. Set the mixture aside to cool.

Beat the crème fraîche and the icing sugar into a light cream, stir in the coffee essence and fold the whole very carefully into the stiff egg whites.

Butter a piece of greaseproof paper and completely surround the outside of a 20-cm (8-inch) soufflé dish (butter side inwards) so that the paper stands about 3 cm (1 inch) proud of the top rim of the dish. It may be necessary to hold the paper in place with string. Fill the dish with the soufflé mixture up to the level of the top of the paper and put the dish in a freezer for at least 3 hours.

Just before serving, remove the paper band and decorate the surface with chocolate (imitation) coffee beans.

ORANGE SOUFFLÉE
Orange soufflé

PREPARATION TIME: 25 minutes
COOKING TIME: 40 minutes
FOR SIX

3 egg yolks	For the orange custard:
75 g (2½ oz) caster sugar	500 ml (17½ fl oz) milk
25 g (scant 1 oz) flour	4 egg yolks
½ teaspoon cornflour	150 g (5 oz) caster sugar
250 ml (scant 9 fl oz) milk	grated orange peel
2 oranges	1 small glass orange liqueur
4 egg whites	
6 sponge biscuits	
150 ml (5 fl oz) orange liqueur	

Begin with the orange custard. Boil the milk; put the egg yolks and the caster sugar into a saucepan and whisk them together. Gradually add the milk, still whisking. Put the pan over heat and stir the mixture continuously while it thickens into a cream. Do not let the mixture boil and take it off the heat when it is thick enough to coat the back of a spoon. Let it cool, then stir in the grated orange peel and the orange liqueur. Remove to the refrigerator.

To make the soufflé, begin by whisking the 3 egg yolks and the caster sugar together with an electric egg beater. Sift in the flour and cornflour, mix and while still beating, slowly pour in the hot milk. Put over heat, bring just to the boil, take off the heat, leave to cool, and then stir in the grated peel of the oranges and the juice of one of them. Whisk the egg whites until stiff and fold carefully into the mixture.

Butter a 20-cm (8-inch) soufflé dish and line the bottom with 2 sponge fingers quickly soaked in orange liqueur. Add a layer of soufflé mixture, then 2 more soaked biscuits, another layer of soufflé mixture, the remaining biscuits, and finish up with the rest of the mixture. Cook in a very hot oven (230°C/450°F/Gas Mark 8) for 25–30 minutes. Serve straight from the oven with the orange custard presented separately.

GÂTEAU AUX MYRTILLES
Bilberry cheesecake

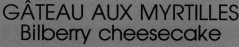

PREPARATION TIME: 1 hour
COOKING TIME: 25–30 minutes
FOR SIX

*1 jar 400 g (14 oz) preserved
  bilberries
300 g (10½ oz) fromage blanc
2 egg yolks
½ lemon
125 g (4½ oz) caster sugar
6 leaves of gelatine
300 g (10½ oz) whipped crème
  fraîche*

*For the Genoese sponge:
2 eggs
100 g (3½ oz) caster sugar
30 g (1 oz) vanilla sugar (see
  p.16)
100 g (3½ oz) flour
1 tablespoon ground almonds*

Begin by making the sponge. Beat the eggs, the caster sugar and the vanilla sugar together until the mixture pours in an unbroken ribbon. Sift in the flour and the ground almonds little by little, beating vigorously.

Line the bottom of a round sponge tin (21-cm/8½-inch diameter) with a piece of buttered greaseproof paper, pour in the sponge mixture and spread it evenly with a spatula. Cook in a hot oven (220°C/425°F/ Gas Mark 7) for 20 minutes. Turn out the sponge and leave it to cool.

The filling is made by first mixing the fromage blanc with the egg yolks, grated peel of half a lemon, sugar and the gelatine. The gelatine should have been soaked in cold water, drained and melted in a double boiler. Finally stir in the whipped crème fraîche.

Line the edges of the sponge tin with a strip of greaseproof paper. Split the sponge into two halves and put one-half, cut side upwards, into the sponge tin. Spread it with a thick layer with the whole of the cream–cheese mixture, leave for 5–8 minutes then add a layer of drained bilberries. Squeeze the juice of ½ lemon over the fruit, then finish off with the second sponge slice. Press it down with the palm of the hand and leave in the refrigerator (not in the freezer) for at least 1 hour. Turn out the cheesecake, remove the paper and serve.

DÉLICE AUX POMMES
Apple delight

PREPARATION TIME: 30 minutes
COOKING TIME: 10 minutes
FOR SIX TO EIGHT

*1 Genoese sponge (21 cm/8½
  inches in diameter) (see facing
  recipe)
50 ml (1¾ fl oz) white rum
icing sugar*

*For the filling:
1 kg (1¾ lb) firm eating apples
50 g (scant 2 oz) raisins
100 ml (3½ fl oz) white rum
100 g (3½ oz) butter
50 g (scant 2 oz) caster sugar
250 g (scant 9 oz) redcurrant jelly*

*For the crème pâtissière:
3 eggs
100 g (3½ oz) caster sugar
15 g (½ oz) vanilla sugar (see
  p. 00)
50 g (scant 2 oz) flour
500 ml (17½ fl oz) milk
salt
100 g (3½ oz) butter
50 ml (1¾ fl oz) white rum*

Begin by making the crème pâtissière: mix 2 egg yolks and the sugars thoroughly together. Sift in the flour, add the third egg, whole, and beat to a smooth cream. Boil the milk with a pinch of salt and pour it into the mixture, beating continuously. Put the pan on the heat and go on stirring to prevent the mixture sticking to the bottom of the pan. Let the mixture bubble a few times, remove from the heat and allow to cool a little. While it is still warm, whisk in the butter, cut into small pieces. Flavour with the white rum and put to one side.

For the filling, soak the raisins in rum. Peel and core the apples and cut them first into quarters, then into thin slices. Warm the butter and sugar in a pan, add the apple and let it cook lightly. Drain the raisins and add them to the apple.

Halve the sponge and sprinkle the cut surfaces with the 50 ml (1¾ fl oz) rum. Spread the lower half with half the apple and raisin. Next add a layer of redcurrant jelly, then all the crème pâtissière. Follow with another layer of redcurrant jelly, the rest of the apple and finally the top slice of sponge. Sprinkle with icing sugar before serving.

GÂTEAU AU CARAMEL
Nut-cream cake

PREPARATION TIME: 35 minutes (24 hours in advance)
COOKING TIME: 40 minutes
FOR SIX

8 eggs, separated
500 g (generous 1 lb) shelled hazelnuts
750 g (generous 1½ lb) caster sugar

50 g (scant 2 oz) flour
30 g (1 oz) vanilla sugar (see p.16)
250 g (scant 9 oz) butter

Whisk the egg whites until very stiff. Chop half the hazelnuts in a blender, mix with 250 g (scant 9 oz) sugar and the flour and fold the whole with a spatula into the egg whites. Divide the mixture into halves and put them into two buttered sponge tins about 23 cm (9 inches) in diameter. Spread into even layers and cook in a fairly hot oven (200°C/400°F/Gas Mark 6) for about 40 minutes.

Put the egg yolks, 250 g (scant 9 oz) sugar and the vanilla sugar into a heavy iron casserole. Put over a gentle heat and thoroughly beat the mixture, adding the butter, knob by knob. The aim is a thick creamy mixture: remove from the heat from time to time while beating. When ready, put to one side.

Just cover the remaining sugar with water and melt it into a syrup over a low heat. Roughly chop the rest of the hazelnuts and stir them into the syrup. Then mix the nuts into the creamy mixture, stirring briskly: the pieces of hazelnut should crystallise as they cool.

Turn out the two sponges and spread half the nut–cream mixture evenly on one of them. Cap it with the second sponge and decorate the whole outside with the rest of the nut–cream. Refrigerate before serving: the cake will be at its best if it is chilled for 24 hours.

(CONTINUED)

Decorate all round the edge with whole hazelnuts. Chop up those nuts remaining and sprinkle them over the sides and top of the cake. Chill thoroughly before serving.

NOISETINE
Hazelnut cake

PREPARATION TIME: 1 hour
COOKING TIME: 40 minutes
FOR SIX

150 g (5 oz) grilled whole hazelnuts
100 g (3½ oz) ground hazelnuts
100 g (3½ oz) flour
5 eggs
160 g (5½ oz) caster sugar
30 g (1 oz) vanilla sugar (see p.16)

For the butter-cream:
200 g (7 oz) caster sugar
3 egg whites
300 g (10½ oz) butter
50 g (scant 2 oz) ground hazelnuts

Sift together the flour and the 100 g (3½ oz) of ground hazelnuts. Beat the 5 eggs, the caster sugar and the vanilla sugar in a bowl over a pan of hot water. When the mixture is frothy, take the bowl from the hot water and continue to beat as the mixture cools. Add the flour–hazelnut mixture and turn the whole into a round buttered cake tin about 23 cm (9 inches) in diameter. Cook in a fairly hot oven (200°C/400°F/Gas Mark 6) for 5 minutes, lower to a moderate heat (180°C/350°F/Gas Mark 4) and leave the oven door ajar. Continue cooking until a sharp pointed knife can be withdrawn clean. Remove from the oven, turn it out onto a wire rack and leave to cool.

For the butter-cream, moisten the 200 g (7 oz) sugar with water and make a syrup. Allow it to thicken up to the point where the syrup poured from a spoon does not break up into separate drops.

Whisk the egg whites until stiff and beat in the hot syrup in a thin stream. Continue to beat while the mixture cools. Soften the butter by working it with a fork and add it little by little to the egg whites, together with 50 g (scant 2 oz) ground hazelnuts.

Divide the cake horizontally into three equal slices. Spread one-third of the butter-cream on the lowest slice, put the second slice on top and in turn put on another layer of one-third of the cream. Cap with the final slice and decorate the cake with the rest of the cream.

(CONTINUED OPPOSITE)

ROCHER AU CHOCOLAT AMER
Bitter chocolate cake

PREPARATION TIME: 30 minutes
COOKING TIME: 25 minutes
FOR SIX TO EIGHT

6 egg whites
200 g (7 oz) caster sugar
100 g (3½ oz) ground almonds
100 g (3½ oz) ground hazelnuts
1 level tablespoon flour

250 g (scant 9 oz) bitter chocolate
1 litre (1¾ pints) whipping cream
450 g (1 lb) icing sugar
125 g (4½ oz) plain chocolate

Using an electric beater, whisk the egg whites until foamy. As they begin to stiffen, add first, little by little, the caster sugar, then the ground almonds, the ground hazelnuts and the flour, sifted in. Divide the mixture into three parts and make three rounds about 10-mm (⅖-inch) thick, on a buttered baking sheet. Cook in a moderate oven (180°C/350°F/Gas Mark 4) for about 20 minutes. As soon as they are cooked, take them off the baking sheet and place them on top of one another. Trim them so they are all the same size and evenness.

Break up the bitter chocolate and melt it slowly in a double boiler, stirring frequently. Whip the cream with a hand whisk and divide in half. Stir half the icing sugar into one portion of whipped cream, give it a few turns of the electric beater and put to one side.

Mix the second portion of cream with the melted chocolate and the rest of the icing sugar. Put the cake together with plain cream on one layer and chocolate cream on the other: decorate the top and sides with the remainder of the chocolate cream.

Cover overall with flakes of chocolate, coarsely grated in a vegetable Mouli, and keep the cake in a cool place up to the moment of serving.

From the 'Hôtel Moderne' in Brioude in the Auvergne: the chef suggests that a chilled Sauternes should accompany this rich cake.

FONDANT AUX POIRES
Pear and chocolate gâteau

PREPARATION TIME: 1 hour (4 hours in advance)
COOKING TIME: 25 minutes
FOR SIX TO EIGHT

3 pears
250 g (scant 9 oz) caster sugar
1 lemon
4 tablespoons kirsch
100 g (3½ oz) whipping cream
25 g (scant 1 oz) caster sugar
30 g (1 oz) vanilla sugar (see p.16)
200 g (7 oz) plain chocolate

For the Genoese sponge:
2 eggs
100 g (3½ oz) caster sugar
100 g (3½ oz) flour
30 g (1 oz) vanilla sugar (see p.16)

For the crème pâtissière:
1 tablespoon cocoa powder
125 g (4½ oz) caster sugar
250 ml (scant 9 fl oz) milk
3 egg yolks
5 leaves of gelatine
400 g (14 oz) crème fraîche

Make the Genoese sponge as on p.179 (omitting the almonds).

Peel and core the pears and poach them for 10 minutes in a syrup made with the sugar, 250 ml (scant 9 fl oz) of water and the juice of the lemon. Remove, drain and cut up into largish pieces.

For the crème pâtissière, stir the cocoa powder and the sugar into the milk, bring to the boil and pour it over the beaten egg yolks. Beat over a moderate heat, without allowing the mixture to boil, until a smooth cream results. Add the gelatine leaves, pre-soaked in cold water, and stir while they dissolve. Let the crème pâtissière cool and, as it begins to stiffen, fold in the whipped crème fraîche.

Split the sponge horizontally into halves and sprinkle the cut surfaces with kirsch. Line a soufflé dish (the same size as the sponge) with greaseproof paper and put one piece of sponge, cut surface upwards, in the bottom. Spread on a layer of pears with the crème pâtissière on top. Add the second piece of sponge and refrigerate for about 4 hours. Turn out the gâteau and decorate with piped cream, whipped with the two sugars, and with coarsely-grated chocolate.

CRÊPES À LA FRAMBOISE
Raspberry pancakes

PREPARATION TIME: 35 minutes
COOKING TIME: about 20 minutes
FOR SIX

For the batter:
250 ml (scant 9 fl oz) milk
2 eggs
50 g (scant 2 oz) flour
50 g (scant 2 oz) clarified butter

For the filling:
either
800 g (1¾ lb) fresh raspberries
100 g (3½ oz) caster sugar
or
500 g (generous 1 lb) frozen
  raspberries
300 g (10½ oz) caster sugar
and
raspberry eau-de-vie
  (Framboise)
icing sugar

Make a pancake batter in the usual way with the ingredients given and cook 6 thin pancakes.

If you are using fresh raspberries, push them through a sieve and thoroughly mix the pulp and the caster sugar. With frozen raspberries, mix them with the sugar in a saucepan, bring to the boil, stirring from time to time. Pass through a sieve.

Fill each pancake with a good portion of raspberry pulp, roll it up and turn under the ends. Bring to the table in a dish and pour flaming eau-de-vie over the pancakes just before serving, and sprinkle with icing sugar.

<u>From 'Le Coq Hardy' restaurant in Bougival outside Paris:</u> the cele-brated chef says that your best Sauternes should be served with these delicious pancakes.

CAPRINETTES
Goat's cheese pancakes

PREPARATION TIME: 20 minutes (1 hour in advance)
COOKING TIME: 3–4 minutes per pancake
FOR SIX

250 g (scant 9 oz) fromage blanc
  (goat if possible)
50 g (scant 2 oz) white flour
50 g (scant 2 oz) wholewheat
  flour
2 eggs
30 g (1 oz) melted butter

50 ml (scant 2 fl oz) white Loire
  wine
1 pinch of salt
100 g (3½ oz) butter for cooking
caster sugar

Thoroughly drain the fromage blanc. In a bowl, make the pancake batter by mixing together the flours, the eggs, the cheese, the melted butter, the white wine, an equal volume of water and a pinch of salt. Leave to rest for at least an hour.

Heat a knob of butter on a pancake griddle and, as it froths, pour on a portion of batter. Cook each one on both sides, as with ordinary pancakes, and as they are done keep them warm in an oven with the door ajar. Sprinkle with sugar just before serving.

PAPANAS
Roumanian pancakes

PREPARATION TIME: 10 minutes (1 hour in advance)
COOKING TIME: 5 minutes each serving
FOR SIX

500 g (generous 1 lb) fromage
  blanc
4 eggs, separated
chopped fines herbes

200 g (7 oz) flour
200 ml (7 fl oz) cooking oil
crème fraîche

Turn the fromage blanc out into a sieve and let it drain for 1 hour.

Beat the yolks of the eggs and mix them with the cheese, the *fines herbes* and the sifted flour. Whisk the egg whites to a stiff foam, and with the aid of a spatula, carefully fold them into the cheese mixture.

Heat the oil in a frying pan and pour in small portions of batter to give pancakes about the size of drop scones. Cook in batches on both sides and keep each lot warm as they are done. Serve hot with crème fraîche.

PETITS GÂTEAUX AU FROMAGE
BLANC
Cheese buns

PREPARATION TIME: 20 minutes (2 hours in advance)
COOKING TIME: 20 minutes
FOR 20 BUNS

200 ml (7 fl oz) milk
120 g (scant 4½ oz) sugar
½ teaspoon salt
35 g (1¼ oz) fresh yeast
600 g (generous 1¼ lb) flour
2 beaten eggs
100 g (3½ oz) melted butter

For the filling:
400 g (generous 14 oz) crumbly
  fromage blanc
2 egg yolks
1 teaspoon grated lemon rind
2 tablespoons chopped rind of
  preserved lemons (see p.16)
1 tablespoon lemon juice
1 tablespoon sugar
1 tablespoon raisins

Warm the milk, stir in the sugar and the salt until they are dissolved. Crumble the yeast into 100 ml (3½ fl oz) warm water.

Sift the flour into a bowl, make a well and put in the yeast. Then slowly pour in the warmed milk, add the beaten eggs and the melted butter. Work everything together into a dough: it should be firm and supple and come away easily from the sides of the bowl. Roll the dough, put into a bowl, cover with a damp cloth and leave to rise in a warm place for 1½ hours.

During this time, make the filling. Mix the thoroughly drained cheese with the egg yolks, the lemon rinds, the lemon juice, the sugar and the raisins. Put to one side.

Lay the dough out on a lightly-floured board and divide it into 20 balls. Arrange them all on a greased baking sheet and leave to rest for 15–20 minutes. Hollow them out with the thumbs and put 2 spoonfuls of cheese mixture in each one. Cook in a fairly hot oven (200°C/400°F/Gas Mark 6) for about 20 minutes.

GÂTEAU PUNCH
Toby cake

PREPARATION TIME: 1 hour
COOKING TIME: 25–30 minutes
FOR SIX

3 eggs
100 g (3½ oz) caster sugar
100 g (3½ oz) flour
rum for flavouring
500 g (generous 1 lb) apricot jam

For the crème pâtissière:
4 egg yolks
125 g (4½ oz) caster sugar
30 g (1 oz) vanilla sugar (see p.16)
50 g (scant 2 oz) cornflour
500 ml (17½ fl oz) milk

For the icing:
200 g (7 oz) caster sugar
4 egg whites

Begin with the sponge. Break the 3 eggs into a round-bottomed bowl, stir in the sugar. Over a very low heat, beat the eggs and sugar until they have doubled in volume. Remove from the heat and continue beating while the mixture cools. Add the sifted flour, mix thoroughly and turn the whole out into a buttered and lightly-floured 20-cm (8-inch) cake tin. Cook in a cool oven (150°C/300°F/Gas Mark 2) for 20–35 minutes. The cake will be ready when a skewer comes out clean. Turn out onto a wire rack, leave to cool.

Next make the filling. Beat the egg yolks with the two sugars and the sifted cornflour. Boil the milk and stir it into the mixture, return the pan to the heat, bring just to the boil and remove from the heat. Allow to cool.

Split the sponge horizontally into two equal parts and sprinkle the two cut surfaces with rum. Spread the lower piece with the filling then top with the other piece of sponge.

Put the apricot jam through a blender and then boil it to reduce to a thick purée. Cover the top and sides of the cake with the apricot purée.

(CONTINUED OPPOSITE)

NOISETIER AU MIEL
Honey and hazelnut cake

PREPARATION TIME: 20 minutes
COOKING TIME: 40 minutes
FOR SIX

200 g (7 oz) clear honey
200 g (7 oz) shelled hazelnuts
3 whole eggs, separated
60 g (2 oz) caster sugar
100 ml (3½ fl oz) cooking oil

200 g (7 oz) flour
1 pinch of salt
2 egg whites
icing sugar

Finely chop the hazelnuts. In a bowl, mix egg yolks, honey and sugar together, then add the oil, the chopped nuts, the sifted flour, the pinch of salt and, finally, the egg whites whisked until stiff.

Butter and lightly flour a 20-cm (8-inch) round cake tin and pour the mixture into it. Cook in a fairly hot oven (200°C/400°F/Gas Mark 6) for 40 minutes. Check the progress of the cooking: the cake will be done when a skewer comes out clean.

Turn the cake out onto a wire cake rack while it is still hot. Allow to cool and decorate with icing sugar before serving.

Elle says this delicious cake goes well at elevenses or tea-time.

(CONTINUED)

Finally, make the icing. Moisten the sugar with a little water and bring it to the boil to make a syrup. Whisk the egg whites until stiff and pour in the syrup in a thin stream, beating continuously while the mixture cools. Pile the icing onto the top of the cake and form it into a dome with a spatula. Smooth it carefully and with a clean hot poker, burn a design, as shown, all round the cake.

DÉLICIEUX À L'ARMAGNAC
Brandy delight

PREPARATION TIME: 25 minutes
COOKING TIME: 45 minutes
FOR EIGHT

4 eggs, separated
125 g (4½ oz) caster sugar
125 g (4½ oz) flour
1½ teaspoons baking powder
30 g (1 oz) vanilla sugar (see
  p.16)

For the sauce:
250 g (scant 9 oz) butter
250 g (scant 9 oz) caster sugar
50 ml (1¾ fl oz) Armagnac

Beat the 4 egg yolks and the caster sugar together until the mixture pours from a spoon in an unbroken ribbon. Sift on the flour without mixing, whisk the egg whites stiff, put them on top of the flour and fold everything together with a spatula. Add baking powder and vanilla sugar.

Pour the mixture into a 23-cm (9-inch) cake tin and cook for 40 minutes in a moderate oven (180°C/350°F/Gas Mark 4). When cooked, turn out onto a wire cake rack placed in a dish of the same size (or larger).

Make the sauce by melting the butter over a low heat with the sugar and 200 ml (7 fl oz) water. When everything is melted, stir in the Armagnac and pour the sauce over the cake. The sauce must be very hot if it is to soak in thoroughly. Pour any spare sauce collecting in the bottom of the dish back into the saucepan, reheat it and pour this over the cake. Continue this operation until all the sauce is absorbed by the cake.

BRIOCHE LORRAINE
Puff cake

PREPARATION TIME: 15 minutes (the day before)
COOKING TIME: 30 minutes
FOR EIGHT TO TEN

375 g (generous 13 oz) flour
50 g (scant 2 oz) caster sugar
3 eggs
150 g (5 oz) crème fraîche

1 pinch of salt
20 g (⅔ oz) fresh yeast
100 g (3½ oz) butter

The day before, mix together flour, sugar, eggs, crème fraîche, salt, and the yeast dissolved in a little warm water. Leave to stand overnight.

The following day, sprinkle the dough with a little extra flour. Flour a pastry board and roll out the dough into an oblong shape. Dot the surface with the butter cut into knobs, fold the dough over to enclose the butter and roll it out once more. Now fold it in three and again roll it out. Repeat this last operation twice more and finally roll out the dough to an oblong about 60 cm×40 cm (24×16 inches). Roll the pastry into a long sausage from its longer edge and cut it into slices about 5 cm (2 inches) long.

Arrange the slices on end in a buttered cake tin, about 2 cm (¾ inch) apart. The top of the slices should be about on a level with the rim of the tin. Cook in a fairly hot oven (190°C/375°F/Gas Mark 5) for 30 minutes.

The brioche is most delicious when warm.

GÂTEAU COCOTTE
Rum cake

PREPARATION TIME: 10 minutes
COOKING TIME: 45 minutes
FOR SIX

200 g (7 oz) flour	*3 eggs*
2 teaspoons baking powder	*2 tablespoons rum*
200 g (7 oz) caster sugar	*100 ml (3½ fl oz) milk*
½ teaspoon salt	*100 ml (3½ fl oz) peanut oil*

Sift flour and baking powder together in a bowl, add the sugar and the salt. Make a well in the middle of the flour and break the eggs into it. Mix thoroughly, stir the rum into the milk and add to the bowl, followed by the oil.

Butter a round ovenproof glass dish 20 cm (8 inches) in diameter, and pour in the mixture. Cover with lid and cook in a fairly hot oven (200°C/400°F/Gas Mark 6), without lifting the lid, for 45 minutes.

Check that the cake is cooked by inserting a skewer: it should come out clean. Turn out onto a wire cake rack and leave it to cool.

<u>Elle advises</u> that the cake will be at its best if made the day before and eaten at the end of the meal accompanied by a rich dessert wine.

GÂTEAU DU GERS
Raisin cake

PREPARATION TIME: 15 minutes (plus soaking the raisins for 1 hour)
COOKING TIME: 25 minutes
FOR SIX TO EIGHT

100 g (3½ oz) raisins	*100 g (3½ oz) butter*
100 ml (3½ fl oz) Armagnac	*200 g (7 oz) flour*
750 ml (generous 1¼ pints) milk	*5 eggs*
100 g (3½ oz) caster sugar	

Remove the stalks from the raisins and put them to soak for 1 hour in half of the Armagnac. Bring the milk and the sugar to the boil. Cut the butter into knobs to soften it.

Sift the flour into a bowl, break the eggs into it and add the rest of the Armagnac. Work in the softened butter and moisten the cake mixture little by little with the hot milk.

Butter an ovenproof dish. Drain the raisins and sprinkle half over the bottom of the dish. Pour in the cake mixture and arrange the rest of the raisins over the surface. Cook in a very hot oven (230°C/450°F/Gas Mark 8) for 25 minutes. Serve warm or cold.

<u>Elle advises</u> that the dish should not be filled to the rim with mixture as the cake will rise during cooking.

SABLÉS CROQUANTS
Ice-box biscuits

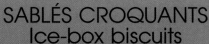

PREPARATION TIME: 10 minutes (12 hours in advance)
COOKING TIME: 15 minutes
FOR SIX

300 g (10½ oz) flour	1 egg
125 g (4½ oz) granulated sugar	2 extra tablespoons granulated
200 g (7 oz) butter	sugar

Mix the flour and the 125 g (4½ oz) of sugar together. Add 175 g (generous 6 oz) softened butter, work it in with the fingertips, then break in the egg. Knead just long enough to produce a supple dough.

Spread the 2 extra tablespoons of sugar onto a pastry board. Form the dough into a sausage shape about 5 cm (2 inches) in diameter and roll it in sugar. Wrap it completely in kitchen foil and refrigerate for 12 hours.

Cut the dough into round slices about 10 mm (⅖ inches) thick. Arrange them with space between on a buttered baking sheet and cook for 15 minutes in a moderate oven (180°C/350°F/Gas Mark 4).

The cooking should be checked from time to time. The biscuits are ready when they are a light golden-brown.

MADELEINES AU MIEL
Honey madeleines

PREPARATION TIME: 15 minutes (1 hour in advance)
COOKING TIME: 10 minutes
FOR 24 CAKES

1 large tablespoon clear honey	100 g (3½ oz) flour
100 g (3½ oz) ground almonds	8 egg whites
250 g (scant 9 oz) icing sugar	250 g (scant 9 oz) butter

Take a bowl and thoroughly mix together the ground almonds, the icing sugar and the flour. Mix in the egg whites, one by one.

Melt the butter in a small pan and heat until it turns nut-brown. Pour it into the mixture and work everything together. Stir in the honey and put the mixture into the refrigerator for 1 hour.

Divide the mixture evenly between the buttered moulds of a madeleine tray. Cook in a hot oven (220°C/425°F/Gas Mark 7), check progress and remove from the oven when the madeleines are golden-brown.

These delicious cakes are best eaten while still warm.

Elle advises that you use the smallest moulds available: this will improve the flavour and the crispness.

GALETTES AUX NOISETTES
Hazelnut biscuits

PREPARATION TIME: 20 minutes (half an hour in advance)
COOKING TIME: 10–15 minutes
FOR ABOUT 60 BISCUITS

100 g (3½ oz) shelled hazelnuts	*9 egg yolks*
200 g (7 oz) butter	*500 g (generous 1 lb) flour*
240 g (8½ oz) caster sugar	*1 pinch of salt*

Take the butter out of the refrigerator well ahead, to make it easier to work. Mix it with the sugar into a paste, work in 8 of the egg yolks one by one, sift on the flour, add a pinch of salt and mix well. Roll the dough into a ball and leave it to rest for half an hour.

Lightly flour a pastry board and roll out the pastry to a thickness of 3 mm (⅛ inch). Cut the pastry into diamonds of a suitable size and arrange them on a buttered baking sheet. Beat the last egg yolk and brush the biscuits. Draw crosses on them with the tines of a fork.

Skin the hazelnuts and crush them briefly in a blender. Sprinkle a pinch of chopped nut onto each biscuit and cook in a cool oven (150°C/300°F/Gas Mark 2) for 10–15 minutes.

<u>Elle says</u> that these biscuits keep well in a closed tin.

PAVÉS AU CAFÉ
Coffee knobs

PREPARATION TIME: 15 minutes (2 hours in advance)
COOKING TIME: 15 minutes
FOR 60 PIECES

20 g (⅔ oz) instant coffee	*4 egg yolks*
10 g (⅓ oz) leaf gelatine	*2 egg whites*
12 sugar lumps	*25 g (scant 1 oz) cocoa powder*
500 ml (17½ fl oz) full-cream milk	*50 g (scant 2 oz) lump sugar*

Soak the gelatine in cold water for 5 minutes. Put the sugar lumps into the milk and bring to the boil, stirring to dissolve the sugar lumps.

Beat the egg yolks in a bowl and, beating continuously, slowly add the hot milk. Make a concentrated essence with the instant coffee and a little hot water and stir it into the mixture. Let it all thicken over a low heat, then dissolve the drained leaf gelatine in it.

Whisk the egg whites until stiff and vigorously beat them into the mixture. Pour it into a shallow cake tin and refrigerate for at least 2 hours.

Cut up into small squares, mix the cocoa powder and sugar together and roll each piece in it so that it is completely covered. Put the coffee knobs into individual paper cases and return to the refrigerator until they are to be served. They will keep perfectly well for 2–3 days under refrigeration.

FRAISETTE
Strawberry sherbet

PREPARATION TIME: 10 minutes (1 hour in advance)

COOKING TIME: nil

FOR SIX

300 g (10½ oz) strawberries	150 g (5 oz) caster sugar
2 oranges	100 ml (3½ fl oz) still water
1 lemon	sparkling water

Wash and hull the strawberries and put them through a blender to make a fine purée. Squeeze the oranges and the lemon and mix the juices into the strawberry purée, together with the sugar and the still water. Keep stirring until all the sugar is dissolved, then put into the refrigerator.

When serving, divide the liquid among tall glasses and top up with well chilled sparkling water.

<u>Elle says</u> that this cooling drink is delicious on a hot day and, being non-alcoholic, is particularly suitable for children.

GLOGG
Glug-Glug

PREPARATION TIME: 10 minutes (the day before)

COOKING TIME: 10 minutes

FOR SIX

1 teaspoon grated ginger	1 bottle red wine
1 teaspoon crushed cardamom	200 g (7 oz) caster sugar
3 sticks of cinnamon	15 g (½ oz) vanilla sugar (see
20 cloves	p.16)
100 ml (3½ fl oz) rum	peel of 1 orange
100 ml (3½ fl oz) brandy	100 g (3½ oz) shelled almonds
100 ml (3½ fl oz) vodka	100 g (3½ oz) raisins

Into a bowl, put the grated ginger, the crushed cardamom, the sticks of cinnamon, and the cloves. Pour in the rum, the brandy and the vodka and leave to stand overnight.

The following day, strain the liquid through a sieve into a saucepan, add the red wine, the caster and vanilla sugars, the orange peel, the almonds and the raisins. Put over a low heat, warm through but do not let the mixture boil. Serve very hot.

<u>Elle says</u> that, if available, an equal volume of aquavit may be substituted for the three other spirits.

Index